Allen Ginsberg
AT&T Bell Labs
Holmdel, New Jersey

Automatic Refinement of Expert System Knowledge Bases

Pitman, London

Morgan Kaufmann Publishers, Inc., San Mateo, California

PITMAN PUBLISHING
128 Long Acre, London WC2E 9AN

First published 1988

Available in the Western Hemisphere from
MORGAN KAUFMANN PUBLISHERS, INC.,
2929 Campus Drive, San Mateo, California 94403

ISSN 0268-7526

British Library Cataloguing in Publication Data
Ginsberg, Allen
Automatic refinement of expert system knowledge bases.
1. Expert systems. Design
I. Title II. Series
006.3′3

ISBN 0 273 08794 0

Library of Congress Cataloging in Publication Data
Ginsberg, Allen.
Automatic refinement of expert system knowledge bases/Allen Ginsberg.
P. CM.

Bibliography: p.

ISBN 0-934613-96-6 (Morgan Kaufmann)
1. Expert systems (Computer science) 2. Database management.
I. Title.
QA76.76.E95G55 1988
006.3′3—DC19

Reproduced and printed by photolithography
in Great Britain by Biddles Ltd, Guildford

Contents

1 Introduction 1

1.1 Automatic knowledge base refinement 1
1.2 Designing automatic refinement systems 5
1.3 An overview of SEEK2 9
1.4 Metalanguage and methodology 14
1.5 Some assumptions 17
1.6 Accomplishments 18
1.7 Synopsis 19

2 Related Research 21

2.1 Expert systems, knowledge base refinement and pattern recognition 21
2.2 Relation to automatic knowledge acquisition 23
2.3 Relation to learning 24
2.4 Relation to discovery 28
2.5 Summary 29

3 Formal Elements of Knowledge Base Refinement 31

3.1 Formal account of refinement operators 31
3.2 Semantic properties of refinement operators 36
3.3 Semantic properties of refinement operations 38
3.4 Radicality and plausibility 45

4 Heuristic Refinement Generation 49

4.1 Frequently used RM primitives 50
4.2 The paradigm 51
4.3 First-order vs. higher-order refinement 53
4.4 Soundness and completeness of refinement generators 56
4.5 A general architecture for heuristic refinement generation 57
4.6 First-order case analysis 61
4.7 Cost of case analysis 80
4.8 Refinement knowledge: heuristics for first-order refinement 82
4.9 Failure of refinability, component/rule addition, and failure-driven higher order analysis 90
4.10 Summary 93

5 Strategy and Tactics 95
5.1 Integration of the three strategic components 95
5.2 Fault localization 96
5.3 Verification and selection 99
5.4 Selection criteria 107
5.5 Searching the universe of knowledge bases 108
5.6 Conclusion 119

6 A Metalanguage for Knowledge Base Refinement 121
6.1 RM primitives 122
6.2 Designing R-functions and heuristics 129
6.3 Designing refinement strategies 132
6.4 Domain-specific metaknowledge in RM 135
6.5 Incorporation of failure-driven higher-order refinement 136
6.6 Summary 142

7 Conclusion 145
7.1 Research significance 145
7.2 Future directions 158
7.3 Concluding remarks 160

I List of RM Primitives and Some Constructs 161

II Generic Atomic Refinement Operators for EXPERT 167

III A Grammar for the Canonical Rule Representation Language 171

References 173

List of Figures

Figure 1.1 Knowledge and metaknowledge for knowledge base refinement 4
Figure 1.2 Elements of a refinement system design problem 7
Figure 1.3 Structure of a knowledge base 10
Figure 1.4 Basic SEEK2 cycle 13
Figure 1.5 SEEK2 refinement experiment example 14
Figure 1.6 SEEK2 session example 15
Figure 1.7 Role of refinement metalanguage 16
Figure 3.1 Refinements as transformational operators 33
Figure 3.2 Rule-contexts 34
Figure 3.3 The on-target relation 40
Figure 3.4 A partial radicality ordering 47
Figure 4.1 Heuristic generation of on-target refinements 53
Figure 4.2 First vs. higher-order refinement 54
Figure 4.3 Architecture of heuristic refinement generator 59
Figure 5.1 Multiple-generation system 106
Figure 5.2 Comparison of selection procedures 117
Figure 6.1 A portion of an outcome-vector 141
Figure 7.1 Train and test experiment 147
Figure 7.2 Train and train again experiment 150

Preface and Acknowledgements

In 1982 - the year I began graduate study in computer science at Rutgers University - I defended my doctoral dissertation in philosophy [14]. That I would go on to defend another one in computer science would have struck me as extremely unlikely at the time. It is only because of the efforts of Sholom Weiss and Casimir Kulikowski in providing support and encouragement for this work that it exists at all. Moreover, if this work makes any significant contributions to the study of heuristic refinement generation, this is only because the basic idea had already been formulated by Peter Politakis and Sholom Weiss [30,31]. It has been a privilege and a pleasure to work with Sholom Weiss, the chairman of my thesis committee, in the advancement of this research program.

Thanks mainly to Robert Weingard - my thesis advisor in philosophy, who encouraged me to study physics and the philosophy of physics - most of my work in philosophy was of a more technical nature than is usually associated with this field in the popular imagination. To what extent my experience in philosophy has influenced *this* work, and whether it adds to or detracts from it, I leave to the reader to decide. In reviewing and preparing this work for publication, however, two philosophical dicta came to mind. The advice given Socartes by the Oracle at Delphi - "know thyself" - may be taken as the motto of this work. I have, in the first place, tried to explain things to *myself* in terms that I understand. I hope that this has been done in such a way that others will be able derive some use or insight from it. Another hope is that this work has been able to acheive a reasonable balance between theory and practice. A contemporary understanding of Kant's famous remark in the *Critique of Pure Reason* - "concepts without intuitions are empty; intuitions without concepts are blind" - is a succinct way of expressing a belief in the vital link between theory (concepts) and experimentation (intuitions) as the driving force in scientific progress. A theory that neither predicts nor explains any empirical results is not science; the significance of empirical results can be evaluated only with respect to some theoretical understanding.

I thank Alex Borgida, Peter Politakis, and Saul Levy, for their help in weeding out errors, improving the clarity of the presentation, and pointing out problems and possibilities that would otherwise have gone unrecognized. I also thank Jack Mostow for discussions that were helpful in designing the experiments described in Chapter 7, and N. S. Sridharan for useful criticisms of the original and revised versions of the manuscript.

Thanks also to Kevin Kern, for programming work on SEEK2, Hobbit, for dealing with VMS, Keith Williamson, for comments on an earlier draft, and Jack Ostroff, for answering questions to which no one else seemed to have the answer. I especially thank Angela DiCorrado for always having a word of encouragement, and usually having the best advice on the vicissitudes of life.

My dear wife, Gail, and our wonderful son, Alexander, are responsible for making it all worthwhile. My only regrets concerning this work are the times it kept me from being with them. My greatest thanks go to my parents and brother for their lifelong moral support.

This work was supported in part by the National Institutes of Health under grant P41 RR02230.

April, 1988
AT&T Bell Laboratories, Holmdel, NJ

To my mother and father

Abstract

Knowledge base refinement involves the generation, testing, and possible incorporation of *plausible refinements* to the rules in a knowledge base with the intention of thereby improving the empirical adequacy of an expert or knowledge-based system, i.e., its ability to correctly diagnose or classify the cases in its domain of expertise.

The research presented here is concerned with the development of useful knowledge base refinement systems - both at the concrete level of system design, implementation, and testing, and also at the "meta-level" of development of tools and methodologies for pursuing research in this area. At the concrete level this work gives a detailed account of the fundamental concepts and principles embodied in an automatic refinement system, SEEK2, a system that generalizes and extends the *empirical-heuristic* approach to knowledge base refinement developed by Politakis and Weiss. With SEEK2 this approach has been made applicable to a more powerful rule representation language, and heuristics encompassing a larger class of refinement operations have been incorporated. Ideas for future extensions to SEEK2 are also discussed in some detail.

Relative to the meta-level of tools and methodology, a high-level *Refinement Metalanguage*, RM, allowing for the specification of a wide variety of alternative refinement concepts, heuristics, and strategies, has been designed and implemented. In addition to allowing for the growth of refinement systems by facilitating experimental research, RM also provides a means for refinement system customization and possible enhancement through the incorporation of domain-specific metaknowledge. The use of a formal metalanguage for specification of automatic refinement systems is an extension of the traditional model of an expert system framework, and is a step in the direction of more powerful, robust, and self-improving expert system technology.

1 Introduction

In this chapter we give an overview of the problem of knowledge base refinement and a general account of the knowledge and subsystems required by refinement systems. The overview includes a description of the SEEK2 automatic refinement system, as well as a discussion of the role and content of a metalinguistic framework for experimental research in the field of knowledge base refinement. We conclude with a summary of the main research contributions of this work and a synopsis.

1.1 Automatic Knowledge Base Refinement

1.1.1 Knowledge Acquisition and Knowledge Base Refinement

The problem of constructing an efficient and accurate formal representation of an expert's domain knowledge, the *knowledge acquisition problem*, is a key problem in artificial intelligence(AI). As a practical matter, the most time consuming aspect of expert system design is the construction of the knowledge base; the rate of progress in developing useful expert systems is directly related to the rate at which it is possible to construct knowledge bases whose level of performance is comparable to that of an expert's in the field.

Conceptually it is worthwhile to view the knowledge acquisition process as consisting of three main types of activities. One activity involves the "elicitation" [2] of rules or rule sets for one or more conclusions of interest from the expert. The second activity involves the attempt to elicit what we shall call *case knowledge* from the expert. This is an important concept in our work, and in expert systems research generally, so we will have more to say concerning it below (section 1.1.2). For now it suffices to say that case knowledge is a set of "problem scenarios" or cases for each of which the expert's conclusion(s) is known. The third knowledge acquisition activity - *knowledge base refinement* - involves the attempt to test and, if necessary, revise the knowledge base in an effort to minimize its estimated rate of error. This is a process that is driven by comparison of the "answers" of the knowledge base with that of the expert's over the total available case knowledge.

The construction of a knowledge base may involve several or many cycles of interleaved instances of the three activities just described. For example, whenever a set of newly elicited rules, R, is to be integrated into a existing knowledge base, KB, one would like to test the system KB+R for possible "correctness" problems, i.e., cases in which KB+R and the expert disagree. In the earlier phases of knowledge base construction it is more likely that correctness problems will be overcome by addition of new rules rather than revision of existing ones. In the later phases, however, one is more likely to find correctness problems that arise as a result of unanticipated interactions among the existing rules. Typically the types of revisions required at this point will involve the sorts of knowledge base refinement actions studied in this work.

1.1.2 Case Knowledge

There is no question that an important part of what *makes* someone an expert in a *domain of expertise*, is the ability to "perform correctly" in *cases* that fall within that domain. Depending on the sort of domain we are talking about, a *case* can be anything from a patient exhibiting certain observable or measurable symptoms, to a set of equations that must be solved or used in some way to calculate the expected value of some physical quantity in a given situation, etc. Any interesting domain of expertise will have a very large, and often potentially infinite, set of distinct cases associated with it. Any expert will have the ability to "perform correctly" in a certain subset of this infinity of potential cases; we call this set of cases the *expert's complete case knowledge*. *Case knowledge* is any subset of the expert's complete case knowledge. When we talk about a *case* c in this work, we think of the expert's "evaluation" (conclusion) or "performance" in c as being part of it.

Expert systems research is concerned with the construction of systems that yield high-performance in "real world" problems, or certain aspects of such problems. Thus part of what gives one the right to call a computer program an *expert system* is the ability of the program to perform well in cases within the given problem domain. The basic source of evidence that such a program *does* perform well over cases in its domain, is its ability to reproduce an expert's performance. Case knowledge, therefore, is not just something that we may or may not want to gather in order to help us in the knowledge acquisition task: it provides the only direct way of validating the adequacy and accuracy of the expert system's performance. One expects, therefore, that any serious effort to construct an expert system will involve an attempt to gather case knowledge and use it as both a guide towards improved performance as well as a measure of current performance.

1.1.3 Conservatism and Radicality - Refinement and Optimization

Abstractly, a knowledge base refinement scenario may be characterized as follows. Let kb_0 be a given knowledge base, let C be the currently available case knowledge for the domain of expertise in question. We assume that kb_0 is not a high-performance knowledge base at this time, and we expect this fact to be reflected in kb_0's performance over the cases in C. That is, we expect that kb_0 will not completely reproduce the expert's judgments over C.[1]

The job of a refinement system is to discover, test, and possibly (tentatively) incorporate modifications to the rules in kb_0, with a view towards improving the *empirical adequacy* of the knowledge base, i.e., making it capable of reproducing the expert's performance in more cases. At the same time the refinement system must try to avoid the recommendation or incorporation of refinements that will not meet with expert approval. In order to do this the refinement system will make use of various sources of knowledge and *metaknowledge*, and case knowledge is *only one* of these. Case knowledge will be used both as a *source of evidence* for generating refinements, as well as a *source of test cases* for determining the expected gain in empirical adequacy of the refinements generated.[2] The general idea is that by making good use of *all* the sources of knowledge and metaknowledge available, the process of generating refinements that improve kb_0's performance over C, has a good chance of generating some refinements that improve the empirical adequacy of the knowledge base in general, and that do not simply reflect "statistical fluctuations" in C.

While some sources of knowledge and metaknowledge may be unavailable in particular cases, there is one important source of knowledge that must always be available. This is simply kb_0 itself (see figure 1-1). We are assuming that kb_0 has been obtained through interaction with an expert - at the very least, the expert has assented to the truthfulness of the rules contained in kb_0. This does not mean that the rules *must* be correct as they are; there would be no need for refinement if they were. This does mean that kb_0 represents "sensible," more or less accurate, knowledge concerning the domain of expertise. Moreover, the more domain knowledge captured by kb_0, the more likely it is that the knowledge base possesses the requisite degree of generality, i.e., it should be capable of dealing with a wide variety of cases in the domain of expertise. Under these assumptions, a *conservative* refinement strategy may be wise, where this is one that obeys certain general, and possibly domain-specific, constraints or intuitions

---

[1]Note that we are not making any assumptions concerning the availability of information pertaining to the underlying probability distribution of cases; we therefore do not assume that C necessarily represents a statistically valid case population. One would expect that in working with a *particular* expert, the knowledge engineer will be able to extract a representative sample of the "local" case population confronting the expert within some period of time. Clearly if we are in possession of useful and accurate statistical information, there is good reason to apply statistical techniques to the problem of constructing and refining a knowledge base. Since, however, expert systems approaches tend to be applied precisely in domains where either little reliable statistical information is available, or where the dimensionality of the underlying "feature space" is so large as to make the use of statistical methods computationally impractical, we do not expect that such information will be available to us in the refinement phase [40].

[2]In keeping with accepted statistical practice, disjoint sets of case knowledge should be used for the purposes of refinement generation and testing. In terms of the approach taken in SEEK2, this would mean dividing C into a "training set" and a "testing set," using the former in the actual run of SEEK2, and then seeing how well the resulting knowledge base performs on the latter. Such an experiment has been performed; the results are encouraging, and are reported in chapter 7.

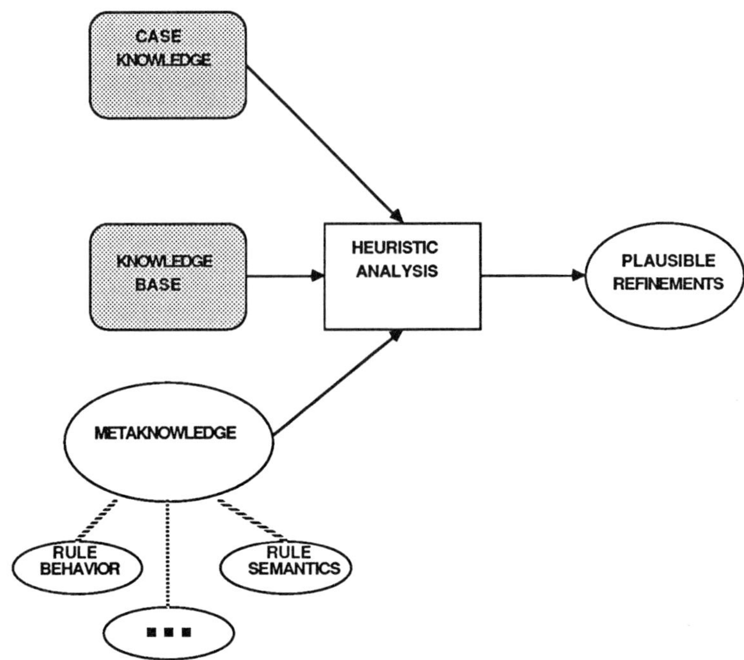

Figure 1-1: Knowledge and Metaknowledge for Knowledge Base Refinement

concerning the "radicality" of refinements to the knowledge base. A conservative strategy is one that attempts to improve the empirical adequacy of kb_0 while making the least radical changes to kb_0 possible.

Clearly, the notion of the radicality, or relative radicality, of a refinement is an important notion in this overall conception of knowledge base refinement. A formal general understanding of radicality can be given. In chapter 5 we will see how, given a kb_0, one can define a mathematical construct called *kb-space* whose points represent all the possible refined versions of kb_0. Given any two points in kb-space there will be a way, perhaps several ways, of "refining" one into the other. If one could define a (path independent) distance function over kb-space, in the same way that one talks about the (pythagorean) distance function defined on points in physical 3-dimensional space, then one would *ipso facto* have defined a *radicality metric* on refinements. That is, if kb is a refined version of kb_0, then the radicality of kb with respect to kb_0 is the distance in kb-space from the one to the other. The goal of knowledge base refinement could then be stated as the attempt to find the points in kb-space *closest* to kb_0 that give the greatest improvement in empirical adequacy over C, i.e., as a search for the closest local maxima of a certain "objective function" defined over kb-space.

Looking at the problem in the way just indicated, we see that knowledge base refinement resembles both mathematical optimization problems and search problems in certain ways. The objective function to be optimized in knowledge base refinement is simply the number of cases in C in which the knowledge base performs correctly. However since the underlying search space, kb-space, is not a Euclidean vector space, it is impossible to apply the techniques of linear or dynamic programming to this optimization problem [1]. In kb-space one cannot take the gradient of a function at a point in order to determine the direction of its greatest ascent; in order to get this information one would have to sample all of the point's closest neighbors in kb-space.

But there is an even greater obstacle in applying mathematical optimization methods to knowledge base refinement. We have shown how radicality may be thought of as a distance function on kb-space, and we could even define such a metric. The problem is that there are *many* metrics that could be used, and, in contrast to the situation in mathematics and physics, the question "which metric is the right one?" cannot be answered by means of empirical observation. While there seem to be several general reasonable "axioms" that any such metric should obey (see chapter 3), and certain non-controversial intuitions concerning the relative radicality of certain refinement operations - e.g., deleting *two* components from a rule r is generally more radical than deleting only one component from r - these axioms and intuitions do not determine a unique radicality metric. Instead of picking a metric by *fiat* as the "right" one, it is wiser to leave unspecified those things whose specification is properly consigned to the level of a domain-specific refinement problem. In other words, it belongs to the theory of knowledge base refinement to think about the *general forms* in which radicality information may be expressed, and how such information may be used in the refinement process, but it belongs, for the most part, to the knowledge engineer or domain expert to supply the actual information itself.

For this reason, we simply cannot proceed under the assumption that an accurate radicality metric will always be available. Without such a metric the idea of the closest neighbors of a point in kb-space is not well-defined, and, therefore, in such a case there is even a larger gap between mathematical optimization and knowledge base refinement.

1.2 Designing Automatic Refinement Systems

So far we have not explicitly stated any assumptions concerning the nature of either the *expert system frameworks*, or the domain problems we expect to consider. The discussion has been somewhat tendentious, in that we have mainly spoken about the expert's *conclusion* or judgment in a case, instead of, for example, the expert's *performance* or *plan of action* in a case. This is in keeping with the fact that this work is focused on expert system frameworks that are designed to deal with *classification problems*. But, from a general point of view, there is nothing in the notion of an expert system that requires such a system to deal solely with classification as opposed to, say, planning problems.

We can capture this level of generality by talking about *refinement system design problems.* Such a problem is defined by providing a *formal specification* of an expert system framework, where in order to give such a specification one must formally specify the syntax and semantics of the items that can appear in a knowledge base, and the nature of the mechanisms that will be applied to these items by the expert system. Assuming that we are dealing solely with rule-based systems this is equivalent to specifying a) a rule representation language, and b) an inference and control mechanism that determines which rules will be applied in any context. A formal specification of such an expert system framework need not, however, be an *exact* specification of any actually existing framework.

Given an expert system framework specification ES, there is a corresponding *refinement system design problem*: design a generic refinement system for ES. That is, design a refinement system that will be of use in refining *any* knowledge base that can be written in the rule representation language of ES.

As is shown in figure 1-2, there is a general structure to refinement systems design problems. To design a refinement system one must specify how *metaknowledge* concerning the expert system framework's rule, case, and inference structures will be incorporated and used by the refinement system. In other words a knowledge representation problem must be addressed: find effective ways of representing formal knowledge *about* the expert system framework in question. One must also provide the actual *refinement metaknowledge* that will be used by the system. At the design level this means that one must specify *generic* refinement metaknowledge (that will be useful in refining any knowledge base written in ES), as well as *general forms* for expressing domain specific metaknowledge that may be deemed to be of use - and hopefully available - in dealing with some of the actual domains of expertise that are to be modeled by knowledge bases written in ES. Finally one must specify the *strategic subsystems* of the overall refinement system in such a way that it is clear how the system will make use of its metaknowledge in achieving its aim.

Detailed descriptions of the generic refinement metaknowledge that is used in SEEK2 will be given in chapter 4, and some examples will be given in section 1.3 below. Put simply, generic refinement metaknowledge is knowledge that relates certain observable or measurable features of rule behavior to possible corrective refinement actions. It may be viewed as a body of theoretical knowledge concerning how knowledge bases can fail.

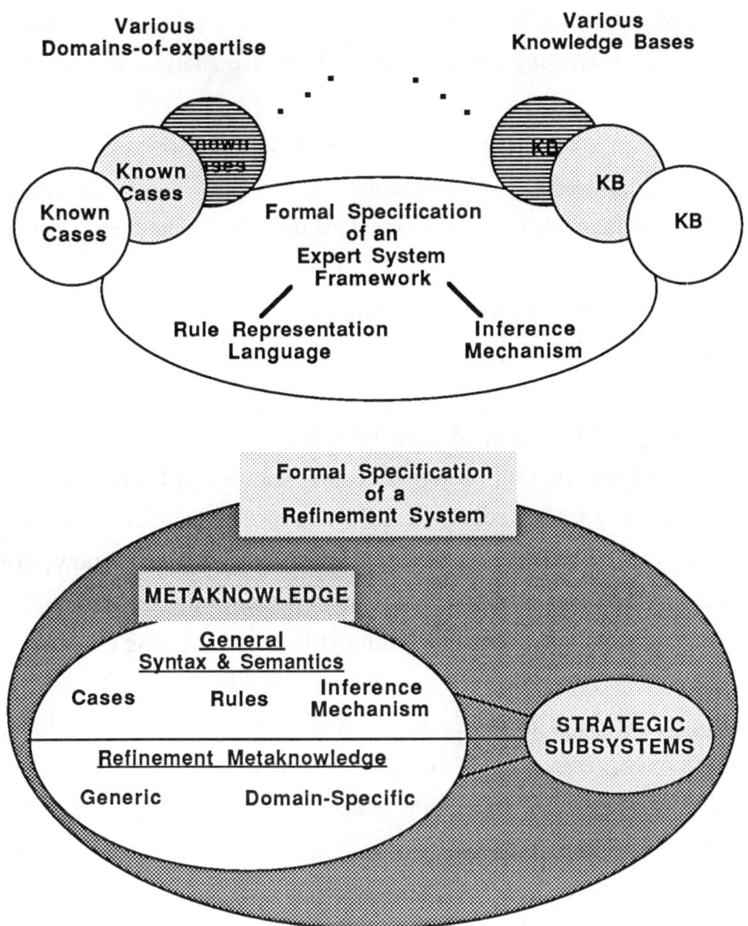

Figure 1-2: Elements of A Refinement System Design Problem

1.2.1 Strategic Subsystems

There are four issues that must be addressed by any automatic refinement system; we say that there are four strategic subsystems of such a system.

In the first place the refinement system must address the issue of *localization*. This refers to the process of determining that a certain subset of rules, R, in the knowledge base is the likely cause of a certain subset, M, of the currently misdiagnosed cases. We call the pair <R,M> a *refinement-situation* or *r-situation* for short. The localization module of a refinement system is responsible for dividing up the overall problem of improving the knowledge base's empirical adequacy into r-situations that can then be addressed independently.

The next issue that must be addressed is *refinement generation.* Given an r-situation <R,M>, the problem is to generate specific *plausible* refinement suggestions involving the rules in R with the intention of correcting the cases in M. In this work a refinement is said to be *plausible* if it "has a chance" of correcting certain cases. A precise analysis of this notion is given in chapter 3.

A refinement system must have a *verification* procedure for testing the efficacy of the refinements that are suggested by its refinement generator. It may also require a *selection criterion* for determining when a refinement should be tentatively incorporated in the knowledge base.

Finally, these subsystems must be integrated into a coherent overall procedure by the refinement system's *control strategy.*

1.2.2 Refinement System Design: A Special Case

The research presented here focuses on refinement system design for expert system frameworks that are intended to be used to solve classification problems. In particular, we focus on frameworks whose rule representation languages have the expressive power of propositional logic, conjoined with certain special "surface forms," and confidence factors. Such frameworks do not, for example, allow for the dynamic binding of variables during run-time.

The term *classification problem* is a technical term in this work, and we use it as a "shorthand" for a whole set of assumptions concerning the nature of the knowledge bases we expect our refinement systems to be dealing with. Many of these assumptions will be clear from the context of the discussion, but some, especially those that are important in understanding how SEEK2 works, must be made explicit at this point. Additional assumptions of a more technical nature are discussed below (see section 1.5).

1. The knowledge base is a collection of *rules of inference* that include many that are *inductive* in nature, i.e., the truth of the premises of a rule does not logically entail the truth of the conclusion. This means that one counterexample to a rule of this type does not invalidate it.

2. The knowledge base has been obtained *via* interaction with a domain expert. This supports the wisdom of taking a conservative refinement strategy.

3. The problem domain and knowledge base are such that a complete, fixed, and finite set of possible "endpoints," i.e., conclusions, can be specified, and is in fact given to the automatic refinement system. The expert's conclusion in any case must be one of these endpoints.

4. The knowledge base will be considered to have performed correctly in a case if its conclusion matches the expert's for that case, otherwise it has performed incorrectly. What matters is the knowledge base's answer, not how it reached it. If the knowledge base employs *confidence factors*, then its conclusion in a given case will be taken to be the conclusion with the highest confidence factor.

1.3 An Overview of SEEK2

In this section we present a brief overview of SEEK2. This automatic refinement system - the result of a collaborative effort involving myself, S. Weiss, P. Politakis, with programming assistance from K. Kern - grew out of an ongoing effort at Rutgers University on the topic of knowledge base refinement. As the name implies, SEEK2 is the successor of a previous system, viz., SEEK [31]. In order to appreciate the specific research progress represented by SEEK2, we briefly compare it with its immediate predecessor SEEK.

SEEK is a purely *interactive* system, and thus does not address the full complement of issues involved in doing *automatic* refinement. SEEK presents the user with a list of refinement suggestions with respect to an r-situation. If requested by the user, SEEK will calculate the results of incorporating any one of these refinements in the knowledge base. But it is up to the user to decide 1) which r-situations to investigate, 2) which suggested refinement experiments to attempt, 3) which refinements to incorporate in the knowledge base, and 4) when to stop the current refinement process. SEEK2, on the other hand, makes these decisions on its own.

SEEK works only with knowledge bases that employ a specialized rule representation format known as *criteria tables*. All of the refinement operations, metaknowledge concepts and heuristics used in SEEK are well-defined only in relation to this mode of representation.

SEEK2, on the other hand, will work with any knowledge base written in the EXPERT rule representation language [39], and thus - since any criteria table knowledge base can easily be "translated" into EXPERT, but not conversely - is a more general refinement system than SEEK. In designing SEEK2 an effort was made to generalize the refinement concepts and heuristics of SEEK in appropriate ways whenever possible. However, certain primitive refinement operations that were not included in SEEK are utilized in SEEK2, e.g., shifts of boundaries on numerical ranges, and there are other operations that, though of minimal utility in SEEK, are of more importance in SEEK2 in virtue of the fact that new concepts and heuristics for these operations have been devised, e.g., alteration of confidence factors.

Finally, SEEK2 makes uses of a partial radicality ordering (see chapter 3) in its selection regime. The idea of using a radicality ordering on refinement operations is entirely new to SEEK2.

1.3.1 Localization

Any knowledge base that meets our assumptions must have a definite hierarchical structure that will help in devising localization principles (see figure 1-3). The localization mechanism employed in SEEK2 is a *divide and conquer* strategy and depends upon certain reasonable assumptions concerning the logical structure of the knowledge base. As we said above, we assume that the expert and knowledge engineer can identify a finite set of *final diagnostic conclusions* or "endpoints;" these are the conclusions that the expert uses to classify the given cases. One can then confine one's attention to the refinement of rules that are involved in concluding a particular endpoint, e.g., if the domain is Rheumatology one may decide to work on refining those rules involved in concluding the single final diagnosis Systemic Lupus. This is the major divide and conquer part of the strategy; it means that at any given moment the system is applying the refinement heuristics only to a proper subset of the rules in the domain knowledge base, and only to a proper subset of the misdiagnosed cases, viz., those that are either a false positive or a false negative for the endpoint in question.

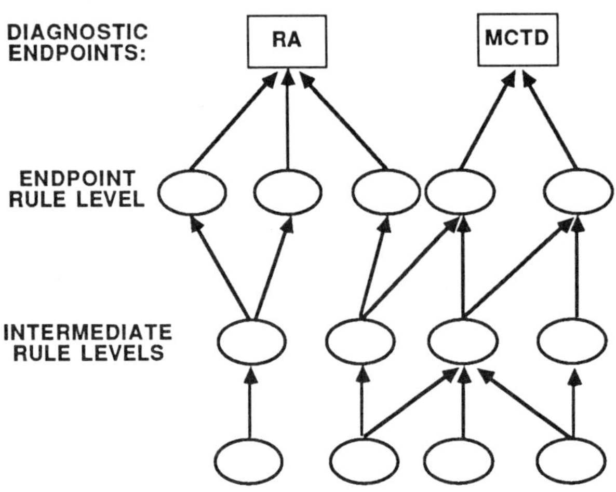

Figure 1-3: Structure of A Knowledge Base

Even within this chosen subset, however, another localization mechanism, based upon the *chaining* pattern of the rules in the knowledge base, serves to constrain the refinement generation process. If our chosen endpoint is Systemic Lupus, for example, we begin by applying the heuristics to all the rules in the knowledge base that directly conclude Systemic Lupus, i.e., rules whose right hand side is this conclusion. A rule that directly concludes some endpoint - we call these *endpoint-rules* - will, in general, have components on its left hand side that themselves are the conclusions of some other rules; such components are called *intermediate hypotheses,* and the rules that conclude them are called *intermediate rules* (see figure 1-3). The rules that conclude intermediate hypotheses may themselves include components that are intermediate hypotheses. Whenever the refinement heuristics suggest modifying an intermediate hypothesis IH, such as deleting it from some rule, the rules that conclude IH are thereby implicated as candidates for refinement.

1.3.2 Heuristic Refinement Generation

In terms of their semantic properties, many refinements of production rules may be thought of as falling in one of two possible classes: *generalizations and specializations* [30]. By a rule generalization we mean any modification to a rule that makes it "easier" for the rule's conclusion to be accepted in any given case. A generalization refinement is usually accomplished by deleting or altering a component on the left hand side of the rule or by raising the confidence factor associated with the rule's conclusion. By a rule specialization we mean modifications to a rule that make it "harder" for the rule's conclusion to be accepted in any given case. A rule specialization is usually accomplished by adding or altering a component on the left hand side or by lowering the confidence factor associated with the rule's conclusion.

On the side of evidence for rule generalization, one of the concepts we have employed in SEEK2, a concept originating in SEEK, is a statistical property of a rule computed by a function that we call *Gen(rule).* Gen(rule) is the number of cases in which (a) this rule's conclusion *should have been reached but wasn't*, (b) had this rule been satisfied the conclusion would have been reached, and (c) of all the rules for which the preceding clauses hold in the case, this one is the "closest to being satisfied." A measure of how close a rule is to being satisfied in a case, based on the number of additional findings required for the rule to fire, is easily computed given the case data (for details of the algorithm used by SEEK see [30]; SEEK2's closeness measure is essentially the same, see chapter 4).

On the side of evidence for rule specialization, one of the concepts we have defined is a statistical property of a rule that is computed by a function we call *SpecA(rule).* SpecA(rule) is the number of cases in which (a) this rule's conclusion *should not have been reached but was*, and (b) if this rule had *failed to fire* the correct conclusion would have been reached, i.e., the correct conclusion was the "second choice" in the case (due to its having the second highest confidence), and the only circumstance preventing its being the "first choice" is the fact that this rule is satisfied. If there is *more than one satisfied rule* that concludes the incorrect first choice then none of these rules has its SpecA measure incremented; instead we have defined an additional concept to cover this situation called *SpecB(rule)*: each of these rules has its SpecB measure incremented.

To get a feeling for the sort of heuristics employed by SEEK2 suppose that for a certain rule r it has been found that Gen(r) > [SpecA(r) + SpecB(r)], in other words the evidence suggests that it is more appropriate to generalize than specialize r. Another piece of information would help us decide *which component of r* should be deleted or altered, viz., the *most frequently missing component*, i.e., the component of r that has the lowest frequency of satisfaction relative to the cases that contribute to Gen(r). The function that computes this statistic is called *Mfmc(rule).* Mfmc(rule) also tells us the *syntactic category* of this most frequently missing component. For example, one sort of component often used in medical diagnostic systems is called a *choice component.* These have the form [k: C_1, ..., C_n], where k, *the choice number* is a positive integer and the C_i's are components (findings or hypotheses, but not choices). A choice component is satisfied *iff* at least k of its C_i's are satisfied. If we know that the rule r should be generalized and that Mfmc(r) is a particular choice component, then a natural thing to do is to *decrease the choice number of that choice component.* Being conservative we decrease the choice number by 1.

To summarize the discussion in this section we now display in full the particular heuristic we have described.

```
If:  Gen(rule) > [SpecA(rule) + SpecB(rule)] &
     Mfmc(rule) is  CHOICE-COMPONENT C

Then: Decrease the choice-number of
      CHOICE-COMPONENT C in rule.

Reason: This would generalize the rule so that it
        will be easier to satisfy.
```

This heuristic and the concepts it references are examples of what we are calling *generic refinement metaknowledge.*

1.3.3 Verification, Selection, and Control Strategy

SEEK2 first obtains a performance evaluation of the initial knowledge base on the data base of cases. This is done by "running" the initial knowledge base on each of the cases in the data base, and then comparing the knowledge base's conclusion with the stored expert's conclusion. The performance evaluation consists primarily of an overall score, e.g. 75% of cases diagnosed correctly, as well as a breakdown by final diagnostic category of the number of cases in which the system agrees with the expert in reaching a particular diagnosis, i.e., "true positives," and the number of cases in which the system reaches that diagnosis but the expert does not, i.e., "false positives."

The system must then decide on the ordering in which it will consider the endpoints in order to generate refinements for them. (Since SEEK2 always considers every endpoint in a cycle, the ordering could be arbitrary.) In the current implementation, SEEK2 orders the endpoints in descending order according to a simple measure on the number of "false negatives" and "false positives," information that is given by the performance evaluation phase. Then the system generates and tests refinements for each endpoint in the ordering in turn; when an endpoint is under consideration it is said to be the current "GDX" or "Given DX."

When SEEK2 tests a refinement it does so by running the proposed refined version of the

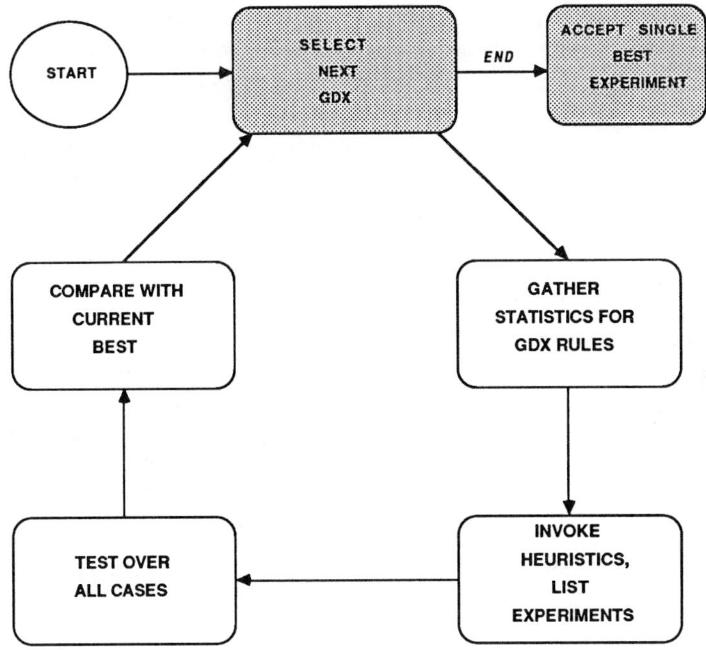

Figure 1-4: Basic SEEK2 Cycle

knowledge over *every case in the data base of cases*(see figure 1-4). Out of all the experiments attempted SEEK2 "accepts" only one, the one that gives the greatest *net gain* in knowledge base performance for *all* final diagnostic conclusions. An internal record of the accepted refinement is kept; and then the next automatic pilot cycle begins. If the current automatic pilot cycle is such that no attempted experiment leads to an actual net gain, SEEK2 stops. Figure 1-5 shows an example of the output SEEK2 produces in the course of running a refinement experiment.

The automatic pilot algorithm just described is a quasi-hill-climbing procedure: at each step SEEK2 is guided totally by the "local" information as to which proposed refinement on the current knowledge base results in the best improvement, i.e., leads in the direction of "steepest ascent."

1.3.4 Session Example and Performance

Figure 1-6 shows the "before and after" performance breakdowns for an actual SEEK2 run. The endpoints are listed in their mnemonic form, i.e., "RA" is short for "Rheumatoid Arthritis", etc. SEEK2 currently has ten statistical concepts and nine heuristics for generating refinements. Working in automatic pilot mode on this Rheumatology knowledge base of approximately 140 rules with 5 final diagnostic categories, and using a data base of 121 cases, SEEK2 was able to

Figure 1-5: SEEK2 Refinement Experiment Example

```
TESTING EXPERIMENT:

 In rule 3.7 (the seventh rule in rule-table 3) decrease the choice
 number of choice component 1

Estimated net gain of this refinement:  16 cases

 Choose  3 of the following  5:
        147         [H(RAYES,0.9:1)
        148         [F(SWOLH,T)
        149         [F(SCLDY,T)
        150         [F(DCO,0:69)
        151         [H(MYOSS,0.9:1)
        ->        H(MCTD,0.4)

  Before----------------------         After----------------------

   True Positives  False Positives  True Positives  False Positives
MCTD    9/ 33  ( 27%)       0          17/ 33  ( 52%)       0
  RA   42/ 42  (100%)      11          42/ 42  (100%)      10
 SLE   12/ 18  ( 67%)       4          12/ 18  ( 67%)       3
 PSS   22/ 23  ( 96%)       4          22/ 23  ( 96%)       2
  PM    3/  5  ( 60%)       1           3/  5  ( 60%)       1
Total 96/121  ( 79%)                 105/121  ( 87%)
```

---

increase the overall performance of the system from a value of 73% (88/121) to a value of 99% (120/121). It used approximately 18 minutes of Vax-785 cpu time. The total number of experiments tried was 112, out of which 9 were accepted.

1.4 Metalanguage and Methodology

There is no magic formula or algorithm for designing useful concepts and heuristics for knowledge base refinement. As with any empirical theory, discovery of such concepts and heuristics involves a combination of common sense, insight, and trial-and-error. SEEK2, for example, has undergone several substantial changes in concepts and heuristics, changes that were suggested by experimentation.

It is apparent, therefore, that progress in the field of knowledge base refinement would be facilitated by a system that gives a researcher the ability to conduct such experiments with relative ease. Such a system, called RM, - for Refinement Metalanguage - has been designed and implemented. A detailed account of this system is given in chapter 6, however, since RM concepts are used throughout this work, an appendix listing the main primitives of RM is provided (see appendix I).

RM is based upon a methodology and metalinguistic framework that was actually used in the design phase of SEEK2, albeit "by hand." As we shall see in chapter 4, every refinement concept used in SEEK2, e.g., Gen(rule), has a straightforward definition in RM. RM makes such definitions possible because it allows the user to focus entirely on the "essential" content of the concept he has in mind: one only needs to be concerned with *what* one wants done, not

Figure 1-6: SEEK2 Session Example

Initial Performance by Endpoint

	True Positives*	False Positives**
RA	42/ 42 (100%)	11
MCTD	9/ 33 (27%)	0
SLE	12/ 18 (67%)	4
PSS	22/ 23 (96%)	4
PM	3/ 5 (60%)	1
Total	88/121 (73%)	

Final Performance by Endpoint

	True Positives	False Positives
RA	42/ 42 (100%)	0
MCTD	32/ 33 (97%)	0
SLE	18/ 18 (100%)	1
PSS	23/ 23 (100%)	0
PM	5/ 5 (100%)	0
Total	120/121 (99%)	

**Cases in which the knowledge base's conclusion matches the given correct conclusion. Thus the figure 9/33 in the second row in the initial breakdown, for example, means that out of 33 cases having as correct conclusion MCTD, the knowledge currently diagnoses 9 of them correctly.*

***Cases in which the knowledge base's conclusion is not identical to the given correct conclusion. Thus the figure 11 in the first row of the initial breakdown, for example, means that the knowledge base has incorrectly reached the conclusion RA in 11 cases.*

---

with *how* it is to be done.

A useful refinement metalanguage should allow for the coding of both *general and domain-specific metaknowledge*. The refinement concepts employed by SEEK2 - for example, Gen, Mfmc, SpecA, and SpecB and the heuristics that employ them, are examples of *general metaknowledge*, i.e., general knowledge about the conditions under which rules should be considered for refinement. Other examples of general metaknowledge in knowledge acquisition would include concepts and strategies for extracting domain knowledge via interaction with an expert [5, 21], as well as concepts needed to encode knowledge concerning the strategic role of rules within the overall classification or diagnostic process [4]. An example of *domain-specific metaknowledge* [4, 33] is that certain rules in a knowledge base are definitional and should never be modified. Such knowledge involves properties of a knowledge base that are not ascertainable by means of a general a priori procedure.

The role envisioned for RM is illustrated in figure 1-7. We see that the refinement metalanguage plays a role in the specification of both the methods of heuristic analysis applied by a refinement system, and the overall control strategy. The figure is also meant to convey the idea of RM being used not only as a tool for experimental research, but also as a device for customizing refinement systems.

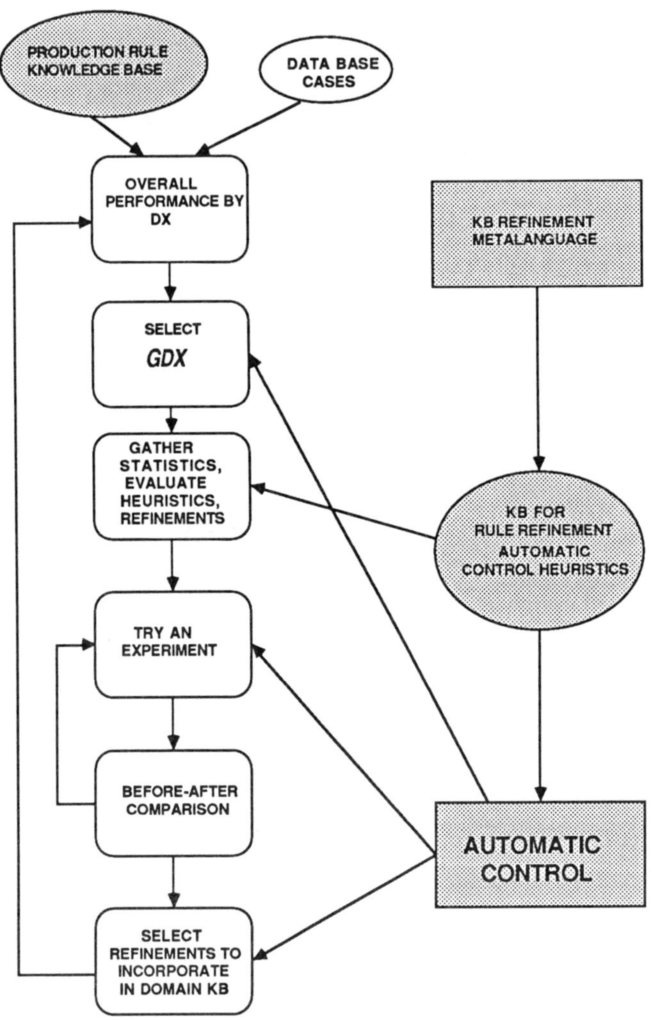

Figure 1-7: Role of Refinement Metalanguage

The basic thrust of the methodology behind RM can be put in a nutshell thusly: find a set of high-level primitives powerful enough to represent the space of possible solutions to the given refinement system design problem. The necessary primitives fall into several categories:

1. **Primitive Refinement Operators:** Given the formal specification of the rule representation language, one must select and represent a set of primitive generic rule modifications or operators, such that all intuitively reasonable rule refinements can be expressed using them. Thus the system should be of use not only in finding or fine-tuning heuristics for refinements that are currently in use, but also offer the possibility for designing heuristics that suggest heretofore

unused refinement operations.

2. **Primitive Refinement Concepts:** These are a set of concepts whose interpretation is based upon our understanding of the entities, knowledge, metaknowledge, etc. that comprise the domain of knowledge base refinement. For example, corresponding to the fact that knowledge base refinement involves modifying rules in a knowledge base, in RM we provide a high-level primitive variable *rule*, which ranges over the set of all rules in the given knowledge base. One must also postulate primitive refinement functions which enable a user to access or describe any important component or "behavioral feature" of the pertinent objects. For example, in RM, the function *rule-conclusion(rule)* returns the conclusion of rule, the function *satisfied(rule,case)* returns true if and only if *rule* is satisfied in *case*, else it returns false (*case*, of course, is a primitive variable over the data base of cases). These primitive refinement concepts form the building blocks out of which sophisticated generic refinement concepts, e.g., Gen(rule), are constructed in RM.

3. **Primitive Metalanguage Operators:** In order to allow for the construction of sophisticated refinement concepts out of primitives, and for the definition of heuristics, one must also specify primitive operators belonging to the metalanguage *per se*. Most of the RM primitives belonging to this category are familiar from simple set theory, logic, and arithmetic.

4. **Primitive Constructive Actions:** Certain primitive actions must be provided by a metalinguistic framework for knowledge base refinement. Among these are actions such as the following: creating a definition of a set of objects, creating a new variable of an already defined type (e.g. let r be a variable of type *rule*), creating a new function or heuristic, creating a refined version of a knowledge base, etc. In other words, the system must allow the user to *create* entirely new objects by defining them out of primitives and previously defined objects, as well as to create new instances of previously defined objects.

5. **Primitive Manipulative Actions:** Certain primitive ways of using or manipulating both primitive and defined objects must be provided. Among these we have, for example: evaluating definitions and heuristics, trying a refinement experiment, accessing a version of the knowledge base. It must also be possible to combine primitive actions into procedures, so that complete automatic refinement systems can be designed and tested.

1.5 Some Assumptions

An expert system framework is more than a rule representation language, it is also a *way of using* linguistic representations to reach conclusions. Therefore we need, as it were, a canonical form for the "inferencing mechanism" of such a system. We try to avoid biasing our account in favor of any current approach to inductive inference; the theory of refinement ought not to exhibit a preference for one approach over another.

We assume the existence of two data structures *evidence space*, and *hypothesis space*, such that the following assumptions are satisfied:

1. The evidence pertaining to a case is presented in its entirety once and for all, at the start of the "consultation," and recorded in *evidence space*. The expert system

must be run in a non-interactive mode, e.g., no questioning of the user occurs, no changes in the evidence occurs. (This is an implementation constraint.)

The evidence includes the following sorts of items: 1) the truth-values of propositions - not necessarily limited to a two-valued logic; 2) numerical values, or ranges associated with quantitative properties. Possibly, confidence values or ranges associated with *hypotheses* in the knowledge base may be presented initially as well. These may represent prior probabilities, or default values, or may simply be volunteered information pertaining to the specific case, and are deposited in *hypothesis space.* In addition, it is possible that items in categories (1) and (2) are also presented with associated confidence values or ranges indicative of the user's degree of belief in the evidence, and these values are deposited in *evidence space* along with the associated findings.

2. Initially, the expert system makes all inferences that it can on the basis of the contents of *evidence space alone*, i.e., every rule is evaluated using the evaluation conventions of the particular expert system framework, and if satisfied the resulting inference (including confidence, and rule identification) is recorded in *hypothesis space*, which is a separate space from evidence space.

3. At this point control is passed to a *global inference agent* whose job it is to review and revise the current state of hypothesis space according to the rules of confidence combination, etc. that are used by the particular expert system framework.

4. Control is now passed back to each rule in turn ("local inference agents"), which are now re-evaluated with reference to the current state of hypothesis space, as well as evidence space. Only rules that go from being previously unsatisfied to currently satisfied are of interest. Any such rules will deposit their conclusions in hypothesis space as before.

5. Steps (3) and (4) are repeated until hypothesis space reaches a stable configuration, i.e., does not change from one pass through the loop to the next. Clearly, it is possible to construct "pathological" rule sets that will prevent hypothesis space from ever reaching a stable condition in this sense. We take the position that the detection and/or prevention of such situations falls, however, within the province of expert system framework design, and is not a proper concern for the theory of refinement (viewed as a species of knowledge acquisition).

1.6 Accomplishments

From a broad perspective, this research deals with two related issues. The first issue concerns the possibility of automating knowledge base refinement at all: can practical and effective automatic refinement systems, capable of dealing with large-scale knowledge bases, be constructed? The second issue concerns the question of what methodology should be utilized in order to formulate and pursue a reasonable research strategy for making progress in the design and implementation of such systems.

This work addresses these issues within the context of an ongoing research program in knowledge base refinement at Rutgers University, a program whose first major milestone was the SEEK system [30], [31]. In terms of this ongoing effort, the research presented here makes the following three concrete advances:

- We have *generalized and extended* the empirically-grounded *heuristic* approach to refinement generation that was originally developed in conjunction with SEEK. The generalized approach is now incorporated in a new system, SEEK2 [17]. Whereas SEEK's refinement concepts and heuristics are applicable only to knowledge bases written in a specialized rule representation scheme called *criteria tables*, SEEK2's refinement concepts and heuristics are applicable to any knowledge base written in the more general EXPERT [39] rule representation language. SEEK2 is an *extension* of SEEK in the sense that it includes concepts and heuristics pertaining to types of refinement operations that were not incorporated in SEEK.
- An *automatic* knowledge base refinement system, SEEK2, has been designed, implemented, and, to a limited degree, tested. The results of these tests provide evidence that the heuristic approach to refinement generation can form the foundation of successful large-scale automatic knowledge base refinement. In addition, analyses of various refinement strategies, as well as a description of the nature of the types of heuristics and knowledge required to implement them in an automatic system, have been provided.
- A *Refinement Metalanguage*, RM, that enables a researcher to easily formalize and test concepts, heuristics, and strategies for knowledge base refinement, has been designed and implemented. This system has been instrumental in revising and debugging SEEK2, e.g., the discovery of new refinement concepts has been facilitated by RM.

Finally, this work attempts to formulate, and as far as possible, formalize, a general theoretical understanding concerning knowledge base refinement.

1.7 Synopsis

Chapter 2 is a brief summary of other work in knowledge base refinement and related fields. Chapter 3 introduces the necessary formal elements for giving a precise characterization of the goals and methods of knowledge base refinement. This involves a treatment of the formal syntax of refinement operations, and a discussion of some semantic properties of refinement operations. In particular a precise definition of the relevant sense of the notion *plausible refinement* is given. This chapter also addresses the problem of radicality measures on refinement operations.

In this work we will delve into the foundations of the heuristic approach to knowledge base refinement, and we will show that a reasonable general architecture for refinement generation based upon the use of heuristic analysis can be devised. This general architecture is not merely descriptive of the current system, but also has implications for the directions of future research. This discussion is given in Chapter 4. This chapter also contains a detailed description and analysis of the refinement concepts and heuristics used in SEEK2.

Alternative control strategies and various verification and selection regimes for refinement systems are discussed in chapter 5. This chapter also shows how knowledge base refinement may be viewed as a search problem over a space of knowledge bases.

SEEK2 is a milestone within a more ambitious ongoing research program. Two of the goals of this program are to formulate ever more powerful heuristics and strategic principles for dealing with refinement problems - potentially involving richer rule representation languages. In this work we will exhibit a methodology and an associated metalinguistic framework for facilitating progress in this endeavor. Specifically, in chapter 6 we present a metalanguage for the design and testing of concepts, heuristics, and strategic principles for automatic knowledge base refinement.

Chapter 7 concludes the work with a summary of research significance and possible future directions for research. Certain experiments that provide evidence for the feasibility and validity of the heuristic approach to knowledge base refinement are introduced and discussed in this chapter.

2 Related Research

This chapter is a brief survey of research of relevance to the problem addressed in this work. Depending on how narrow or broad one's scope is, the amount of research of relevance is either very small or very large: if one asks about automatic knowledge base refinement, *as we have defined it here*, there is very little research that has taken this as its primary focus; if, however, one relaxes the assumptions made above in certain ways, or looks at the problem from a broader point of view, then one can see automatic knowledge base refinement as being a special case of automatic knowledge acquisition, and as being related to such AI fields as "learning" and "discovery." Therefore, in each of the subsections below I first show how automatic knowledge base refinement is *conceptually related* to one of these other fields; I then refer to those parts of the existing literature in that field that are of greatest relevance to the proposed research.

First it must be noted a good deal of the research presented here is a direct descendant of the SEEK project of Politakis and Weiss. A discussion of SEEK and its relationship to SEEK2 may be found in [17], and in chapter 4.

2.1 Expert Systems, Knowledge Base Refinement, and Pattern Recognition

In order to avoid misunderstandings concerning our view of knowledge base refinement and the techniques we advocate for doing it, it is worthwhile to briefly draw some important distinctions between what we are doing and approaches to modeling decision-making and problem-solving based on statistical pattern recognition techniques [7].

While our approach makes significant use of some of the key features of statistical pattern recognition work, namely, an emphasis on optimizing the *overall performance* of the classification system, and the use of disjoint sets of cases for training and testing [12], there are important differences. The main difference between our work and statistical pattern recognition approaches to the design and refinement of classification systems, is the use of symbolic representations - exemplified by a knowledge base of rules - as opposed to more traditional mathematical formalisms, e.g., linear vector spaces. Refining rules is simply a very different problem than optimizing a classifier. Of course, this difference is a distinguishing feature of many, if not all, AI approaches in dealing with classification systems.[3]

A related difference between knowledge base refinement and pattern recognition techniques lies in the comparative role and value they each accord to the various components of the expert's knowledge. The goal of knowledge base refinement is not merely to revise a set of rules so that performance will be optimized, it is to *do so in a manner that is likely to meet with the approval of the expert whose knowledge we are trying to capture in constructing an expert system in the first place.* While the expert's *case knowledge* can be said to drive our techniques, without the *initial knowledge base* acquired from the expert, there is simply nowhere to go. Moreover, the *constraints of conservatism*, both the general constraints that we as knowledge engineers feel justified in imposing and the domain-specific constraints the expert may be able to provide, limit the impact that the particular case knowledge we have available to us can have on knowledge base during a refinement session, i.e., in a real sense the initial knowledge base itself is a major determining factor of the direction in which refinement will proceed. The more substantial and reliable the constraints, the less likely it becomes that biased case knowledge can lead us astray. Finally, when a refinement system presents an expert with certain refinement suggestions, not only is the expert the final judge of their validity, this sort of judgment is one that presumably falls within the expert's competence to make.

Pattern recognition, on the other hand, is not limited by such concerns. It is a much more general set of mathematical techniques that seeks to *do whatever can in principle be done, given whatever knowledge is available.* For example, while certain pattern recognition techniques rely on what we call *case knowledge* - which means knowing the important features of cases in general, and having a data base of correctly classified cases - some of them can be used even when no cases with known classification are available, e.g. clustering. Moreover, while additional knowledge beyond case knowledge is welcome and useful, e.g., knowledge of prior or conditional probabilities, pattern recognition can get along without it, and as a practical point, the gathering and validation of such knowledge is not an important part of the methodology of the field. And it is not clear that the ability to make judgments concerning probabilities in a domain is necessarily a part of expertise in a domain, e.g., while it is natural to expect an expert in Rheumatology to be able to judge whether a certain finding is consistent with or indicative of Arthritis, it is much less clear that it falls within *his* expertise to judge the conditional probability of that finding given Arthritis. Given that neither the expert nor the data

---

[3]It is important to note, however, that recent work in the field of *syntactic pattern recognition* (see, for example, [10]) does allow for the use of formalisms, e.g., semantic networks, grammars, etc., that are more usually associated with AI. Moreover, there is a strong analogy between the problems of automating knowledge base refinement and a fundamental learning problem in syntactic pattern recognition, viz., the "grammatical inference" problem [19].

usually available can give us reliable estimates of prior and conditional probabilities, pattern recognition often makes use of techniques that are entirely driven by case knowledge.

There is a difference in the nature of the optimization processes used in pattern recognition and the optimization process in knowledge base refinement. In a typical pattern recognition scenario the optimization of the classifier (or set of classifiers) tends to be a global affair in the following sense. At every point in the process *any and every* coefficient is subject to "refinement"; furthermore, the concept of a radicality measure on refinements has little or no point in mathematical optimization procedures, since adjustment of coefficients is usually the major type of refinement contemplated.

In knowledge base refinement, on the other hand, even ignoring for the moment the assumption that the knowledge base truly represents useful expert knowledge, the very fact that the items in the knowledge base are complex objects, e.g. rules, the components of which can be altered in a wide variety of ways, makes the notion of a radicality ordering on refinements an interesting and rich idea. But when we add on the assumption that the given knowledge base represents useful domain knowledge, it is quite clear that the desire to construct an optimized version under the "constraints of conservatism," is not only a worthwhile thing to do, but is essential to the success of the enterprise. While there are many more refinements than adjusting weights possible in refining knowledge bases, there are also more dangers and liabilities, and hence less willingness to tamper with what is given.

Knowledge base refinement is a "local" optimization problem in the sense that it is assumed that "large" portions of the knowledge base will be left unchanged by the process. While it is true that we want to improve the performance of the knowledge base as a whole, this does not mean that "anything goes." Although we cannot know in advance which portions of the knowledge base will escape refinement, unless of course we have domain-specific directives from the expert on this score, we do insist that a "knowledge base" whose final form is not expected to bear an overwhelming resemblance to the current form, is not one that is ready for refinement. To put the difference in the nature of the optimization processes into a nutshell: in classical pattern recognition techniques the emphasis is on the actual *construction* of an optimal classifier, while in knowledge base refinement the emphasis is on correcting a small number of flaws in a complex structure that is assumed to be largely correct.

2.2 Relation to Automatic Knowledge Acquisition

In contrast to knowledge base refinement, which we view as dealing mainly with modifications to components of existing rules, knowledge acquisition deals with actions intended to bring entirely new rules into the knowledge base. Knowledge base refinement "merges" into knowledge acquisition if we allow refinement operators that increase the number of rules in the knowledge base.

Even within knowledge acquisition, however, one should draw a distinction between what we may call "raw" knowledge acquisition and "contextual" knowledge acquisition, i.e., between the process of acquiring new rules, presumably with the help of an expert, when initially nothing about the concepts used in the new rules is known, and the process of acquiring new rules when one already has some rules containing the same concepts. Knowledge base refinement is thus very closely related to contextual knowledge acquisition, since the former is concerned with refinements to existing knowledge in the context of an existing knowledge base. Knowledge base refinement tends to merge into contextual acquisition, not raw knowledge acquisition. It seems likely that the framework and techniques we find useful in knowledge base refinement will have extensions that are useful for contextual knowledge acquisition.

Relevant work in the field of contextual knowledge acquisition includes Davis' approach to interactive contextual knowledge acquisition [5], and the automated approach of Drastal and Kulikowski to contextual knowledge acquisition, using structural and causal knowledge in conjunction with case knowledge, and raw knowledge acquisition, using only case knowledge [6]. More general knowledge acquisition issues are addressed in [2, 21, 8].

2.3 Relation to Learning

If we agree that a system that improves its performance with respect to its task domain can be said to have learned something, then there is an obvious connection between learning and automatic knowledge base refinement, viz., if S is the automatic refinement system and K is the object-level expert system, then the combined system S+K is one that learns.

There is a deeper sense, however, in which the S+K system is a learning system. While improved performance over time is a *sign* that a system is capable of learning, it is, in my opinion, not a logically sufficient condition for predicating that accolade of a system. Learning, in the deep sense, is the ability of a system to successfully construct or modify representations of some aspect of reality in order to achieve some purpose. Production rule expert systems, whether we regard them as "direct" representations of aspects of the object domain, or as representations of some aspects of an expert's representations of the object domain, are clearly representations of some aspect of reality. An automatic refinement system can be viewed as endowing an expert system with the capacity to modify such representations in the light of empirical evidence in order to achieve a better match with the reality they purport to represent. A consequent improvement in performance may be viewed as evidence that the refinement responsible for it in fact does make the knowledge base a better match to reality.

In terms of traditional AI work in machine learning, the problem of knowledge base refinement may be viewed as a special case of the *concept learning* problem [26]. The knowledge base we start with may be viewed as a system that already has partial descriptions of the concepts that are to be learned. That is, the classificatory categories for the problem domain in question may be thought of as the concepts to be learned, and the rules that conclude them may be thought of as partial description of these concepts. The problem is to refine these descriptions so that a better match with the given case data, or "instances," is obtained.

While the refinement of rules is analogous to the refinement of partial descriptions - indeed many rule refinement operations are identical to concept description construction/refinement operations (see [25]) - this analogy should not be pushed too far. This is especially true for classification systems that deal with uncertainty. Machine learning research in concept learning has focused on applications in which it is natural to assume that it is always possible to know with certainty whether an instance falls under a particular concept. Our work in refinement is partially motivated by the problems that arise in dealing with domains in which this assumption is generally unwarranted , e.g., medical diagnosis. In such domains, a concept description that is not, when considered in isolation, an optimal description, may nevertheless form part of a set of concepts, i.e., the entire knowledge base, that does optimize performance.

Another connection with the area of learning is apparent if we relax assumption 4 (see page 8 above) which concerns the criterion of correctness for knowledge base performance. Suppose that we adopt a criterion of correctness which involves the idea that the *way* in which the expert system reaches its conclusion must meet a given standard, e.g., it must take the most efficient path, or its reasoning must match an expert's. We may further assume that the *control regime* of the object knowledge base is accessible to and modifiable by to the automatic refinement system, i.e., the latter has an understanding of *how* the object expert system uses its knowledge base to reach conclusions. In attempting to maximize performance under these assumptions, a refinement system would be concerned not only with adjustments to the object knowledge base but also with adjustments to the object level control structure [11].[4] Much of the work in learning has been concerned with exactly this question, viz. How can a problem solving system learn to improve its problem solving abilities?

A final connection to research in learning is the idea of applying a knowledge base refinement system to *itself* in order to refine its own rules and associated knowledge for doing knowledge base refinement [24]. Taking the liberty of regarding ourselves as the experts from whom the knowledge has been extracted, we may regard the concepts and heuristics we use in our refinement system as itself an initial "knowledge engineering" knowledge base for the domain of knowledge base refinement. The problem now is to refine this knowledge base into

---

[4]Of course it is possible that the object level control structure is itself partially embodied in its own production rule knowledge base.

a better one. The required data base of cases for this application would be a collection of cases of the following schematic form:

Case Findings:

1) a knowledge base kb, and associated cases
2) the item x in kb that is being considered for refinement
3) the information available to the refinement system concerning the behavior of x over the data base of cases

Conclusion of the knowledge engineering knowledge base:

The refinement operation recommended for x by the refinement system

Expert Conclusion

The action prescribed for this rule by the knowledge engineer/expert in this case. Alternatively, the system could use the results of its own testing as a feedback mechanism, i.e., did the refinement lead to a net gain in this case?

There are two problems with this idea. First, it is extremely doubtful that there is anyone who is really qualified to play the role of the expert in compiling this case knowledge; therefore we would be forced to rely on the purely empirical feedback as mentioned above. Secondly, if the refinement system's heuristics and associated knowledge are poor to begin with, then it seems rather unlikely that they would suggest good experiments for modifying themselves. Assuming that the knowledge engineering knowledge base is pretty good to begin with - this is after all something we assume about the ordinary knowledge bases to be refined - it is conceivable that this approach could yield some worthwhile results of a limited nature but the value of these ends may not justify the cost of the means. This is a possible avenue of future research.

Some of the relevant work in learning includes Mitchell's work on concept and rule learning [27, 28], and recent work by Fu and Buchanan on the learning of metarules for guiding the invocation of object level rules [11].

2.3.1 Explanation-Based Learning and Knowledge Base Refinement

Recent *explanation-based* approaches in machine learning assume that it is possible to *prove* that an instance falls under a concept using a, presumably infallible, *domain theory* [29]. This proof may then be generalized to yield a general concept description. There have been a number variations on this theme [32, 20], including the use of explanation-based techniques for the purpose of rule refinement [33]. All of these explanation-based approaches share one feature: they are *knowledge intensive*, in the sense that they depend upon knowledge - the domain theory - over and above the known instances (cases), the primitive concepts of the domain, and "rules of thumb" that can be acquired from domain experts.

Our approach to knowledge base refinement is designed to be used in conjunction with applications in which such domain theories are either unknown, inherently uncertain or statistical in nature, or too complex to be useful given current technology. For such domains it is either impractical or simply impossible to design a refinement mechanism that generates refinements that are *guaranteed* to be theoretically valid or lead to an improvement in overall performance (even over the training cases). This is why we employ a *heuristic* refinement generation procedure, and why we *test* a candidate refinement for its effect on the *overall* performance of the classification system. However, our approach is compatible with, and can be improved through, the use of knowledge intensive techniques when additional knowledge is available.

In a recent paper Reid Smith et.al [33], discuss an approach to knowledge base refinement for "learning apprentice" systems that makes use of explanation-based learning ideas. In contrast to an expert system, a learning apprentice system is not expected to (initially at least) perform at expert levels of competence, but is supposed to function as an "apprentice" to an expert. Such a system "interactive and gradually refines its knowledge through experience gained during normal problem solving [33]."

While there are certain similarities between the approach discussed in [33] and the approach taken by SEEK2, there are also major differences. For example, a key element in our approach is to generate refinements by looking for patterns over potentially large sets of cases in a case data base; a key element of a learning-apprentice approach is to generate refinements "on the fly" one case at a time, as a problem arises. This fundamental difference makes it seem as though the two approaches are really addressing two different problems.

Forgetting about this fundamental difference, however, there are features in the approach to *refinement generation* described in [33] that we can focus on as a basis of comparison. The learning-apprentice approach relies upon the "justification structure" of a knowledge base rule r in order to generate refinements for r. A justification structure "explicitly records the assumptions and approximations involved in the derivation of a shallow rule [33]," where a "shallow" rule is simply a rule in the expert system knowledge base. Since such a structure encodes knowledge over and above the knowledge in the expert system rules, we may call this approach a *knowledge intensive* approach.

The basic idea is that if we want to refine r in case c, we look at r's justification structure to determine the "assumptions and approximations" that are false or unjustified in the circumstances of c. At that point one looks at ways of altering these implicated elements of the justification structure so that c will be diagnosed correctly. This may be a matter of altering a default assumption concerning a parameter value - in this case the rule r is itself left unchanged - or it may be a change in a component in a "justifier belief" that will "propagate" through the justification structure and entail a change in a component of r.

In terms of the nature of the refinement generation analysis carried out by the knowledge intensive approach, it seems that the goal is to find refinements that *actually* correct the currently misdiagnosed c. In terms of the dimensions of refinement generator classification (see chapter 3) we say that the goal is to generate *exact refinements* with respect to the currently misdiagnosed case. The focus of SEEK2, on the other hand, is to generate refinements that "have a chance" of correcting a certain subset of the current set of misdiagnosed cases, we call such refinements *plausible refinements* (see chapter 3).

As is discussed in chapter 3 the *informal* notion of the *plausibility* of a refinement to some piece of knowledge involves a number of aspects, one of which is the idea of the *expected empirical utility* of the refinement, i.e., how great an improvement in the empirical adequacy of the knowledge base do we expect to see by making a certain refinement? Another aspect of the informal notion is raised by the question of the *theoretical acceptability* of the refinement, i.e., does a refinement "make sense" in terms of the underlying domain theory? In SEEK2 we attempt to increase the likelihood of generating plausible refinements, in the second sense, by adopting a conservative strategy. Also, at various places throughout the work we indicate ways in which certain varieties of domain-specific metaknowledge would contribute towards this aim.

It is clear that the approach taken in [33] focuses on the generation of refinements that are plausible in the sense that they have theoretical acceptability. Since the SEEK2 approach deals mainly with *one* aspect of the informal notion of plausibility, and the knowledge-intensive approach deals mainly with *another* aspect of this notion, there is no incompatibility in their fundamental models of refinement. Since the ideal goal of a refinement system is to produce refinements that meet all the criteria associated with the informal notion of plausibility, we would expect an "ideal" refinement system to incorporate aspects of both approaches.

2.4 Relation to Discovery

To my mind, discovery is what happens when someone learns something that is, up until that time, unknown (relative to an appropriate reference class of intelligent agents). Therefore, having established a connection between automatic refinement and learning, we have *ipso facto* established a connection with discovery. While discovery of object level knowledge is not the primary goal of an automatic refinement system, it seems likely that the more sophisticated the refinement system is, the more likely it is to discover connections among object level features that have hitherto escaped the attention of experts, and hence the more likely it is that the system will make discoveries.

Relevant work done under the rubric of discovery includes Lenat's approach to discovery and modification of heuristics [24], and the work of Langley, Bradshaw, and Simon concerning "discovery" of laws stating empirical regularities in natural science domains [22].

2.5 Summary

Previous research on knowledge base refinement, in the sense defined here, has been limited. Refining a large scale knowledge base is clearly a complex undertaking. Related empirical machine learning work in concept learning has concentrated on the learning of entire rules from case data and hierarchical descriptions [26], rather than the incremental refinement of rules acquired from a human expert. Because numerous expert systems are actively under development, in recent years there has been increased interest in more immediate results in easing the knowledge acquisition task. While restricted to relatively simple knowledge bases and representations, a few papers have appeared on empirical refinement [23, 41].

The forms of empirical analysis described in this work do not exclude other forms of analysis that are useful in knowledge acquisition. For example, systems that employ concepts and strategies for extracting domain knowledge via interaction with an expert have seen renewed interest among researchers [5, 21, 8]. In addition, researchers working on the Programmer's Apprentice have reported some progress in improving knowledge acquisition in programming tasks by combining algorithmic fragments stored in software libraries with intelligent editing facilities [38]. While these efforts may be viewed as alternative techniques for knowledge acquisition, they may also be viewed as complementary to an empirical approach to refinement.

3 Formal Elements of Knowledge Base Refinement

In this chapter we will be concerned with formal issues that must be addressed in the design and construction of both automatic refinement systems, and the design and construction of meta-level systems for the specification of the former.

The key questions may be posed as follows: What sort of thing is a refinement?, How are they specified?, and What sorts of properties do they have? We will see that, given a grammar for a rule representation language, refinements may be viewed as transformational operators on the parse-trees accepted by the grammar. This analysis will also lead to a canonical form for specifying generic refinement operators. We then discuss some of the important well known semantic properties of such operators, e.g., the notion of generalization and specialization. After this, semantic properties that are crucial from the point of view of knowledge base refinement are discussed and, as far as possible, defined, i.e., the ideas of *plausibility* and *radicality*.

3.1 Formal Account of Refinement Operators

We can think of the rules in a knowledge base as formal objects whose syntactic structure is totally defined by their parse-trees in a grammar for the rule representation language we are employing. We may then think of refinements as *operators that map complete parse-trees into complete parse-trees*, similar to Chomsky's transformational operators [3].

3.1.1 The Rule Representation Language

To carry out this program we need to decide on a rule representation language. In order to keep the discussion at the most theoretically useful level of generality, our policy is to work with a *canonical* rule representation language, rather than any particular expert system rule language. The grammar for this language is given in appendix III.

There are two points to be made concerning our canonical language. First of all, it has the expressive power of first-order logic. The second point is that it contains what we call *specialized surface forms*. These are forms that, logically speaking, do not increase the expressive power of the language, but that represent convenient short-hand notations for certain useful constructs. Experience has shown that specialized surface forms may not only be more readable than their corresponding "deep" forms, but also sometimes have *naturally corresponding, useful, and well-understood refinement operations* associated with them. In such cases we prefer to incorporate the specialized form in our rule representation, rather than insist on a translation that would necessitate complicating the definition of the corresponding refinement operations.

To illustrate these remarks let us consider choice-components, a type of rule component used in EXPERT. A choice-component has the following syntax: **[<Choice-number>: <choice-list>]**, where the *choice-number* is a positive integer, and *choice-list* is list of finding/hypothesis components. A choice-component is satisfied just in case at least *choice-number* of the components in its *choice-list* are satisfied. As we shall see, there are a number of natural generic refinement operations associated with such components, e.g., one can raise or lower the choice-number.

Another useful surface form allowed by our canonical language is the notion of a *range*. Ranges are of two sorts: 1) numerical ranges associated with findings that correspond to a quantity, and 2) confidence ranges for hypotheses. Thus, for example, the form **(Temp [0:50])** can be used to represent the proposition "the temperature is between 0 and 50." The form **(Battery-is-Dead [.5:1])** can be used to represent the proposition "the hypothesis that the battery is dead is supported to a degree between .5 and 1." Again there are natural generic refinement operators associated with such components, e.g., raise or lower the value of one of the range boundaries.

3.1.2 Generic Refinement Operators

Figure 3-1 (p. 33) shows how the refinement operation of altering a choice-number can be viewed as a transformational rule on parse-trees.

An important distinction between refinement operators has to do with the way in which the parse-tree transformation defining the refinement is specified. If the transformation is specified without reference to any nodes in the parse tree *containing terminal symbols*, then the operator is *generic*, otherwise it is *non-generic*. (Note that symbols for logical operators and punctuation that are special symbols required by the language, e.g., '&', ':', '[', etc., are not terminal symbols in the sense we have in mind here.)

To clarify this definition we define a *complete rule-context* as a sequence of non-terminal, and possibly terminals symbols, i.e., symbols actually belonging to the canonical language, such that there is a parse-tree (possibly incomplete) with these symbols as its tip or leaf nodes. See figure 3-2 (p. 34) for an example of a complete rule-context and its corresponding parse-tree. Now a *rule-context* in general, is either a complete rule-context, or a sequence of symbols that can be obtained from a complete rule-context by removal of symbols corresponding to certain tip nodes in the parse-tree for the complete rule-context. See figure 3-2 (p. 34) for an

RULE

[2: p [.9:1], q, r, d [0:69], s] & (F a) $\longrightarrow$ C [.4]

Parse Tree & Transformation

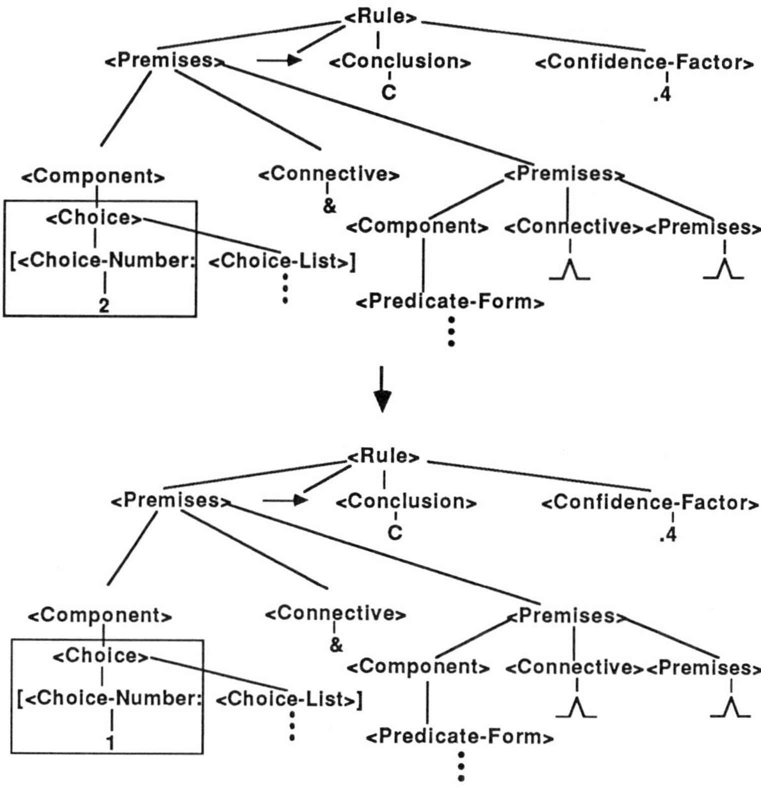

Figure 3-1: Refinements As Transformational Operators

example.

Thus instead of viewing refinement operators as transformations on parse-trees we may view them as transformations on rule-contexts. To specify such a transformation it is usually sufficient to exhibit the initial and resulting rule contexts, together with a set of conditions that define the way in which the elements in the two contexts are related as a result of the transformation (see appendix II). Now we say that a refinement is *generic* if the *initial and resulting rule-contexts* contain no terminal symbols of the canonical language, otherwise it is *non-generic*.

In general we work only with generic refinement operators since their conditions of applicability in no depend upon the literal content of a specific knowledge base. However some

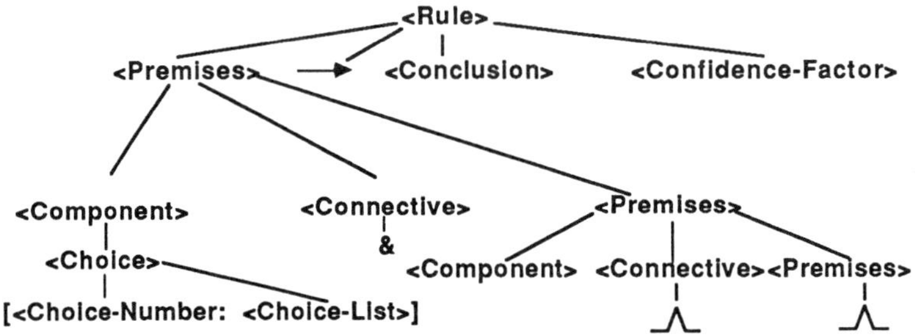

Corresponding Complete-Rule-Context

[<Choice-Number>:<Choice-List>]&<Component> → <Conclusion> ><Confidence-Factor>

A Rule-Context Derived From The Above

. . .[<Choice-Number>:<Choice-List>]. . . → <Conclusion> ><Confidence-Factor>

Figure 3-2: Rule-Contexts

non-generic refinements involve symbols of such wide use that they could, for all intents and purposes, be viewed as being generic. For example, consider the refinement operation:

```
...(= <term> <term>)...  →  ...(> <term> <term>)...
```

This transformation is specified using the terminal symbols "=" and ">," but it is clearly one that has potential applicability to many knowledge bases.

3.1.3 Primitive vs Complex Refinement Operations

In order to complete our formalization of the notion of refinement it is necessary to actually designate a set of *primitive refinement operators* for our language, such that for every possible rule the set of all possible refinements to that rule can be generated by the sequential application of primitive refinement operators. I have specified such a set of primitive operations only for a subset of the canonical language (see appendix II), since, at this time, our research deals only with a subset of this language.

The primitive refinement operations we will be using have some nice properties that we will discuss later. For now I want to point out that these operations appear to have a truly "primitive" or "atomic" nature, in the sense that they all involve making a single modification to a single rule component. More complex changes to a rule would involve either application of a composition of two or more operators in tandem, or, equivalently, the sequential application of two or more operators. A particular refinement operation γ will be said to be an *nth-order* refinement operation, for some $n \geq 1$, where n is the number of primitive operators used in γ. A first-order refinement system, such as SEEK2, will suggest and attempt refinements operations all of which involve the application of a single primitive operator.

3.1.4 Operators vs Operations

For the purposes of the discussion below it is important to draw a distinction between refinement *operators* and refinement *operations*. An operator is a general abstract mathematical object which may or may not have *parameters*. A parameter is a variable that must be given a value before the operator can actually be applied to an object. An operation is an instance of the application of an operator. For example the operator that raises the value of a numerical boundary is parameterized by a real variable which is intended to be assigned the value of the increment to the original value, or simply the new value. Application of this operator to a particular rule component with a specific increment is an example of an operation.

All the *semantic properties* we shall discuss are, in the first instance, properties of refinement *operations*. However, when a refinement *operator* is such that every one of its instances possesses a certain property, then we say that the operator also possesses the property. In section 3.2 we deal with properties that do apply to operators in this sense; in section 3.3 we deal with properties that can only be predicated of *operations*.

3.1.5 Expressive Completeness

As we shall see in section 5.5.1, every knowledge base implicitly defines a space of possible refined versions of itself. To put the point in a somewhat different and abbreviated way, given a rule representation language, L, *together* with sets of predicates corresponding to findings, F, and hypotheses (including endpoints), H, one can precisely define the set of all knowledge bases that can be formed in L using the items in F and H as the basic building blocks in the rules; we call this set of knowledge bases *kb-space*. A given knowledge base is represented by a unique point in kb-space.

A set of refinement operators O will be said to be *expressively complete* iff for any two distinct points in an arbitrary kb-space, kb_1 and kb_2, there is a sequence of operations drawn from O that transforms kb_1 into kb_2.

The current version of SEEK2 does not employ an expressively complete set of refinement operations.

3.2 Semantic Properties of Refinement Operators

An important semantic trichotomy exists among refinement operations: any refinement operation must be either a *generalization*, *specialization*, or neither of the two.

Intuitively, a generalization refinement to a rule is one that makes it "easier" for that rule's premises to be satisfied in any given case, or one that makes the rule reach a "stronger" conclusion on the basis of exactly the same premises. In precise terms, for our purposes a generalization refinement operator is one whose application always results in a rule being transformed into one of its generalizations, where in order for a rule **r′** to be a generalization of another **r** it must at least be the case that i) it is logically impossible for the premises of **r** to be satisfied without the premises of **r′** being satisfied, and ii) the confidence factor for **r′** is equal to or greater than the confidence factor of **r**.

This definition implies that if two rules are completely identical except for their confidence factors then the one with the greater confidence factor is a generalization of the other. This accords with the idea that a refinement that keeps a rule's premises constant but allows it to reach a stronger conclusion in the logical sense is to be considered a generalization. This implication is warranted, of course, only if having a higher confidence factor is indeed consistently interpreted as meaning that the conclusion is more strongly warranted; but that is one of our assumptions.

Intuitively, a specialization refinement to a rule is one that makes it "harder" for that rule's premises to be satisfied in any given case, or one that makes the rule reach a "weaker" conclusion on the basis of exactly the same premises. In precise terms, for our purposes a specialization refinement operator is one that *always* transforms a rule into one of its specializations, where in order for a rule **r′** to be a specialization of another **r** it must at least be the case that i) it is logically impossible for **r′** to be satisfied without **r** being satisfied, and ii) the confidence factor for **r′** is equal to or less than the confidence factor of **r**.

It is easy to give examples of refinement operations that are neither generalizations nor specializations. For example, suppose a rule has a component of the following form:

$$\ldots(\text{Predicate}\ldots\langle\text{constant}_1\rangle\ldots)\ldots \rightarrow \ldots(\text{Predicate}\ldots\langle\text{constant}_2\rangle\ldots)\ldots$$

An instance of this "constant switching" operation would be changing (F a) to (F b). There are no interesting logical relationships between these two forms *per se*, so the operator is neither a generalization nor a specialization operator. Yet one can imagine instances, *that can be specified in domain-independent fashion*, in which such a refinement would be reasonable. For example we may mistakenly start out believing that a's possession of the property F is important in inferring some hypothesis that has *observable consequences* O. By examination of cases we find, however, that there are many cases in which a is observed to have F but O is not observed. On the other hand, in every case that O is observed, b is also observed to have F. In the situation described we have case evidence that (F a) should be changed to (F b), and it would not be unreasonable for a refinement system to offer this refinement suggestion if it led to an increase in empirical adequacy. Moreover, in light of the description I have just given, it is plausible to assert that a general heuristic concerning the conditions under which this refinement should be attempted can be formally specified.

Our work to date has focused on primitive refinements that are either generalizations and specializations, and complex refinements that can be formed by composition of these primitives. Focusing on these two fundamental modes of refinement has been fruitful, because we have an intuitive general understanding of what sorts of "faults" in rule or component behavior call for the application of a generalization or specialization refinement (see chapter 4). However, as the second example above indicates, there is good reason to hope that detailed investigations into the semantics of certain operations in the third category may yield useful results.

3.2.1 Rule Addition and Deletion

Operations that either add a single rule or delete a single rule from the knowledge base can also be viewed as parse-tree transformations: rule addition maps the null parse-tree into a parse-tree for the rule in question; rule deletion maps the parse-tree for the rule in question into the null parse-tree.

Intuitively, addition/deletion of a rule for a conclusion H is typically a generalization/specialization operation with respect to H. To accommodate this intuition, the definitions of generalization/specialization given above (p. 36) must be modified. To see this, suppose that the knowledge base consists of the single rule a $\rightarrow$ H [.3] Now suppose we add the rule b $\rightarrow$ H [.3]. Since a and b are logically independent, no generalization/specialization relationships hold between the two rules. Intuitively, however, adding the second rule is a generalization. But a generalization of what? To put it in somewhat vague terms: it is a generalization *of the set of conditions under which the knowledge base will assert a particular conclusion*, viz., H [.3]. Under this interpretation, rule addition operations are generalizations of the conclusions they reach; similarly rule deletion operations are specializations of the set of conditions under which their conclusions will be reached. The notion of the "set of conditions under which the knowledge base will assert a conclusion" can be made precise [15, 16]. However, since this work is more concerned with rule transformation rather than rule addition/deletion, the definitions given above are sufficient for our purposes.

3.3 Semantic Properties of Refinement Operations

Informally speaking, an important semantic property of any contemplated refinement operation is whether or not it is a "good" refinement with respect to a given knowledge base and data base of cases. Obviously one can define a "good" refinement as one that corrects some error in the knowledge base, or that corrects currently misdiagnosed cases; but this is a useless definition from an operational point of view. For a semantic property of refinement operators to be useful in the *actual generation* of refinements, it must be one that a) can be evaluated by the refinement system itself, and b) does not involve simply testing the refinement for its effect on the known cases.

In this section we will formulate a precise, operationally significant sense in which a refinement may be said to have a certain degree of *plausibility*.

3.3.1 Aspects of the Informal Notion of Plausibility

There are several aspects to the "common sense" notion of plausibility. First, there is the degree to which the refinement is *theoretically acceptable* given our (i.e., the experts') current understanding of the domain. This involves the issue of the meaning or *semantic content* of the rules in the knowledge base insofar as they are representations of laws or facts in the object domain. To determine whether, and to what degree, a contemplated refinement is plausible, in this sense, generally requires a much richer representation of domain laws, processes, etc. than is contained in a knowledge base. For this reason we do not deal with this sense of plausibility in this work[5].

Secondly, there is the degree to which the refinement is likely to improve the empirical adequacy of the knowledge base. In ordinary and scientific usage, the fact that a refinement to a theory corrects or is believed to have a chance of correcting some currently incorrect predictions of the theory, is *in itself* taken as evidence of the plausibility of the refinement. Indeed, it can happen that a "refinement" that can explain or predict empirically verifiable results which would otherwise remain unexplained, will tend to be adopted no matter how *a priori* implausible it seems on the basis of current theory, e.g., Einstein's special theory of relativity. It is this aspect of plausibility, what we may call the *expected empirical utility* of a refinement, that we are most concerned with in this work, and that we will be defining below.

There is, however, a third aspect to the common sense idea of plausibility that must concern us. This is the degree to which a refinement represents a departure from what is currently believed to be an acceptable theory, or law. This is what we have termed the *radicality* of a

---

[5]The approach to refinement discussed in [33] would seem to provide a way of capturing this aspect of plausibility.

refinement. We have already seen that the operational goal of knowledge base refinement (for expert system knowledge bases) is to improve the empirical adequacy of a knowledge base under the constraints of conservatism (see chapter 1). One of the constraints of conservatism is to prefer less radical refinements to more radical refinements, other things being equal. How general intuitions as well as domain-specific metaknowledge concerning radicality can be captured will be discussed below.

3.3.2 Expected Empirical Utility of A Refinement Operation

The plausibility of a refinement is directly proportional to its expected empirical utility, where the latter is the number of currently misdiagnosed cases that the refinement *has a chance* of correcting. In order to formulate an operational notion of plausibility, we must therefore understand exactly what is meant by the idea of a refinement's "having a chance" of correcting a case.

3.3.2.1 On-Target Refinement Operations: Intuitive Picture

Given any knowledge base kb, a case m currently misdiagnosed by kb, and any refinement γ to one or more rules in kb, the incorporation of γ in kb will either cause kb to correct its diagnosis for m or not. Talk of γ's *having a chance* of correcting m is meaningful, therefore, only when one brings another term into the relation, viz., what is known (by the relevant agent or system) concerning the state of affairs involving the misdiagnosis. In other words, the question 'Does γ have a chance of correcting m?' is meaningful only when posed in relation to a body of knowledge (or beliefs) concerning the relevant r-situation, and since different agents or systems may possess distinct knowledge concerning the *same* r-situation, the answer to the question may vary from system to system.

Let C be the data base of cases. We may think of <kb,C> as a "combined system" that can be in any one of a number of completely specified states called *microstates*. A formal account of these will be given below. For the time being it suffices to think of a microstate as being a "complete" characterization of the behavior of every rule and rule-component in kb vis-a-vis every case in C, i.e., the behavior of any item or combination of items in kb relative to any case in C can be deduced from the information in the microstate.

The knowledge that a system has concerning an r-situation <R,M> - where R contains those rules in the knowledge base that are suspected of causing the misdiagnosed cases in M - will be called the system's *View* of the r-situation. Such a body of knowledge will be thought of as specifying a *macrostate* of the combined system <kb,C>. Again these will be defined formally below. For the time being it suffices to think of a macrostate as being a *partial specification* of the actual microstate of <kb,C>. In other words, in general, being in a macrostate is consistent with being in any one of a number of *accessible* microstates.

Given a view V of <R,M>, let us designate the set of microstates accessible relative to V as $\mu(V)$. Relative to V, a refinement γ to R will be said to be *On-target* with respect to mcases$\subseteq$M if and only if there is at least one microstate $\sigma \in \mu(V)$ such that, if σ is the actual microstate of the <kb,C> system , the refinement γ corrects every case in mcases. Thus, for γ to have a chance of correcting a case m, is for γ to be On-Target with respect to m (relative to the system's view).

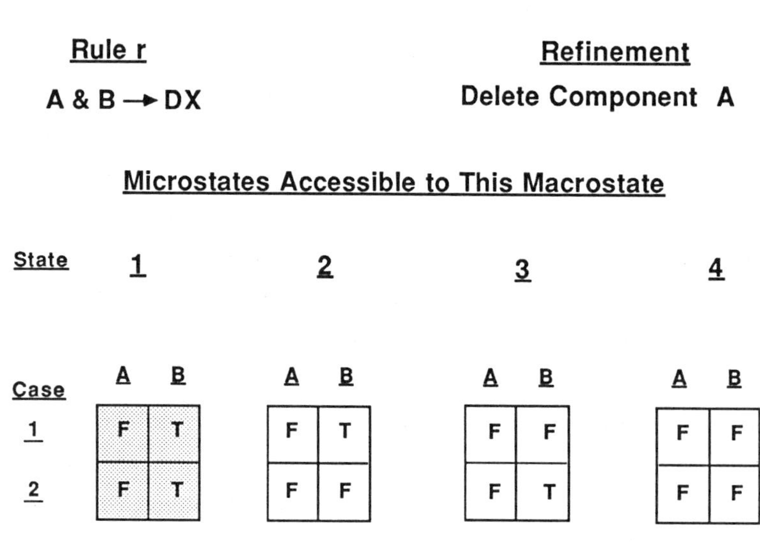

Figure 3-3: The On-Target Relation

A simple example will help in drawing an intuitive picture of these notions. The reader should refer to figure 3-3 for this example. Let kb and R consist of a single rule r, as illustrated (we ignore confidence factors in this example). Let C and M consist of two (misdiagnosed) cases, 1 and 2, whose correct conclusion DX is also the conclusion of r. In addition to this information, assume that the system's view of this r-situation contains only the information that the first component of r is unsatisfied in both cases. The accessible microstates for <kb,C> are as diagramed in figure 3-3. Note that while there is a microstate, number 4, in which deletion of component A from r will result in no gain, there is also a microstate, number 1, in which this refinement will correct both cases. Intuitively, from the system's point of view, this refinement has a chance of correcting these cases because, relative to the system's view, microstate 1 is accessible (can obtain). We say that deletion of component A from r is on-target with respect to these cases. (Note that deletion of component B from r is *not* on-target for either case, and note that the system can *know* this on the basis of the information in its view.)

A refinement γ is said to be *exact* with respect to mcases$\subseteq$M if *every* microstate that is accessible relative to V is one in which application of γ causes every case in mcases to be diagnosed correctly by the knowledge base. Given an r-situation <R,M> and a view V, the set of refinements that are exact is a subset of the set of refinements that are On-target. This work is concerned only with the generation of On-Target refinements.[6]

3.3.3 On-Target Refinement Operations: Formal Explication

This section shows how the intuitive picture drawn in the preceding section can be justified by means of precise mathematical constructions. This section may be skipped without loss of continuity.

3.3.3.1 R-Phase Space and Microstates

First we need to define the notion of a microstate of the system <kb,C>. We shall introduce a mathematical construct called *r-phase space*. A microstate will be any point in this space.

Assuming that kb does not vary, a point in the r-phase space corresponding to the microstate of the system <kb,C> is determined by specifying the value of every *feature* for every case in the data base of cases. By a feature we mean the "real world" fact or quantity that determines the value of some finding component in the knowledge base. For example, if KB contains a finding component of the form *temperature of patient in range 100...103*, then the corresponding feature will be a quantity corresponding to the given patient's temperature. True/false finding components, such as, *Patient has swollen hands*, correspond to features that take on the value 1, if the feature obtains, a value of 0 if the feature is known not to obtain, and some designated third value if it is not known whether the feature obtains or not. Formally, if there are m features f_i, $1 \leq i \leq m$, and n cases, then the dimensionality of r-phase space is $(m+1)\times n$, where the increment in the feature count represents the feature corresponding to the stored expert's conclusion of a case k (what we call the PDX(k) in RM), and will be designated f_0^k. A point in r-phase space (a *microstate*) will then have the following form:

---

[6]See [15, 16] for recent work by the author which indicates that exact refinement generation is sometimes feasible and effective for fairly complex "real world" knowledge bases.

$$\langle kb, f_0^1, \ldots, f_i^j, \ldots, f_m^n \rangle$$

where the subscript is an index on the features, and the superscript is an index on the cases.

As we said above, the microstate of the <kb,C> system is supposed to be a complete characterization of the system. The definition of microstates given has this property in virtue of the fact that all satisfaction properties of a knowledge base are determined once an initial set of findings is posited as input.

For later purposes it will be useful to define the notion of a *feature-vector corresponding to a case* [7]. Given a microstate specification σ, as above, and a case with index k, then the feature-vector corresponding to this case is given by the following "sub-vector" of σ:

$$\langle f_1^k, \ldots, f_m^k \rangle$$

and will be denoted by the notation $\mathbf{f}(\sigma,k)$.

Note that this account may be generalized to deal with knowledge bases that employ the full power of the predicate calculus by associating a distinct feature to every object in the domain of discourse when necessary. For example, if the knowledge base contains a finding component of the form *Patient x has temperature in range 100...103*, then for every "patient object" in the domain of discourse there is a feature that corresponds to the temperature of that patient. In general, we may presume that the domain of discourse is finite. However, even if the domain of discourse is infinite, the current approach will still be applicable.

We should note that the account given here is essentially an application of some of the basic ideas of statistical mechanics (for example, see [35]; these are ideas that are also important in information theory). Given a macrostate, we may think of the number of microstates accessible to it as a measure of its *entropy*. The less (more) we know about the microstate of the r-system, the more (less) accessible microstates there are, and therefore the higher (lower) the entropy. Clearly higher (lower) entropy views will generate a greater (fewer) number of on-target refinements.

3.3.3.2 Specifying Macrostates: Intuitive Picture

A macrostate encapsulates a certain body of knowledge concerning an r-situation. We may think of a macrostate involving a particular r-situation as being expressed by the *values of certain functions* as applied to the given r-situation; we will call these *r-functions*. In other words, the r-functions in question are generally applicable to any r-situation that might be encountered by the refinement system, and the knowledge that the system will gather concerning any r-situation can be no greater than the knowledge expressed by the application of these r-functions to the r-situation. While a single system's knowledge-gathering capabilities, and hence its associated set of r-functions, are fixed, one system's knowledge-gathering capacity and depth of analysis may be greater than another's. This difference would be mirrored by the relative power embodied in the two differing sets of r-functions associated with the two agents.

In order to say precisely what the *content* of any *possible* r-function can be, yet still maintain the requisite degree of generality and flexibility, one must specify certain *primitive r-functions* and *primitive operations for combining them*, i.e., one must specify a *metalanguage* for the construction of such functions. An r-function will be any function that can be constructed from the primitive r-functions by means of the primitive operations. Primitive operations are taken from logic, simple set theoretic operations, arithmetic, and certain algorithmic constructs. The primitive r-functions used in RM are described in appendix I; their use is demonstrated throughout chapter 4, and they are discussed in detail in chapter 6. This discussion is not repeated here; for present purposes it suffices to assume that a sufficiently rich metalanguage for r-function construction is a given.

Let Φ be the set of r-functions associated with a refinement system. By the notation $\Phi(<R,M>)$ we designate the act of applying every $\phi \in \Phi$ to every possible argument for ϕ in the r-situation <R,M>, as well as the collection of resulting values. We call this collection of values the refinement system's *view* of the r-situation, and we call Φ the *viewfinder*.

3.3.3.3 Microstates Accessible to A Macrostate

Let $V=\Phi(<R,M>)$ be a refinement system's view of a particular r-situation. V may contain objects of many different sorts, e.g., numbers, sets of objects, sequences, etc. However for the purposes of analysis it is most useful to view each $v \in V$ as a *proposition* that expresses the information yielded by the corresponding application of the r-function in question. For example, if f is an r-function on pairs <r,C> - where r is a rule and C is a set of cases - and f returns the number of cases in C in which r is satisfied, then ordinarily f returns a number as its value. But we may view it as returning a proposition P of the form, "The number of cases in C in which r is satisfied is n." V as a whole, therefore, may be regarded as a collection of propositions concerning the objects in the knowledge base and the data base of cases.

Similar remarks apply to microstates: the elements of a microstate can be regarded as representing propositions concerning the values of features in cases (including the expert's conclusion).

Given a $v \in V$ and a microstate σ, there are two possibilities of interest: the values of the features in σ are consistent with the truth of v or they are not. For example if v is the proposition that a (non-numerical) finding component c is unsatisfied in case m, then microstates in which the feature corresponding to the value of this finding in case m has the value 1 (true) are inconsistent with the truth of v; all other microstates are consistent with the truth of v.

A microstate σ is *accessible relative to a view* V if and only if σ is consistent with the truth of the set of $v \in V$, otherwise σ is *inaccessible* relative to V.

Before defining the On-target relation it will be useful to discuss some preliminaries. We define the notion of an *endpoint-vector* as follows. Assume the set of endpoints, DX, of the domain knowledge base is enumerated in some fixed order, i.e., $dx_1, \ldots dx_n$. Then an endpoint-vector is a vector of confidence-factors of length n. Intuitively, the *i*th entry in an endpoint-vector corresponding to a case m is the confidence accorded to dx_i by the knowledge base in case m. We may therefore regard a knowledge base kb as defining a *partial function* from feature-vectors to *endpoint-vectors*: let **f** be a feature-vector, and let **e** be an endpoint-vector; then we say that kb(**f**)=**e** if and only if running kb over the data represented by **f** results in final hypothesis confidence factors for the endpoints identical to the values in **e**.

Let V be a view of a given r-situation <R,M>, where $R \subseteq KB$. Let $\mu(V)$ denote the set of microstates accessible relative to V, and let σ be a variable over the members of $\mu(V)$. Let γ be a refinement operation involving (only) rules in R, and let KB′ be the knowledge base that results *after* application of γ to R. Let $m \in M$, and let **f**(σ,m) be the feature-vector corresponding to case m in microstate σ. Then γ is *On-target with respect to m* if and only if *there is a* $\sigma \in \mu(V)$ such that the endpoint-vector **e**=KB′(**f**(σ,m)) accords the highest confidence to PDX(m); if γ is not on-target with respect to m then we say that it is *off-target* with respect to m. A refinement γ is On-target with respect to a *set* of mcases$\subseteq$M if and only if *there is a* $\sigma \in \mu(V)$ such that *for every* $m \in$ mcases the endpoint-vector **e**=KB′(**f**(σ,m)) accords the highest confidence to PDX(m). Note that in the preceding definition the universal quantifier falls inside the scope of the existential quantifier, i.e., in interpreting the definition one should imagine that we first fix σ to refer to a particular microstate and then we would show that γ will correct each m given its feature-vector **f**(σ,m) in σ.

In words, we say the relation On-target(γ,V,M) is true if and only if there is a microstate σ accessible to V relative to which application of γ to kb will correct every case in M.

3.3.3.4 Accuracy of Viewfinders

It is necessary to explicitly state an assumption concerning viewfinders that will be made throughout this work. The assumption is that viewfinders always yield *truths*. A viewfinder may not tell us everything there is to known about an r-system, but what it does tell us is true.

This assumption can be formally expressed within our framework as follows. Let V=Φ(<R,M>), be a view, and let σ be the microstate of the r-system. Then we say that V is *accurate* if and only if $\sigma \in \mu(V)$, where $\mu(V)$ is the set of microstates accessible to V. To say that $\sigma \in \mu(V)$ is just another way of saying that what V tells us is consistent with the actual state of the r-system. We will say that a *viewfinder* Φ is *accurate* if and only if for any r-situation <R,M>, Φ(<R,M>) is accurate.

Obviously truth is a virtue. The reason it is worth mentioning is the following. Let $\sigma \in \mu(V)$, then if γ is any refinement operation on R that corrects mcases$\subseteq$M, then On-target(γ,V,mcases) is true. The proof is trivial: On-target(γ,V,mcases) is true if there is an $\beta \in \mu(V)$ such that for every m$\in$mcases, KB′(**f**(β,m)) produces an endpoint-vector with CDX(m)=PDX(m); but by hypothesis σ is just such a microstate. Intuitively, what this result says is that if V is an accurate view of <R,M>, then if we confine our attention to refinements that are on-target with respect to V we don't have to worry that we might be missing some refinement to R that has a chance of improving empirical adequacy. To put it differently, if a view is *not* accurate then even if we generate and test *all* refinements which *seem* (relative to the view) to have a chance of improving empirical adequacy, we may miss some refinements that do lead to an improvement.

We have therefore proven the following result, which we state here for future reference:

Let Φ be an accurate viewfinder, let <R,M> be an r-situation, let γ be a refinement operation on R that corrects every case in mcases$\subseteq$M.

Then On-target(γ,Φ(<R,M>),mcases) is true.

3.4 Radicality and Plausibility

The basic task of a refinement system is to offer refinements that are known to improve empirical adequacy and that are likely to meet with expert approval. Since the expert has already assented to the rules in the knowledge base, we assume, other things being equal, that he will prefer refinements that tend to preserve the knowledge base in its current form. The radicality of a refinement operation is a property that tells us how great a departure a refined version of a rule (or a kb) is from the initial version.

3.4.1 Radicality Metrics

As we mentioned in chapter 1, a radicality metric on the space of all refined versions of a knowledge base kb can be formally defined. The problem is that many different radicality metrics may be defined, and there is no one of these that is the "correct" one. Moreover, it is not clear what sort of information, even domain-specific information, one can use to make a selection of radicality metric in a particular instance.

On the positive side, there are two points to be made concerning the possibility of arriving at a useful version of such a metric. First, one can specify several natural "axioms" that it would seem reasonable for *any* such metric to obey, e.g., if the radicality of γ=β, then the radicality of γ^{-1}=β, where γ^{-1} is the inverse operation to γ. Secondly, there is a function that obeys these axioms and that can always be used as a metric, viz., the number of primitive operators in γ can be taken as a measure of the radicality of γ. Note that this metric is of no use in doing pure first-order refinement, since it will assign every first-order refinement a radicality of 1.

In any event, if a radicality metric, Rad(γ) is given, then one may use it together with On-target to form a measure of plausibility as follows. Suppose that γ is on-target with respect to the cases μ. Then the *plausibility of* γ is defined as the ratio $|\mu|$/Rad(γ). Intuitively this number may be interpreted as the the *estimated number of cases gained per unit change.*

3.4.2 Radicality Operationalized for First-Order Refinement

The notion of a radicality metric is not only a theoretical ideal, it also has limited practical value in knowledge base refinement. The fact is that if there is some reason to believe that a refinement γ has a chance of correcting a large number of cases, then γ should be tested and, if it does indeed have a dramatic impact on the empirical adequacy of the knowledge base, the system should, at the very least, report this information. This seems to be a desirable mode of operation regardless of the radicality of γ.

Depending on the strategic configuration of the refinement system, radicality information may be useful at various "decision points" or perhaps not at all. A system that does not tentatively incorporate refinements, what we call a *ground-zero* system (see chapter 5), may have no use for such information, since it never has to make a decision concerning incorporation of refinements. A system that does tentatively incorporate refinements, what we call a *generational system* (see chapter 5), e.g. SEEK2, can use radicality information to decide among competing refinements that are known to yield an improvement in empirical adequacy. (In SEEK2 radicality comes into play only when competing refinements yield an *equal* net gain in performance.) We now describe a general scheme for operationalizing radicality for first-order systems.

Given a set of primitive generic refinement operations for (a subset of) our canonical language, we specify a *partial ordering* on these operators corresponding to our (qualitative) intuitions concerning the relation *operator x is more radical than operator y.* Such an ordering - in fact, the one used in SEEK2 - is exhibited in figure 3-4. If x and y are two refinement operators, then if a path can be traced *down* from x to y then y is *more radical* than x; if the reverse is true then x is more radical than y; if neither is true then x and y are noncomparable according to this relation. For us noncomparability means that, other things being equal, there is no reason to prefer one operator over the other in terms of radicality, and we say that the

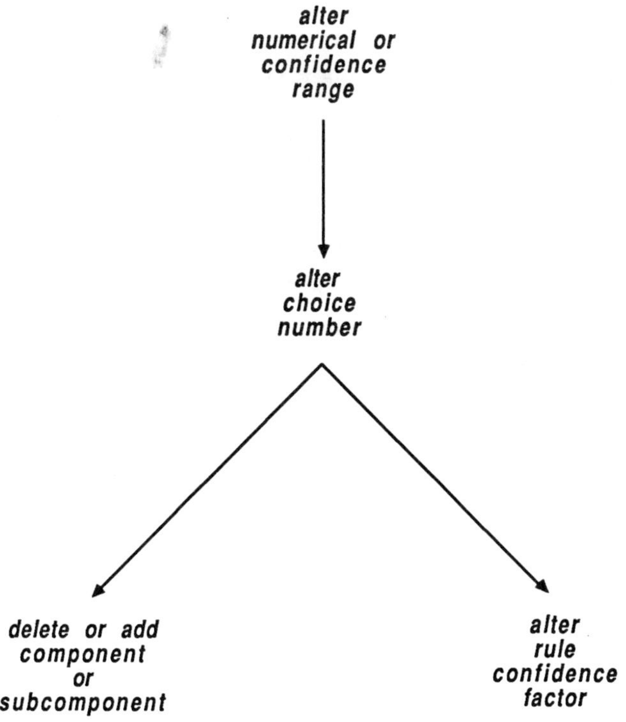

Figure 3-4: A Partial Radicality Ordering

operators are at the same level of radicality.

Note that the partial ordering is an ordering on *operators*. Thus, from the point of view of this ordering alone, there is nothing to distinguish two distinct applications of a confidence raising operator, even if one application involves a greater increase than another. Therefore, for operators that do involve such numerical parameters, a quantitative radicality ordering is imposed on the corresponding *operations* according to the size of the parameter. For example, a confidence increase of .3 is more radical than a confidence increase of .2.

As mentioned above, in SEEK2 the radicality orderings just described come into play only when two or more refinement operations have been found to yield an equal net gain in performance. This is the simplest policy; others can be implemented using the same orderings. Thus, one might insist that as long as any combination of operations from a qualitatively lower radicality level in the ordering can be found that yields an equal improvement to even *one* operation at a qualitatively higher level, then the former should be preferred to the latter. For example, suppose that within a given cycle of refinement generation and testing it is found that *deletion* of component c from rule r yields a net gain of 10 cases (and suppose this is the greatest net gain over all refinements tested). Suppose it has also been found that raising a numerical boundary in component c_1 of rule r_1, yields a gain of 5 cases, and that raising a numerical boundary in component c_2 of rule r_2, yields a gain of 5 cases. Note that we *cannot* assume that the *joint effect* of these two operations will be a net gain of 10 cases. Let us suppose that the two operations are now tested *in tandem* to determine what there joint effect is, and suppose the resulting gain is 10 cases. Then according to the policy we are describing, the system should select these two changes for tentative incorporation in the current cycle, rather than the qualitatively more radical deletion operation.

There are other factors that go into a judgment concerning a proposed refinement's radicality that are not taken account of in this scheme. Some of these factors can be quite sophisticated and difficult to "quantify," such as the desire of avoiding refining components that have survived a long "evolutionary history" intact. Others are easily incorporated, but it is difficult to give any *a priori* (domain-independent) justification on whether and how they are to be employed, e.g., a preference for refining endpoint rules over intermediate rules, or vice versa. At any rate, the incorporation of such factors is a subject for future research.

4 Heuristic Refinement Generation

In chapter 3 we showed that the notion of a refinement's having a certain degree of *plausibility* can be formalized. The basic concept is that of a refinement being *On-Target* with respect to set of misdiagnosed cases, relative, of course, to a given view.

A goal of this chapter is to show that this notion is operationally significant, that is, a refinement system can generate On-Target refinements in an efficient manner, without resorting to brute force methods. The paradigm for refinement generation presented in this chapter is called *heuristic refinement generation*, since it makes use of *rules* or *heuristics* for generating on-target refinements. The term "heuristic" is also applicable because the approach is *not* intended to generate *every* on-target refinement that exists with respect to a given r-situation and view. This is a paradigm that was first developed in the SEEK system [30, 31].

This chapter should also be viewèd as providing the necessary background information and motivation for our future discussion of the metalinguistic approach to refinement system construction (see chapter 6). The refinement concepts and heuristics presented here encapsulate our current state of knowledge concerning heuristic refinement generation. While a good number of the concepts and heuristics to be presented have been discussed elsewhere [30, 31, 17], it is only by reviewing the current situation, and describing possible alternatives and extensions to it that we will have a better understanding of the sorts of capabilities that should be provided in a refinement metalanguage. Moreover, in this chapter all refinement concepts will actually be defined using the metalanguage RM. This exposition will serve to illustrate both the power and desirability of the metalinguistic primitives selected, and will demonstrate the systemization of metaknowledge that can be achieved by applying a metalinguistic approach.

After a discussion of the general heuristic refinement generation paradigm, we will consider the issue of the relative merits and costs of doing first-order vs. higher-order refinement based upon a heuristic approach. This will lead us to the notion of *failure-driven higher-order refinement*, and a proposal for a general architecture for heuristic refinement generation that can accommodate the former. The bulk of this chapter is taken up with the description and analysis of the heuristic generation of *first-order* on-target refinements.

4.1 Frequently Used RM Primitives

In describing refinement concepts and heuristics in this chapter we will make extensive use of the RM metalanguage. An annotated list of the most important RM primitives is given in appendix I. However a list of the more frequently used RM primitives, and some useful defined notions, is provided below.

Variables

case = a variable ranging over cases in the data base

rule = a variable ranging over rules in the model

hypothesis = a variable ranging over hypotheses

dx = a variable ranging over endpoints (note than any dx is a hypothesis by definition)

mcase = a variable over the set of *misdiagnosed cases*.

Functions

```
CDX(case) = knowledge base's highest confidence conclusion
            in case

CDX-2(case) = the knowledge base's second highest conclusion
              in case

PDX(case) = expert's conclusion in case

RuleCF(rule) =  confidence-factor of rule

ModelCF(hypothesis,case) = the confidence accorded to hypothesis
                           by the knowledge base in case

Rules-for(hypothesis) = the set of rules with hypothesis as
                        their conclusion

Satisfied(item, case) = T iff item is satisfied in case
                      = F iff item unsatisfied or unknown in
                        case where item can be a rule, a rule
                        component, or a rule subcomponent.
```

4.2 The Paradigm

Suppose our view V of an r-situation <R,M> consists of the following information: i) r is unsatisfied in mcases$\subseteq$M, ii) for each mcase$\in$mcases r concludes PDX(mcase) with a confidence factor high enough to correct the case, and iii) component c of r is unsatisfied in every mcase$\in$mcases. In terms of our semantic definition, it is clear that deletion of component c from r is on-target with respect to mcases: there is an accessible microstate σ - namely, the one in which every *other* component in r is satisfied in each mcase $\in$ M - such that this refinement corrects these cases relative to their feature-vectors in σ.

This bit of reasoning can be encapsulated in a general "rule of thumb," in a manner that is exactly analogous to typical expert system rules in ordinary applications. Since our goal is to *generate* plausible refinements, the rule is most useful in the following form:

```
If in the current view V,
  there is a rule r with component c such that:

    i) r is unsatisfied in mcases⊆M,
   ii) for each mcase∈mcases r concludes PDX(mcase)
       with a confidence factor high enough to correct the case,
  iii) component c of r is unsatisfied in every mcase∈mcases.

Then

    On-Target(delete c from r,V,mcases)
```

The conclusion of this rule is to be interpreted as making the assertion that deletion of component c from rule r is on-target with respect to mcases. Note that since we have an independent semantic characterization of what it is for a refinement operation to be on-target, we have a criterion by which to judge the truth or falsity of such rules as general principles. From our discussion it is clear that the rule is an example of a true rule.

What makes the rule useful is not only the fact that it is true, but that it is in a form which allows us to see how simple deductive mechanisms can be applied to it so as to generate specific plausible refinement suggestions for a given r-situation <R,M>. Thus imagine that the viewfinder contains the following r-function:

```
F(c^r,M) =
     the set of cases m ∈ M such that
     rule r is unsatisfied in the misdiagnosed case m &
     the conclusion of r = PDX(m) &
     the confidence factor of r ≥ the hypothesis confidence
       of CDX(kb,m) in m &
     component c of r is unsatisfied in m

(Note: the notation c^r designates a variable over the components
  c of rule r)
```

In terms of this r-function the above rule may be rewritten as:

```
If   in the current view V,
     F(c^r,M) = ζ ≠emptyset

Then

     On-target(delete c^r,V,ζ)
```

In gathering the view of <R,M> the value of $F(c^r,M)$ will be computed for every component of every $r \in R$. If for a particular c^r the antecedent of the refinement heuristic is satisfied, then the conclusion is drawn. While a conclusion so drawn tells us something that is true, it also may be thought of as offering a suggestion, viz., deletion of c^r will aid in accomplishing the goal of correcting the cases in M.

Generalizing from our example, we see a familiar paradigm taking shape. Heuristic refinement generation is exactly analogous to the familiar rule-based framework used in ordinary expert systems. A heuristic refinement generator may be seen as consisting of a *viewfinder*, and a *knowledge-base* of heuristics similar to the one we have shown in figure 4-1. In order to avoid confusion, we will call a refinement generator's heuristic knowledge base its *r-knowledge*. The viewfinder is a mechanism for ascertaining the presence/absence or values of useful features concerning r-situations. This is similar to an ordinary expert system in which there is a fixed set of features that can characterize any case in the domain; the values of these features may be ascertained by the expert system itself or by interrogation of a human observer. R-knowledge is a set of principles or rules of thumb that relate the presence of certain complex patterns of features in a view of an r-situation to the existence of plausible refinements for the correction of the misdiagnosed cases in that r-situation. Again this is similar to an ordinary expert system in which the knowledge base contains rules that relate the presence of complex patterns of features to classification endpoints (i.e., diagnoses) or to suggested courses of action (i.e., treatments).

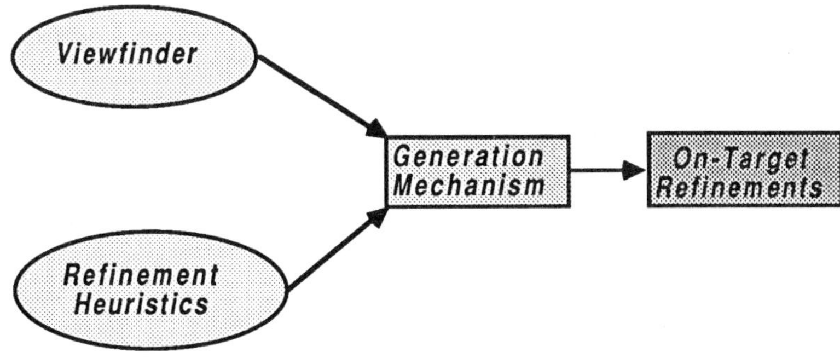

Figure 4-1: Heuristic Generation of On-Target Refinements

4.3 First-Order vs. Higher-Order Refinement

As conceived in this work, heuristic refinement generation is a process driven by *empirical case analysis*: given an r-situation, <R,M>, a refinement generator will gather certain kinds of information by examining the behavior of the rules in R with respect to the misdiagnosed cases in M. This is the process that we have dubbed as *gathering a view V of the r-situation*, or *determining the macrostate of the r-situation*. What enables a refinement system to construct a V for an r-situation is its viewfinder Φ. Φ is a collection of r-functions that, for a given refinement system, is fixed. Case analysis is the application of the r-functions in Φ to the objects in an r-situation in order to construct a view. Once the view is obtained, r-knowledge is invoked to generate specific refinement suggestions.

A first-order refinement system is one that limits its refinement suggestions to operations that involve the application of a *single* primitive refinement operator (see chapter 3). Intuitively, the viewfinder of such a system can be expected to contain r-functions that represent certain patterns of features that are relevant to the application of a single primitive refinement operator. Since primitive refinement operators apply to a single rule component, the r-functions in the viewfinder will be functions of *single rules* and *single rule-components*. Figure 4-2 shows a simple illustration of the point. If we are interested in generating a first-order generalization refinement to a rule r, we will search for the following sort of pattern in the currently misdiagnosed cases: r's conclusion is correct, r's confidence is greater than the confidence of the current incorrect conclusion, etc. This pattern represents a complex property that can be attributed to r, e.g. in SEEK2 we talk about Gen(r) = the number of misdiagnosed cases in which a pattern similar to that just indicated is satisfied by r.

First-Order

Unit of analysis : *single rules, components*

Refinement Type	Pattern
Generalize a rule r	r's conclusion is correct, has confidence > confidence accorded to currently incorrect conclusion by KB • • •

Second-Order

Unit of analysis: *pairs of rules, components*

Refinement Type	Pattern
Specialize a rule r_1 in tandem with Specialize a rule r_2	r_1 & r_2 are both satisfied & conclude incorrect conclusion with confidence > the confidence the correct conclusion is accorded by the KB in this case • • •

Figure 4-2: First vs. Higher-Order Refinement

Now suppose that we were interested in generating *second-order* on-target refinements. Intuitively, the viewfinder of a system capable of generating on-target second-order refinements can be expected to contain r-functions that represent certain patterns of features that are relevant to the joint application of pairs of primitive refinement operators. Establishing the presence of such patterns in a case will require the joint examination of *pairs* of rules and/or rule-components: we say that *second-order case analysis* is required in order to generate second-order on-target refinements. Figure 4-2 again gives a simple example. A second-order specialization refinement to two (endpoint) rules r_1 and r_2 will be on-target only when a certain type of pattern is jointly satisfied by the two rules. For example, both r_1 and r_2 must be satisfied and conclude the incorrect conclusion at a confidence greater than the confidence accorded to the correct conclusion, etc.

4.3.1 Estimate of Cost

An important use of r-functions is to help the refinement generator select prime refinement candidates from the set of initial candidates R. The exact details of how this is done will of course vary from one refinement system to the next. A typical *first-order* refinement generator might start out by calculating the values of certain r-functions of the form f(rule,M) for every rule in R, where M is a set of misdiagnosed cases. For the sake of argument let us make the egregious assumption that the amount of computation required to compute a call to any r-function of any order is constant. Then the cost of the first phase of the typical first-order refinement generator is on the order of |R|*n, where n is the number of r-functions calls made for each rule.

Let us suppose that we have n second-order r-functions of the form $f(<rule_1,rule_2>,M)$ and that our refinement generator is to apply them to each pair of rules in R. The amount of work done on this analysis will be on the order of $|R|^2$*n. Going to the logical limit, there are $2^{|R|}$ subsets of R for which it is conceivable one might wish to calculate some nth-order r-function call, and so the amount of effort expended by such an analysis is clearly exponential in |R|.

Assuming that the first phase of case analysis has produced a set R′ of prime refinement candidates that are either single rules or ordered n-tuples of rules, the next step is to apply further case analysis to each of these items in an effort to find the rule-components, or combinations of rule-components that are prime candidates for refinement. Let m be the total number of components in the rules in R′. If we apply n first-order r-functions of the form f(component,M) to each component, then, by our assumption, the amount of effort expended is on the order of m*n. Application of n second-order r-functions will require work on the order of m^2*n, and since there are 2^m subsets of the set of components in R′, the amount of work required to do a "complete" nth-order analysis is exponential in m.

Even this simple analysis is persuasive: to the greatest extent possible one would like to do first-order case analysis, and revert to higher-order analysis only when indicated. However there are a number of caveats to be made. The first is that while an r-function may be explicitly first-order in form, it may *implicitly* be more or less equivalent to higher-order r-functions in content. Consider for example the first-order r-function:

f(rule,cases) = the <$component_1$,$component_2$> pair in rule that is jointly most frequently satisfied in cases

= Select $<c^r_1,c^r_2>$ with Max Joint-Satisfied-Count($<c^r_1,c^r_2>$, cases)

Clearly a single call to this r-function implicitly involves many calls to the second-order r-function Joint-Satisfied-Count, where the latter is a specially defined r-function that returns the number of cases in which the two components are jointly unsatisfied.

The second caveat, also illustrated by the preceding example, is simply to once more point out that the assumption that any call to any r-function involves the same amount of computation is absurd. The amount of work expended is clearly related to the "length" of the definition of the given r-function, and the complexity of the constructs used therein.

Additional discussion on the cost of case analysis is given in section 4.7.

4.4 Soundness and Completeness of Refinement Generators

We will say that a heuristic refinement generator Γ *suggests* a refinement γ to correct an r-situation <R,M> if and only if, with respect to the view V=Φ<R,M>, there is some satisfied refinement heuristic in Γ that concludes that γ is on-target for some mcases$\subseteq$M. Γ will be said to be *sound* if and only if, whenever Γ suggests a refinement γ to an r-situation, γ *is* on-target with respect to that situation. Γ will be said to be *complete* if and only if, whenever it *is* the case that a refinement γ is on-target with respect to an r-situation Γ suggests γ as a refinement to that r-situation. Note that this definition is relativized to the refinement operators contained in the refinement system. Thus a system that contains only one refinement operator, O, may still be complete: so long as it suggests every on-target refinement involving O, it satisfies the definition.

Let us define the *order of a refinement operation* as the number of primitive refinement operators it is composed of. Then Γ will be said to *nth-order-sound*, for $n \geq 1$, if and only if, whenever Γ suggests an *nth-order* refinement γ to an r-situation, γ is on-target with respect to that situation. Similarly Γ will be said to be *nth-order-complete* if and only if, whenever an *nth-order* refinement γ is on-target with respect to an r-situation then Γ suggests it. Clearly Γ is sound (complete) if and only if it is nth-order-sound (complete) for *all* $n \geq 1$.

There is no excuse for a refinement generator to be unsound (i.e., not sound). (Note that if a refinement generator is so designed that it can *never* suggest nth-order refinements for some n, then it is trivially nth-order-sound for that n). Given the cost of exhaustive higher-order analysis, however, there is good reason why it is unreasonable to expect a refinement generator to be anything *more than* first-order complete.

But is first-order completeness itself a reasonable expectation in practice? This is a question that probably has no single answer. Clearly one factor is the scope of the refinement operators employed by refinement system. For a refinement system that generates refinements for a set of *expressively complete* refinement operators (see section 3.1.5), it will, in general, prove to be computationally intractable to be first-order complete. If the viewfinder of such a system has high "entropy," i.e., tends to produce views that have a large number of accessible microstates, then too many on-target refinements will exist. If we try to design a viewfinder with low entropy - so that fewer on-target refinements will exist - there is a good chance that computing the view will become intractable. However, first-order completeness might not be an infeasible goal for systems - such as SEEK2 - that employ a restricted set of refinement operators.

4.5 A General Architecture for Heuristic Refinement Generation

Every refinement system, whether based on first or higher-order case analysis, has to confront the problem of how to recognize failures of refinability, i.e., r-situations in which rule acquisition, as opposed to rule refinement, is desirable. Now an analogous problem arises for first-order systems, or any system whose order of analysis is not exhaustive with respect to the given r-situations, namely, how do we recognize failures of "first-order refinability," i.e., r-situations in which complex refinement operations, generated by higher-order analysis, are needed? In this section we briefly discuss this question from a general point of view.

Suppose that either within a single cycle, or perhaps over the course of a number of cycles, a first-order refinement generator has generated and tested one or more refinements for a set of misdiagnosed cases, mcases, but with limited or no success, i.e., no matter what the system tries all or most of the mcases remain misdiagnosed. The question is whether, and how, by reviewing the record of its failures concerning these cases, and perhaps gathering additional information via a higher-order case analysis, the first-order refinement generator can temporarily, as it were, operate in a higher-order mode in order to generate complex refinements. This type of temporary higher-order operation is called *failure-driven higher-order analysis*. Concrete examples of scenarios in which failure-driven higher-order analysis is called for, are given latter in this chapter (see section 4.9.2) and in section 6.5.

In this section we present a general architecture for heuristic refinement generation that is powerful enough to accommodate the process of failure-driven higher-order analysis.

4.5.1 Three Types of Refinement Heuristics

We may draw a distinction between r-knowledge heuristics whose premises contain *only* r-function calls (of course, the premises may contain comparisons and mathematical/logical operations on these values), and those whose premises also include components of the form On-target(γ,V,mcases), i.e., contain components that might be concluded from other r-knowledge heuristics. R-knowledge heuristics of the first form will be called *view-to-refinement* heuristics, or *vr-heuristics* for short. R-knowledge heuristics of the second form will be called *refinement-to-refinement* heuristics or *rr-heuristics* for short.

One use for such rr-heuristics is as a way of implementing some aspects of the *constraints of conservatism.* For example, suppose a vr-heuristic is satisfied and recommends *deletion* of a component. In the spirit of conservatism one should try to avoid such an action if a less radical measure is possible. For each component type one might incorporate an rr-heuristic that would act as a "demon" with respect to recommendations concerning components of that type, making sure that whenever a deletion is proposed alternative measures are also tried. For example, one such rr-heuristic would say that if a numerical finding is recommended for deletion, then one might achieve the same goal by extending the associated numerical range of the finding.

The third type of r-knowledge heuristics will be called *control heuristics* or *c-heuristics.* Strictly speaking, the consideration of such heuristics, as their name implies, belongs more with a discussion of the strategic control principles of a refinement system than with a discussion of refinement generation *per se.* However, insofar as issues of control strategy are intertwined with issues in refinement generation, some discussion of c-heuristics is appropriate here.

Whether we think of vr and rr heuristics as stating facts (about what refinements *are* on-target) or as offering advice (about what refinements we *ought* to try), heuristics in these categories have one function, viz., to generate specific plausible refinement suggestions. On the other hand, while the "ultimate" function of c-heuristics is to aid in the generation of plausible refinements, their immediate function is to get the *refinement system* to *take an action* that is indicated in the current situation, e.g., conduct a higher-order analysis of some rules belonging to the current r-situation. In other words, while the conclusion of any vr or rr heuristic is always of the form On-target(γ,V,mcases), the conclusion of a c-heuristic always involves a *directive constructed out of primitive actions* available to the refinement system. Such an action might be, for example, to gather joint dissatisfaction statistics for components in a rule that should be generalized, but for which generalization of the most frequently missing component has failed: this would be an instance of the primitive action *Compute(r-function).* (A list of primitive actions that can be performed by a refinement system is included as part of the specification of a metalanguage for the specification of control strategies (see appendix I)).

In addition, the premises of c-heuristics may contain components that express *feedback* information of two possible types: i) information concerning the effectiveness of refinements that have already been suggested and tested, ii) information concerning the changes that take place *in a view* of an r-situation as a result of incorporating a refinement.

4.5.2 Levels of Analysis

As can be seen in figure 4-3, we may view a refinement generator as being organized into *levels.* Each level has its *own* set of vr, rr, and c-heuristics. At level *n*, we find the items that are to be used in conducting *n*th-order case analysis with the intention of generating refinements applicable to kb-objects of order *n*. C-heuristics that operate *within* a level will be called *tactical c-heuristics*. C-heuristics that are not *part* of any level, but operate *between* levels will be called *strategic c-heuristics*; they are like switches that cause the system to move up or down the various levels of analysis.

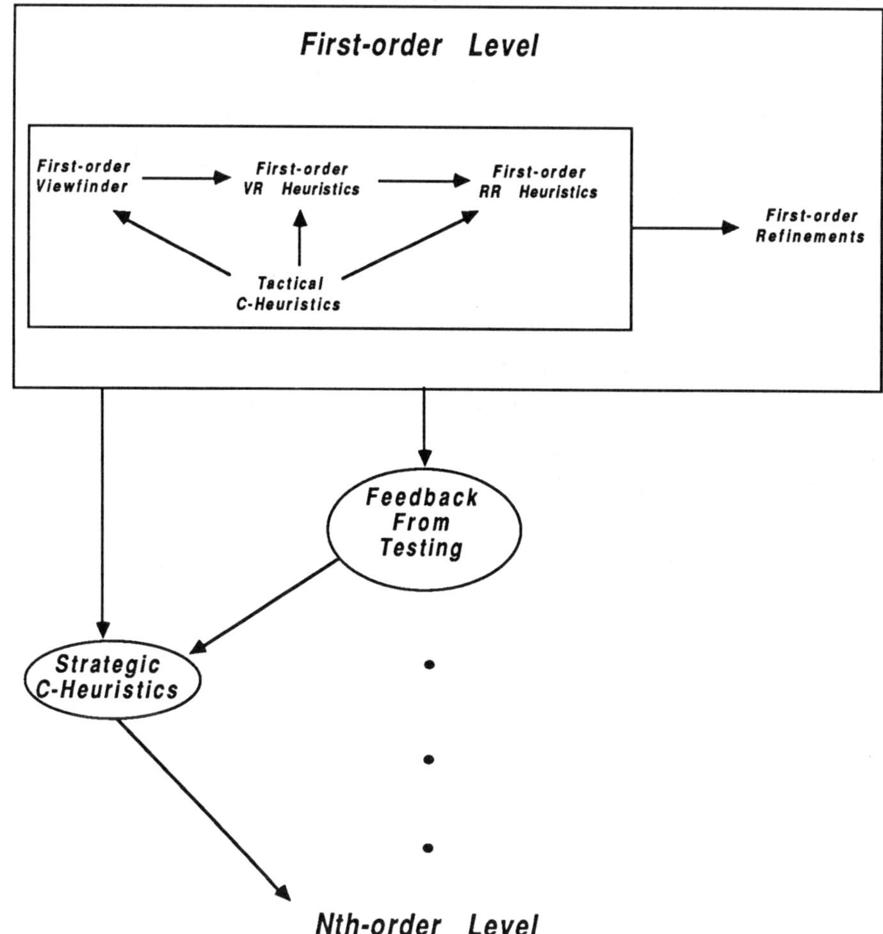

Figure 4-3: Architecture of Heuristic Refinement Generator

As an example of a tactical c-heuristic we cite a control principle that is used in SEEK2. Considered abstractly, SEEK2 may be thought of as dealing with r-situations <R,M> in which R always consists of *all* the rules in any rule-chain leading to a specified dx. The fact is, however, that initially SEEK2 does case analysis and refinement generation only for the *endpoint-rules* that conclude dx. If during the course of this initial generation process a refinement that involves deleting/altering a hypothesis component H in an endpoint rule is generated, then, and only then, is refinement generation initiated for the intermediate rules that conclude H. This "backchaining" on implicated hypothesis components may be iterated.

Giving a realistic example of a *strategic c-heuristic* is not an easy matter, since, to my knowledge, there is no refinement system in existence that makes use of any. For a detailed description of a scenario in which such c-heuristics would be applicable, and what they would say, the reader should refer to the discussion of failure-driven higher-order analysis in sections 4.9.2 and sections 6.5. In this section we will simply give a brief abstract description of the role envisioned for strategic c-heuristics in the overall architecture of a refinement generator.

Given the costs of doing exhaustive higher-order analysis, the idea is to start out by doing exhaustive first-order analysis for the *complete set of r-situations* presented to the refinement generator, including the generation and testing of refinements. Once this has been done, strategic c-heuristics evaluate the feedback and make a determination as to whether or not higher-order analysis of some aspects of one or more of the r-situations is called for. This determination may involve evaluating several features including 1) the overall degree of success achieved by the first-order analysis, and, 2) for mcases that have resisted correction, ascertaining whether refinements that are on-target with respect to these mcases are failing to improve empirical adequacy because they do not correct *them*, or because, while they do correct them, they also cause currently correctly diagnosed cases to become misdiagnosed. The relevance of (1) is obvious: we may find that an adequate overall improvement in knowledge base performance is achieved by first-order refinement. The relevance of (2) is as follows. If a refinement γ does a good job of correcting the mcases it is *intended* to correct - those for which it is on-target - but fails generally because it causes more new misdiagnosed cases μ, then in conducting a higher-order search for complex refinements we will want to examine the cases in μ and the rules R' invoked in those cases. Formally, if $\langle R,M \rangle$ is the r-situation that led to generation of γ, then we would now be doing a higher-order analysis for the *augmented* r-situation $\langle R \cup R', M \cup \mu \rangle$. On the other hand, if γ failed because it simply did not correct its on-target cases, then in moving on to a higher-order analysis we will still be concerned with the *same* r-situation as originally led to generation of γ, but now we will be examining it with a finer-grained analysis.

4.6 First-Order Case Analysis

First-order case analysis is of interest theoretically since it represents the simplest case. Intuitively one hopes that a first-order viewfinder can be implemented so as produce views in roughly linear time, i.e., so that the overall complexity of view construction would be on the order of |R|+|components of the rules in R| in the worst case, where this number is given in terms of two fundamental operations: 1) simple access to values of primitive r-functions, and 2) primitive operations on such values. We address this issue below.

First-order case analysis is also of interest because SEEK2's heuristic refinement generator can be formulated in terms of first-order r-functions. It therefore provides a testbed for questions concerning first-order case analysis, viz., can first-order case analysis be done in linear time, how effective is such analysis in suggesting plausible refinements, etc.

4.6.1 Nature of the R-Situations

For both strategic and theoretical reasons it is important to specify the nature of the r-situations that a heuristic refinement generator will confront. This is done by imposing constraints on R and M. As a matter of strategy such considerations should, and will, be discussed separately from the issue of refinement generation *per se*. However, without making some assumptions about the nature of the r-situations that the refinement generator is to confront it is very difficult to do concrete work.

4.6.1.1 Constraint on M

Our first order of business, therefore, is to constrain the contents of M and R in such a way that the rules in R may be thought of as *possible candidates for refinement* with respect to the mcases in M. This is done by relying on the endpoints of the knowledge base for providing a "principle of division." Specifically, M must consist of *mcases* such that PDX(mcase) or CDX(mcase) is identical to a specific common endpoint dx. Since, by definition an mcase satisfies PDX(mcase)$\neq$CDX(mcase), this means that M consists of mcases whose conclusion should be dx but is not, or whose conclusion is dx but should not be. An mcase in the former category represents a *false negative* judgment on the part of the knowledge base, or an *FN* for short, and an mcase in the latter category represents a *False Positive* judgment, or an *FP* for short. Let FN(dx,mcase) and FP(dx,mcase) be r-functions, actually, r-predicates, that return true or false according as to whether mcase is a FN or FP with respect to dx. Then M(dx) may be defined as an r-function that returns {mcase| FN(dx,mcase) $\vee$ FP(dx,mcase)}, i.e., M(dx) is the set of all FP's and FN's with respect to dx.

The rationale for choosing M(dx) as a principle of division is simple: if all the mcases in M(dx) are corrected then, *other things remaining equal*, the refined knowledge base's performance with respect to the endpoint dx will be perfect (over C of course). Clearly, if the knowledge base has no FN's or FP's with respect to dx, then every time the knowledge base *should* conclude dx it does, and it *never* concludes dx in a case that it should not.

Therefore, unless otherwise stated, the M in an r-situation σ will be understood to be the value of M(dx) for some dx. At the very least M must be a subset of such a M(dx). Therefore we will speak of the *endpoint or dx associated with M,* or that generates M.

4.6.1.2 Constraint on R

Given an M, we now want to state a constraint on the possible members of R, the set of initial refinement candidates with respect to M.

1) An *endpoint rule* r is an *initial refinement candidate with respect to M* if there is an mcase ∈ M such that either

   a) r's conclusion = PDX(mcase) or

   b) r's conclusion = CDX(mcase) *and*
   r is satisfied in mcase, *and*
   r's confidence factor ≥ the final hypothesis confidence factor of PDX(mcase) in mcase.

2) An *intermediate rule* r is an *initial refinement candidate with respect to M* if r is a member of a rule-chain whose last link is an endpoint rule that is an initial refinement candidate with respect to M.

The definition can be viewed as being recursive: rules that do not directly conclude classification endpoints, i.e., intermediate rules, become refinement candidates through their ultimately being connected to refinement candidate rules that do directly conclude endpoints, i.e., endpoint rules.

Some simple ideas and terminology associated with this constraint on R are worthy of comment. An instance of an mcase satisfying clause (1.a) in the definition will be said to *provide evidence that r ought to be generalized,* i.e. have some generalization refinement applied to it, while an instance of an mcase satisfying clause (1.b) *provides evidence that r ought to specialized,* i.e., have some specialization refinement applied to it. Corresponding to these circumstances we will speak of a rule *being a candidate for generalization/specialization.*

While a single mcase m cannot simultaneously satisfy clauses (1.a) and (1.b) *with respect to the same rule r,* m can independently satisfy these clauses with respect to distinct rules, and it is clearly possible for two or more cases to provide evidence that r should be both generalized and specialized. The latter circumstance might indicate that one component of the rule should have a generalization operation applied to it, while a distinct component of the rule should have a specialization refinement applied to it. Given this analysis it might seem wise to adopt a policy of *non-comparability* of these two sorts of evidence in the formulation of refinement generation principles, i.e., refinement generation principles for generalization refinements ought not take account in any way of evidence for specialization and vice versa. However, as we shall see below, there are reasons for taking an approach to refinement generation that allows for the comparability of these two sorts of evidence.

We note that a rule can be a candidate for generalization regardless of its satisfaction status. If r's conclusion=PDX(m)$\neq$CDX(m), and r *is* satisfied, then the only relevant generalization operation is to raise r's confidence factor so its conclusion=PDX(m) can become the endpoint with the highest hypothesis confidence factor in mcase m. On the other hand, rules can be implicated by a case as requiring specialization only if they are satisfied in the case.

Notice that while the definition specifies clearly how intermediate rules, i.e., those that do not directly conclude an endpoint, may become refinement candidates, it does not help us very much in determining whether the evidence indicates a need for generalization or specialization operations for such rules. The reason is that with the introduction of intermediate rule levels the complexity of the problem again mushrooms. We will see below how heuristic refinement principles that reduce the problem complexity can be used to generate refinements for intermediate rules. For now, in order to indicate the nature of the complications introduced by intermediate rules, we point out that one and the same mcase m can implicate a *single intermediate rule r in two different ways* by virtue of the fact that i) m provides evidence that endpoint rule r_1 should be generalized, ii) m provides evidence that endpoint rule r_2 should be specialized, and iii) r's conclusion H occurs in components of both r_1 and r_2. Without further analysis of this specific mcase it is impossible to know whether i) r's refinement candidacy as evidenced by m should be taken seriously at all, i.e., whether we should act upon it, ii) m really supports the generalization of r, or iii) m really supports the specialization of r.

The last example raises a general point, viz., a rule's being a refinement candidate in the sense provided by the above definition, certainly does not mean that *it really ought to be refined in any way*; for one thing other refinements may do a much better job of correcting the problem. For a rule, or any item, to be a refinement candidate means that we have some reason for attempting to generate refinements for it.

4.6.2 First-Order R-functions on Rules: Satisfaction Measures

Given an r-situation σ the first order of business for a first-order refinement generator is to apply r-functions to the rules in R, the set of initial refinement candidates, in an effort to locate a few of them that are *prime* refinement candidates. In this section we discuss first-order r-functions on rules that are intended to aid in accomplishing this task.

One of the advantages of dealing solely with generalization and specialization refinement primitive refinement operators, is that every first-order r-function is naturally "geared" toward providing evidence for the application of one or the other sort of refinement category. Therefore, we can divide our discussion into a consideration of r-functions relevant to generalization operators, and those relevant to specialization operators.

Before doing so however, we discuss a pair of r-functions on rules and rule components of great interest, not only to first-order case analysis, but to case analysis in general. As is the case with the other r-functions, one of the two relates to generalization and the other to specialization. The former is a *measure of how close an unsatisfied rule is to being satisfied*, and the latter *measure of how close a satisfied rule is to being dissatisfied.* These two concepts are useful as a kind of "primary" filter on the set of refinement candidates.

4.6.2.1 Closeness to Satisfaction

To appreciate the potential usefulness of a closeness measure in generating plausible refinements, consider again the following simple scenario. Suppose we know, on the basis of other r-functions, that r_1 is a rule that would correct mcase m if it were to be satisfied in m, and that component $c \in r_1$ is unsatisfied in m. As we have said before this gives us some reason to believe that deletion or some generalization of c could correct m. We can't be sure of this because there may be other components of r_1 unsatisfied in m. Now add the following information to the scenario. There is another rule r_2 for which exactly the same property holds with respect to m, i.e., if satisfied r_2 would correct m, and we know r_2 is missing a component c_2 too. In fact there may be several rules for which exactly the same property holds. Without further information, we have no reason to favor one of these rules over the other.

Short of doing an exact analysis, what further information could help us in distinguishing the "refinement potentials" of these candidates with respect to m? Suppose that we knew in some intuitive sense that r_1 was in fact "very far" from being satisfied in m, but that r_2 was "very close" to being satisfied. Given this information, even if we were told that refinement to c_2 would still not correct mcase, if forced with a choice we would choose to refine c_2 above c_1. The reason is that since r_2 is already closer to satisfaction than r_1, the refinement to c_2 will bring us closer to correcting m than the refinement to c_1. *A fortiori*, if we do not know that the refinement to c_2 is guaranteed to fail, all the more reason to choose it. Another reason to choose the rule closer to being satisfied is that this policy seems to be more in accord with the spirit of conservatism; one may view this rule as the one intended to cover the situation.

Politakis [30] showed how the intuitive idea of closeness to satisfaction could be measured in a quantitative fashion. With minor changes, the same closeness measure is employed in SEEK2. The measure I am going to define here is a revised version of the measure used in SEEK2. The differences between the newer measure and that used in SEEK2 will be pointed out after the definition has been given.

Intuitively one would expect a measure of a rule's closeness-to-being satisfied in m to be related to a measure of the radicality of the least radical refinements necessary to make the rule become satisfied in m. In the presence of a well-defined radicality metric one might opt to take these measures as being identical. The problem, as we have had occasion to point out before, is that the choice of metric can in large part be a measure of taste, or domain-specific considerations.

However, there is a deeper philosophical argument for keeping these two measures distinct. A radicality metric on refinements is supposed to capture some of our intuitions about the "comparative meaning" of rules, i.e., about when rules can be said to be more similar in meaning than others, etc. Radicality metrics are therefore solely a function of objects in the knowledge base, and have no dependence on what the "external world" is like. But this is precisely what a closeness measure on rules is intended to capture, viz., how close is a rule to being satisfied by the current state of the world, i.e., how close is a rule to being satisfied *in terms of the findings given in the current case.* This is intended to be a wholly objective domain-independent measure of an empirically verifiable feature of rules. While it is true that we cannot alter the findings that make a rule unsatisfied, but only the rule itself, it does not follow that the "minimum changes needed" *to make* the rule satisfied are an accurate measure of how close the rule is *to being* satisfied by the case findings. For one thing, since there may be a number of different ways in which a rule can be changed to make it satisfied, in order to specify one as being the "minimum change," one must make a judgment concerning the relative radicality of the alternatives. As we have discussed previously (see chapter 3), radicality judgments may often be a matter of opinion.

Be that as it may, we present a closeness measure on rules over cases that is based on a measure of the minimum number of findings in a case whose values prevent the rule from being satisfied. The *partial satisfaction measure* of a rule in a case, or *PSM(rule,case)* is a recursive r-function that is defined in terms of the partial satisfaction measures of the components in rule. In order to avoid counting the same finding component more than one time, we state the definition in a sort of semi-procedural form, where we start with the first component on the extreme left, c_1, and proceed sequentially to the last component c_n:

1. PSM of a rule

$$\texttt{PSM(rule,case)} = \sum_{c \in rule} PSM(c,case)$$

2. PSM of components

i) If c_i is a truth-valued finding:

PSM(finding,case) = 1 if Satisfied(finding,case) = F *and this component has not already been counted in computing the PSM of a c_j where $j<i$*

= 0 if Satisfied(finding, case) = T, or c_i has already been counted

ii) If c_i is a numerical-valued finding with associated range [l:h], and value v in case:

PSM(finding,case) $= \frac{|Min\{v-l,v-h\}|}{|v-(l+h)/2|}$, **if Satisfied(finding,case)=F**

= 0 if Satisfied(finding, case) = T, or c_i has already been counted

iii) If c_i is an intermediate-hypothesis, Hypo, with associated confidence range [l:h]:

PSM(Hypo,case) = minimum PSM(r,case) of all rules r that conclude Hypo with confidence somewhere in the range [l:h]

iv) If c_i is a Choice, i.e., [k: ch(1),...,ch(n)]:

PSM(c_i,case) $= \sum_{i=1}^{i=k} Min[PSM(ch(j),case)]$

= sum of the k lowest PSM(ch(j),case). *In computing each PSM(ch(j),case) sequentially we again take care not to count the same component more than once.*

One immediate difference between this and the earlier PSMs is the care we have taken to be sure not to count the same finding more than once. This was never explicitly stated in SEEK or in SEEK2, and the fact is that SEEK2's currently implemented PSM will count findings more than once. Whether situations in which findings are over-counted arise depends upon the logical structure of the rule-chain in the knowledge base. Here is a simple schematic example of a realistic situation in which this could happen. Let r_1 be of the form ...H_1&H_2...-> dx, where H_1 and H_2 are intermediate hypotheses. Now suppose that the *only* rules for these two hypotheses are r_{h1} and r_{h2} of the form ...F...-> H_1 and ...F...-> H_2, respectively, where the F that appears in these two rules represents *exactly the same finding component, and occurs as a conjunct at the top level of the rules*. Suppose that in m all three rules are unsatisfied. Then in computing PSM(r_1,m) we will count F twice unless we explicitly take care to avoid counting findings more than once.

This is one way in which the new PSM differs from the previous ones. Another way concerns the definition of the PSM of a numerical-valued finding component, clause (2.ii) of the definition. *The PSM of a numerical-finding F with value v is defined as the ratio of the distance of v from the closest range-boundary to the distance of v from the midpoint of the range.* This ratio is always less than or equal to 1, and approaches 1 asymptotically as v gets further and further away from the closest range-boundary. This behavior is clearly consistent with the desired interpretation of PSM.

The justification for incorporating this new clause in our PSM definition can be easily illustrated by the following example. Let r_1 be a rule that is missing only truth-valued finding component F_1 in case m, let r_2 be a rule that is missing only numerical-valued component F_2 with range [l:h] and value v. According to the earlier closeness measures both rules have a PSM=1. However, suppose that v is "almost" in the range [l:h], whereas the truth value of F_1 in m is simply the opposite of what F_1 says it should be. Intuitively F_2 is closer to being satisfied than F_1.

One could argue, cogently I believe, that whether this sort of PSM on numerical findings is appropriate may depend upon domain-specific, and perhaps even knowledge-base specific considerations. In some cases one is willing to say that being outside the range is simply equivalent to being false, and there is no merit to being closer to a boundary rather than farther away. But in such cases, I would suggest, one thereby shows that one has no intention of allowing refinements to the boundaries in the first place, i.e., one is so confident about the existing boundaries that they are not subject to refinement. Conversely, if one is willing to consider refinements to boundaries then I can see no way of escaping the conclusion, assuming one abides by the spirit of conservatism of course, that being closer to a boundary rather than farther away counts for something. And what it counts for is a measure of how close the component is to being satisfied (as well as a measure of the radicality of the refinement needed to make the component satisfied).

Alternative schemes for dealing with numerical findings are possible. For example, one could measure the distance from v to the closest endpoint or the midpoint against the total size of the range, i.e h-l. This would allow for PSM values > 1, indeed it would allow for unbounded PSMs. This would seem to be an undesirable consequence.

One might wonder why a similar PSM measure for intermediate hypothesis components is not advocated. In other words, instead of or in addition to looking at the the minimum PSM of the rules that conclude the hypothesis H, as described in clause (2.iii) of the definition, why not also look at the distance of the actual knowledge base confidence in H from the closest range-boundary. For example if the component is of the form H [.5:1], and the actual confidence in H in the case is .4, then analogously to numerical findings we compute a PSM = .1/.35 ≈.29.

First of all, it is obvious that we would not want this sort of computation to completely *replace* computing PSMs for rules that conclude H, even though this would result in savings in the complexity of the overall computation. This would result in extremely counterintuitive judgments of closeness, as the reader may ascertain for himself. But even to include this calculation *in any way* as part of the PSM of H, seems to violate the philosophical position outlined above. In the case of a numerical *finding* when we measure distance from satisfaction in the way we have advocated, we are measuring values whose interpretation is a matter of objective empirically verifiable features of the real world - a numerical finding represents an objective feature of the domain of expertise which exists whether or not a given knowledge base mentions it. This is not the case with confidence ranges for intermediate hypothesis. When we measure the distance from H's actual confidence to the closest range-boundary, we are measuring values that have meaning only within the context of a knowledge base of rules together with a method of handling uncertainty. In other words, we are talking about *constructs* that we use to measure *our* confidence in conclusions, constructs whose meaning and use may vary from person to person, as well as from system to system. I am not saying that these constructs have no value, or that they should not be used. What I am saying is that a closeness measure that incorporates the sort of calculation over confidence ranges that we are discussing, is less *objective* than one that does not, i.e., it is less of a direct measure of the degree of match of *case findings* to rule satisfaction.

4.6.2.2 Satisfaction Measures for Complex Forms

Ultimately the PSM of any kb-object in a case will depend upon the satisfaction or dissatisfaction of its "constituent" findings, i.e., the primitive r-function *Satisfied(finding,case)* is an essential ingredient in the definition. In our discussions we haven't said much about the logical form of findings; we know that they are simple-components which in turn can be propositional or predicate forms (see chapter 3). In most real life expert system the findings can essentially be thought of as propositional in nature, even if, as in EMYCIN, their internal structure can be exhibited to a limited degree. But what becomes of the notion of a findings being's satisfied or having a closeness measure if it contains either free or quantified *variables*?

Presumably if an expert system makes actual use of variable x, then it must have access to (a representation of) a domain of individuals that can be the value of x. Therefore when we speak of a form containing x free, e.g., F(x), as being satisfied in a case, we are generally speaking about x as denoting a particular individual in the domain for which F(x) is true. There is no ambiguity about the satisfaction conditions of an existentially or universally quantified form.

Does the notion of closeness to satisfaction make sense for rules containing such forms? Consider the case of free variables first. For rules with free variables the meaning of closeness must be redefined in terms of bindings of the variables in the rules that *minimize* the PSM as defined above. For example, consider the rule schema:

(F x) & (G x) & (H x) -> (I x) **(1)**

Suppose the rule is not satisfied in case c. Now it doesn't make sense to say that **1** has a PSM of n in case c; one must relativize the PSM to a choice of bindings for the variables in the rule. For example suppose case c involves two objects A and B that can each be bound to x. To compute the closeness measure for **1** in case c we have to compute the PSM of the two possible instantiations of **1** using our definition and take the minimum.

The more objects that can be bound to a variable in a case, the more costly the calculation is. Moreover **1** is the simplest case. Consider a revised version:

(F x) & (G y) & (H x) -> (I x) **(2)**

Now we have to compute the PSM for each of he following possible bindings:

x	y
A	A
A	B
B	A
B	B

and take the minimum. Note that if a predicate in **2** is an intermediate hypothesis, then we have to do the same thing for every rule that concludes it before the closeness of **2** can be known.

The closeness of an existentially quantified form is calculated in more or less the same way as for free variables. The case of a universally quantified component or rule is different. Here one has to sum over the PSM of the form for *every* binding of the variable that does not satisfy the form. The closeness of multiply quantified forms can be obtained in similar fashion.

Even for a small universe of individuals, these cases involve considerable computation. The value of computing closeness measures for such forms is questionable, especially when the costs are so large that one is spending more time calculating PSMs than generating and testing refinements. This is an issue that must be left to future research.

4.6.2.3 Closeness to Dissatisfaction

PSM is an r-function that aids in filtering out good generalization candidates. By "symmetry" one is led to wonder whether we can identify *an r-function measuring "closeness to dissatisfaction" of satisfied rules, as an aid in filtering out prime specialization candidates.* Such an r-function was not devised in the original SEEK nor in our work on SEEK2. We will see that such a closeness to dissatisfaction measure or *DSM* can be defined, and that it can have a variety of uses.

At first glance one might think such a notion is misconceived: if a rule is satisfied, then all its components are satisfied; to make it dissatisfied one has only to make *one* of its components dissatisfied, and so every rule will have the same DSM. This would be true if every component of every rule had exactly the same formal structure. But we know this is not so. Consider the following simple example. Let r be a one-component rule whose left hand side is of the form [1: ch(1), ch(2), ch(3)]; r can be satisfied in a case c in virtue of exactly one, or exactly two, or all three of the choice elements being satisfied in c. Intuitively in each case r is closer to being dissatisfied than in the next. The DSM of a choice component will therefore be the sum of the minimum DSMs of the required number of choice elements that need to be dissatisfied in order to make the entire component dissatisfied.

In the case of numerical findings it is also clear that one satisfied finding may be closer to being dissatisfied than another on the grounds that the value in the former case is closer to one of the range-boundaries. In fact the same formula that we used for the PSM of a numerical component can be used in defining its DSM.

The DSM of a satisfied/unsatisfied truth-valued finding is 1/0.

Clearly the DSM of a rule will be equal to the minimum DSM of its components. The DSM of an unsatisfied rule is 0, the DSM of a satisfied rule is a number greater than 0.

These remarks are sufficient to show that a DSM r-function can be defined. Of what use would a DSM be?

At the level of *first-order analysis of endpoint rules* DSM does not have a filtering role analogous to PSM. The reason is that for first-order heuristic analysis the main r-situations of interest in relation to specialization are *SpecA situations* (see section 4.6.4). In a SpecA situation there is a unique rule, the SpecA rule, whose dissatisfaction will correct the mcase. Therefore there is not a *group* of initial specialization candidates from which we want to filter out the best candidate, i.e., the one that is already closest to being dissatisfied. There is only the SpecA rule to worry about. (Similar remarks apply to *SpecB situations*: while we can compare the DSMs of the SpecB rules, the fact is that *every* one of them must be dissatisfied if mcase is to be corrected.)

However, once we move to the level of *intermediate rules*, DSM has a role to play, even in a first-order system. The reason is simple. Suppose a SpecA rule r contains *two or more* intermediate hypotheses, and say, for the sake of argument, that r's left hand side contains only hypotheses. Now if we want to focus our attention on a particular component of r to specialize it makes sense to work with the hypothesis whose DSM in mcase is a minimum, since it is already closest to being dissatisfied in mcase.

There is, however, an important implication of this example: even if the SpecA rule consists entirely of non-hypothesis components, it is worthwhile knowing the DSM of each of its components in order to help us select one of them as a prime candidate for specialization. In other words, what PSM is to rules, DSM is to components. Let r be a rule that we want to specialize, and suppose that r has more than one component. To pick a single component of r to modify we can take the DSM of each component in r, and then generate refinement experiments only for the component with the minimum DSM.

DSMs of *rules* becomes useful when we move on to higher-order analysis. For example in a situation in which it is determined that several satisfied rules are independently sufficient causes of the misdiagnosis, higher-order analysis might be applied to yield a joint generalization-specialization refinement in which we might choose to specialize only those satisfied rules with the minimum DSM.

Finally, in either first or higher-order analysis DSM might be of use as an indicator of a possible failure of refinability of the knowledge base, and therefore as an indicator of a need for renewed knowledge acquisition. As an example of this consider a set of SpecB rules each having components that are extremely "over-satisfied" in mcase, and suppose we have reason to believe that these rules are basically in correct form. Suppose in addition that there was also no good candidate of sufficient confidence for generalization in mcase. It is intuitively appealing to view this situation as calling out for new endpoint rules for PDX(mcase).

4.6.3 Generalization Related R-Functions

4.6.3.1 R-Functions Related to Confidence Boosting

Situations that are amenable to correction by confidence boosting are easy to identify at the endpoint level using first-order analysis. Basically we look for satisfied rules for PDX(mcase), if there are any, then the one whose confidence factor is closest to the value of CDX(mcase) is singled out, since it will require the least boost in confidence to correct the case[7]. This is called a *genCF situation* and the chosen rule is called the *genCF rule.*

If one intends to use confidence boosting as a refinement mechanism, there are two pieces of information that are worth gathering: a) how many times is a rule a gen-cf rule relative to a set of mcases, and b) given this information, how big a confidence boost in the rule will be required for it to correct all/most/some of those cases? The r-functions that return this information are *genCF(rule,mcases) and Mean-CDX-CF(mcases)* and are defined below.

```
(First we define some r-functions used in the definition
 of genCF)

genCF-rule(mcase)
```

[7]Clearly a number of the satisfied rules could meet this specification. One therefore has to decide whether to arbitrarily choose one of them, or consider the whole set of them. We opt for the former policy.

```
        =   the rule such that
                 a) PDX(mcase)=conclusion(rule)
                 b) rule is satisfied in mcase
                 c) of all the rules satisfying conditions
                      (a) and (b) in mcase, none has a greater
                      confidence factor than rule.


        =   Select rule ∈ Satisfied-rules-for(PDX(mcase),mcase)
                    with Max RuleCf(rule).


genCF-mcases(rule,mcases)
            = {mcase∈mcases| rule = genCF-rule(mcase)}

genCF(rule,mcases)
            = |genCF-mcases(rule,mcases)|


Mean-CDX-CF(mcases)
            = the mean value of the confidence of CDX(mcase)
              over mcases

            = Mean(CDX(mcase),mcases)
```

In computing the mean value of CDX(mcase) over the mcases, instead of the maximum, we reveal our intention to try to correct most (raise the genCF rule's confidence to the mean plus, say, two standard deviations) or some (raise to the mean) but not all of the cases. In other words, we want to err on the side of caution.

The situation with intermediate rules is basically the same. The notion of a genCF situation can be extended to apply to intermediate rules in the following way. Let r_g be an endpoint rule that is to generalized, and suppose that the single missing component that is to be generalized is the intermediate hypothesis H_g with range $[\alpha:\beta]$. If there are satisfied rules for H_g then this is a genCF situation, because by raising the confidence of one of these rules to fall within $[\alpha:\beta]$ one will correct the case. Note also that this back-chaining of genCF possibilities could proceed to any intermediate rule level. With minor revisions, therefore, the r-functions defined above can be made to apply to these situations as well. (In the current implementation of SEEK2, however, genCF information is gathered only for endpoint rules).

4.6.3.2 R-Functions Related to Component Alteration

The types of generalization that involve alteration of rule components are far more varied and subtle than simple confidence boosting. Moreover, in the general case an unsatisfied rule may have a number of unsatisfied components. These factors increase the complexity of the problem, sometimes to the point where first-order analysis is not sufficient. Here we are talking about r-functions that are first-order not merely "in name" only, but in spirit as well, i.e., do not involve calls to higher-order r-functions in their definitions. We will elaborate on this point below.

At the endpoint level a *gen situation* is one in which there are unsatisfied rules for PDX(mcase) anyone of which would correct mcase if it were satisfied. In the typical case there will be many such "gen candidates" in a gen situation. This is where our PSM comes in. The *gen-rule* in a gen situation is that "gen candidate" rule whose PSM(rule,mcase) is a minimum. Analogously to genCF situations, if we are to capitalize on the refinement possibilities in gen situations we need to two things: a) how many times is a rule a gen-rule with respect to a set of mcases, and b) which components of the rule ought to be generalized to correct those cases?

The following are the r-functions that provide the answers:

```
gen-rules(mcase)
    = the rules for PDX(mcase) that would correct mcase
      if satisfied

    = {rule∈ Rules-For(PDX(mcase))|
                RuleCF(rule)≥ModelCF(CDX(mcase),mcase)}

      (Note that we do not need to specify that these rules are
      unsatisfied, since that is entailed by the other clauses)


gen-rule(mcase)
   = the rule in gen-rules(mcase) that minimizes PSM(rule,mcase)

   = Select rule∈gen-rules(mcase) with Min PSM(rule,mcase)

gen-mcases(rule,mcases)
   = the subset of mcases in which rule = gen-rule(mcase)

   = {mcase∈mcases| rule=gen-rule(mcase)}


gen(rule,mcases)
    = the size of gen-mcases(rule,mcases)

    = |gen-rule(rule,mcases)|
```

```
Mfmc(rule,cases)
    = the most frequently missing (i.e., unsatisfied)
      component of rule relative to the set of cases

    = Select c∈rule with Min Satisfaction-count(c,cases)
```

An instance of Mfmc of particular interest is:

```
Mfmc(rule,gen-rule(rule,mcases))
    = the most frequently missing component of rule relative to
      the subset of mcases in which rule is the gen-rule.
```

It is easily inferred from these r-functions that we intend to focus attention on the Mfmc of rule in its gen-mcases as our prime refinement target. This approach has its drawbacks - as well as some intuitive appeal - but it has the virtue, as we shall see below, of being first-order in spirit as well as name. The same cannot be said of a more sophisticated approach that would involve use of the following r-function:

```
Mcomp(c^r,cases)
    = the subset of cases in which c^r is unsatisfied

    = {case∈cases| ¬Satisfied(c^r,case)}
```

We could compute the value of this r-function for *every* component of a rule over its gen-mcases, i.e., for each c^r we would have a subset of the gen-mcases in which it is unsatisfied. We would then compile these results to get data of the form "c^r is unsatisfied in gen-mcases x,y,..." Except for the space requirements (to keep track of the subsets), so far the procedure could be done in linear time, i.e., when we examine a gen-mcase we add it to a list for every c^r such that ¬Satisfied(c^r,mcase). However, the idea now would be to "consolidate" the information in these subsets in a useful fashion, which does not come down to simply taking an intersection (but even this would not be first-order in spirit). Rather, one would want to find the *smallest* set of c^r whose *joint dissatisfaction* fully accounts for as many as the mcases in the gen-mcases as possible. As an example, let r be a rule with three components, and let mcases consist of six cases identified by the integers from 1 to 6. Then in the first phase of this analysis we will have gathered information that can be represented in tabular form as follows, where an entry under a component represents the circumstance that the component is unsatisfied in that case:

	Component		
	$\underline{c_1}$	$\underline{c_2}$	$\underline{c_3}$
	1	3	3
Case	2	4	4
	3	5	5
		6	6

Notice that in this example c_2 and c_3 each have equal claim to being Mfmc. While it is only by working on all three components that we can correct all the mcases, the fact is that there is only one mcase, viz. 3, in which all three components actually take *joint* responsibility for the misdiagnosis. By working on c_1 alone we may correct mcases 1 and 2. By working on c_2 and c_3 *together* we may correct 4, 5, and 6. And since we can correct mcases 4, 5, and 6 *only by working jointly* on c_2 and c_3, $\{c_2,c_3\}$ is therefore the smallest set of components whose *joint dissatisfaction* is responsible for the largest share of the mcases.

To produce the analysis given in the preceding paragraph from the above table is easier said than done. In general if r has n components, the corresponding table has n columns, and in the worst case each column will have |mcases| rows. Starting with the first element in the leftmost column, we will have to compare it with every element in each of the other n-1 columns, i.e., we do (n-1)|mcases| comparisons. However, we have to do this for every element in the first column, and since there are |mcases| of them the total cost is on the order of $(n-1)|mcases|^2$, in terms of the number of comparisons. While this is a very coarse-grained analysis, it is enough to show that a sophisticated approach to component generalization is definitely not first-order in spirit.

Before moving on to intermediate rules we discuss two other r-functions geared to the generalization of numerical ranges (or confidence ranges). Let F be a numerical finding with range [L:H] that we wish to generalize with respect to mcases. In order to do this we might wish to lower the value of L or raise the value of H. Here we talk about the r-function related to lowering the value of L; the other case is completely analogous.

```
L-Miss(cr [L:H],cases)
      = the subset of cases such that the value of cr is less
        than L

      = {case∈ cases| value(cr,case) < L}

L-down(cr [L:H],mcases)
      =  the mean value of cr in the mcases in which it falls
```

```
    below L

  = Mean(value(c^r, L-miss(c^r [L:H],mcases))
```

Note that these definitions apply equally well to intermediate hypothesis components.

This brings us to the consideration of intermediate rules. As with genCF situations, it turns out the same r-functions that apply to gen situations with endpoint rules are applicable to intermediate rules. Whether we decide to refine only the Mfmc of an endpoint rule, or some combination of missing components, the fact is that consideration of intermediate rules can be delayed until an intermediate hypothesis H has been targeted at the endpoint level. Once that has happened, we can look at all unsatisfied intermediate rules for H in the appropriate confidence range and take their PSMs over each of the mcases that implicate H, i.e., we can apply a suitably revised version of gen-rule(mcase) to gen situations at the intermediate level. Clearly, therefore we can use gen-mcases(rule,mcases) and gen(rule,mcases) at the intermediate level as well. Obviously each intermediate gen-rule that we identify will have a Mfmc with respect to its gen-mcases. If the Mfmc is also an intermediate hypothesis, the same analysis can be back-chained to the next level of intermediate rules, otherwise appropriate action will be taken just as for the Mfmc of endpoint rules.

4.6.4 Specialization Related R-Functions

First it is convenient to define a subset of the mcases that are relevant to first-order specialization.

```
Spec-Mcases(mcases)
      = the subset of mcases in which PDX(mcase) is the 2nd
        highest knowledge base conclusion

      = {mcase∈mcases| PDX(mcase)=CDX-2(mcase)}

Let spec-mcase be a variable over Spec-Mcases for a fixed set
of mcases

Spec-rules(spec-mcase)
      = the set of satisfied rules for CDX(spec-mcase) with
        confidence factor greater than or equal to
        PDX(spec-mcase)=CDX-2(spec-mcase)

      = {rule∈Satisfied-rules-for(CDX(spec-mcase),spec-mcase)|
           RuleCF(rule)≥ModelCF(CDX-2(spec-mcase),spec-mcase)}

SpecA-mcases(rule,mcases)
      = the spec-mcases in mcases such that rule is the only
        member of Spec-rules(spec-mcase)
```

= {spec-mcase∈ mcases | Spec-rules(spec-mcase)={rule} }

SpecA(rule,mcases)
= the size of SpecA-mcases(rule,mcases)

= |SpecA-mcases(rule,mcases)|

SpecB-mcases(rule,mcases)
= the spec-mcases in mcases such that rule is only one of the members Spec-rules(spec-mcase)

= {spec-mcase∈ mcases | rule∈ Spec-rules(spec-mcase)}

SpecB(rule,mcases)
= the size of SpecB-mcases(rule,mcases)

= |SpecB-mcases(rule,mcases)|

We earlier spoke of the value of DSM in localizing components of SpecA or SpecB rules as refinement targets. Since we currently do not employ a DSM in SEEK2 we will not include it in further discussions, though it is a subject for future research.

One might decide to deal with a Spec situation by lowering a rule's confidence. Analogous to the role of Mean-CDX-CF in genCF situations, we define an r-function:

Mean-PDX-CF(mcases)
= the mean value of the confidence of PDX(mcase) over mcases

= Mean(PDX(mcase),mcases)

so we can know to what value the confidence should be lowered.

Specialization of numerical and confidence ranges can be defined in a way that is somewhat analogous to the generalization of such ranges. For example, the following r-functions can be used in determining when and to what value a lower bound L should be raised:

L-spec(c^r [L:H],cases)
= the subset of cases such that the value of c^r is greater than or equal to L but less than or equal to the midpoint of the range

= {case∈ cases | l≥value(c^r,case)≤(L+H)/2 }

L-up(c^r [L:H],mcases)
= the mean value of c^r in the mcases in which it falls between L and the midpoint

```
= Mean(value(c^r, L-spec(c^r [L:H],mcases))
```

The idea is to specialize the component by raising L to a value closer to the midpoint as determined by L-up.

As with genCF and gen situations, SpecA and SpecB have application at intermediate rule levels in a way that can be detected by first-order analysis. Once an intermediate hypothesis H in an endpoint SpecA rule r has been targeted, for example, then if there is only one satisfied intermediate rule r′ that concludes H with confidence in the specified range, then r′ may be considered a SpecA rule at the intermediate level. If r′ is only one of a number of satisfied rules for H, then r′ is a SpecB rule at the intermediate level, albeit r is a SpecA. (The current implementation of SEEK2 does not gather specialization information for intermediate rules).

4.6.5 R-Functions for Conservation

We have defined an r-situation as a <R,M> pair satisfying certain conditions. We will now see that, for certain kinds of case analysis, this notion of an r-situation must be extended or modified. All the r-functions we have talked about so far are designed to gather information from misdiagnosed cases alone. Do the other cases in C have any role to play in refinement *generation* (it is obvious that they have an important role in refinement *verification*)?

Correct cases, i.e., cases for which PDX(case)=CDX(case), do have a role to play in refinement generation, viz., they can be used to filter out on-target refinements that nevertheless have some chance of degrading the knowledge base performance over currently correct cases. In other words, these cases can be used to guard that only conservative modifications are adopted.

It is worth noting, however, that since we propose to test every generated on-target refinement over the entire data base of cases anyway, if we err against caution in the refinement phase due to a lack of such information, this error will always be detected in the verification phase. However, if we fail to generate a plausible refinement due to such estimates, we may be making an error that we will never detect. It does not pay to be overly conservative in the refinement generation phase.

We will use *ccase* as a variable over correct cases, and *ccases* as a variable over sets of correct cases. There are four r-functions dealing with ccases that have at one time or another found their way into a version of SEEK or SEEK2. Specifically *Hits(rule)* and *Signif(rule)* are generalized versions of concepts originating in SEEK; *Fits(rule)* originated with SEEK2, but is not used in the current implementation; *Signif-Level(rule,cf)* originated with SEEK2 and is an example of a refinement concept that was discovered with the aid of the metalinguistic framework RM. We define them below in order of increasing usefulness.

```
Fit-Ccases(rule,ccases)
    = the subset of ccases in which PDX=CDX and this rule
      is satisfied and concludes CDX

    = {ccase∈ ccases| PDX(ccases)=CDX(ccase)=Conclusion(rule)}

Fits(rule,ccases)
    = the size of Fit-ccases(rule,ccases)

    = |Fit-Ccases(rule,ccases)|


Hit-Ccases(rule,ccases)
    = the subset of Fit-Ccases(rule,ccases) in which rule
      concludes CDX with confidence  ≥ the
      knowledge base's confidence in the 2nd  highest
      ranked conclusion

    = {ccase∈Fit-Ccases(rule,ccases)|
          RuleCF(rule)≥ModelCF(CDX-2(ccase),ccase)}

Hits(rule,ccases)
    = the size of Hit-Ccases(rule,ccases)

    = |Hit-Ccases(rule,ccases)|

Hit-Rules(ccase)
    = the set of rules that are "hits" with respect to  ccase

    = {rule∈Satisfied-rules-for(PDX(Ccase))|
          RuleCF(rule)≥ModelCF(CDX-2(ccase),ccase)}

Signif-Ccases(rule,ccases)
    = the subset of ccases in which {rule}=Hit-Rules(ccase)

    = {ccase∈ ccases| Hit-Rules(ccase)={rule} }

Signif(rule,ccases)
    = |Signif-Ccases(rule,ccases)|

Signif-Level(rule,cf,ccases)
    = the size of the subset of Signif-Ccases(rule,ccases)
      in which the 2nd highest conclusion in ccase has a
      confidence  greater than CF

    = |{ccases∈Signif-Ccase(rule,ccases)|
          ModelCF(CDX-2(ccase),ccase)≥CF}|
```

Intuitively a rule's Signif-Ccases are ccases for which the rule, in its current form, may be said to be the *sine qua non.* In contemplating refining a rule in order to correct a certain number of mcases we want to be conscious of the number of Signif-Ccases that are potentially at stake. Signif-Level is a refinement of this notion that is particularly applicable to contemplated reductions in confidence of a SpecA rule. Clearly in reducing the confidence of a SpecA rule r to gain mcases we want to avoid reducing it to the extent that we lose ccases belonging to Signif-Ccases of r. If CF is the value to which we contemplating reducing r's confidence factor, then Signif-Level(r,cf,ccases) tells us how many Signif-Cases of r's will be lost by doing so.

4.7 Cost of Case Analysis

Our hope has been that a first-order viewfinder would be capable of being implemented so as to produce views in linear time, where the complexity is measured in terms of the number of calls to primitive r-functions and the number of operations on the resulting values.

Consider the following example. A *satisfied* rule is a genCF rule in *mcase* if its confidence for PDX(mcase) is higher than *any* other satisfied rule that concludes PDX(mcase). If an implementation of the genCF idea "mirrored" this intuitive statement, then the resulting complexity would be non-linear. To see this let r_1 and r_2 be two satisfied rules for PDX(mcase) in a genCF situation. Then in calculating genCF(r_1) (genCF(r_2)) according to the preceding specification, we will not only call primitive r-functions with the current argument as value but also for r_2 (r_1) as well. Clearly this represents a duplication of effort that can be avoided by judicious reformulation of r-function definitions. Fortunately there are ways of implementing genCF ideas, as well as all of the other first-order r-functions presented here, so that primitive r-function calls never need to be repeated unnecessarily, and the observant reader will note that we have often structured our formal definitions with this goal in mind. Moreover, it seems reasonable to suppose that any set of r-functions, even of higher-order, can be "optimized" in this fashion, viz., calculations on the values of primitive r-functions can be arranged so that repeat calls are avoided.

This leaves the question of whether in terms of the number of operations performed in the calculations done on the values of primitive r-functions, the first-order r-functions presented here are linear functions of the number kb-objects examined in the given r-situation. In order to deal with this question let us try to determine the most efficient way in which genCF-mcases(rule,mcases) could be determined for every relevant rule in R an r-situation with M=mcases.

By dint of its form we tend to view this process of evaluation of genCF-mcases(rule,mcases) over R as proceeding from a fixed rule in R to a search over the mcases. But this approach definitely entails a duplication of effort as we have seen above. The key to optimizing the process is to view it in an exactly opposing manner, i.e., as proceeding from a fixed mcase to a search of all the rules in R. For every mcase, we find the rule (or rules), if any, that is the genCF rule for that mcase, and increment its genCF "count" accordingly. Every rule looked at will have the same fixed number of operations O applied to it, i.e. a) does conclusion(rule)=PDX(mcase), b) is Satisfied(rule,mcase)=T, c) what is the value of the distance=ModelCF(CDX(mcase),mcase)-RuleCF(rule), and d) is it less than the currently smallest distance? When we have looked through all the rules in this way, we will know which rule is the genCF rule in this mcase. After we have done this for each mcase in mcases we will know the value of genCF(rule,mcases) for every rule. Therefore the total amount of work done *per rule* is O*|mcases|, and the total amount of work overall is |R|*O*|mcases|, i.e., proportional to the number or rules examined.

The preceding argument can easily be repeated for SpecA, SpecB, and the various mean values that are calculated in case analysis. Fits, Hits, Signif, and Signif-Level are r-functions that deal with a rule's correct or desirable behavior, and therefore have a *ccase* or *ccases* argument instead of an *mcase* or *mcases* argument in their definitions. Therefore the cost of evaluating one of these r-functions *per rule* will be O*|ccases|, where ccases is a relevant set of correctly diagnosed cases. If the given r-situation has the form <R,mcases,ccases> then the total cost of analysis will be on the order of |R|*O*(|mcases| + |ccases|), i.e., the overall cost is linear in (|mcases| + |ccases|).

We have not, however, mentioned gen(rule,mcases), a cornerstone of our analysis (nor Mfmc, but the latter is less problematic). The reason is that one might suspect that the complexity of computing PSM(rule,mcase) - which is needed for gen - for every rule in R and mcase in mcases, is not proportional to the *number of distinct components* in R and |mcases|, due to the interleaving of rule-chains. It would seem that we would be forced to duplicate some of our efforts every time the same hypothesis appears in more than one rule-chain.

In order to show that this is not the case, it is sufficient to note the following points. First of all, given an mcase and a knowledge base kb, one can arrange the order of computation of PSM for every component and rule in kb, so that each of them needs to computed exactly once. Of course, this can only be done if we are willing to store PSM values for components and rules. The computation would start by computing PSM for every distinct finding component in the kb. We then use these values in computing PSMs of the components and rules that they are part of, and so on. Essentially, if one views the rules in kb as corresponding to an acyclic digraph, with the various nodes representing the components and rules, and the arcs representing the containment relation, then what we would be doing is to process the PSMs of the nodes in a topological ordering produced by starting with finding nodes (these would have no arc entering them) and ending with the nodes corresponding to endpoint rules. Each node would be visited exactly once, and at the time of its visitation all the information relevant to determining its PSM would already have been computed and stored[8].

The second point needed to demonstrate the linearity of PSM, is that the complexity of computing the PSM of any component or rule, provided it is done in the ordering described, is a function of that kb-object's type and parameters only. In particular, the complexity of computing the PSM of any finding component and any hypothesis component may be viewed as essentially a constant; for a choice component it will depend on the size of the choice-list; for a rule it will depend on the number of components in the rule. In the latter two cases the amount of computation done is therefore variable, but it must be bounded by some finite constant imposed by the maximum number of components that can occur in a choice component or a rule. Therefore as we visit each node in the digraph in turn, the work we do in computing PSM for that node is always bounded by some constant χ. Therefore the total work done in computing PSM for every component and rule in kb is bounded by χ(*number of rules in kb + number of rule-components in kb*).

4.8 Refinement Knowledge: Heuristics for First-Order Refinement

We now know how to do first-order case analysis, the question is what r-knowledge do we need to combine it with in order to generate plausible refinements? Before we delve into the nuances of any particular set of heuristics, it may be helpful to consider some higher level options.

The task of a heuristic refinement generator is to generate on-target refinements. Or is it? The fact is that two attitudes are possible here. We can view the basic driving desire behind refinement generation as being the generation of refinements that *maximize expected gains in performance over the mcases in the given r-situation*. Or we can view this desire tempered by the desire not to degrade performance over cases currently diagnosed correctly, i.e., the goal is generate refinements that *maximize expected gains over the mcases in M, but minimize the expected losses over the set of Ccases*. Let us call the first attitude *max-gain*, and the second *max-gain+min-loss*.

---

[8]To elaborate somewhat, the digraph consists of typed nodes, where the nodes can have elements in them. A node is of one of the following types: 1) finding component, whose elements will either a numerical range or a truth-value, 2) hypothesis component, whose elements will include a confidence range, 3) choice component, whose elements will include a choice-number, 4) rule, whose elements will include a confidence factor. An arc from node α to node β exists if any of the following is true: i) α corresponds to a component that is contained (at the top level) in the rule that corresponds to β, ii) α is a type 4 node that corresponds to an intermediate rule r with confidence factor CF and β is a type 2 node corresponding to a hypothesis component whose range includes CF, iii) α is a node corresponding to a rule component that is a choice-element in the choice component corresponding to β. Note that while identical components may have distinct occurrences in distinct rules, the corresponding rule map has only one node per distinct rule-component. Given our assumptions concerning the logical structure of kb, this digraph must contain both nodes that have no arcs coming into them, and nodes that have not arc leaving them; the former are all the finding nodes (we are ignoring finding-to-finding rules), and the latter are all nodes that correspond to endpoint rules. Moreover, it is clear that the map will contain no cycles. The nodes of such a digraph can be topologically ordered.

This is an issue we have already broached in this chapter (see p.78). To be consistent with what we said earlier - that to be overly cautious in refinement generation is a mistake - it would seem that we should advocate taking a max-gain attitude. However, as we shall see shortly, the r-knowledge in SEEK2 is best understood as resulting from a max-gain+min-loss position. Fortunately, however, it is relatively easy to parse SEEK2's r-knowledge into those parts that implement the max-gain goal and those parts implement the min-loss goal. Therefore once we have understood the structure and content of this r-knowledge it is an easy matter to "strip off" the pieces relevant to min-loss in order to derive a pure max-gain refinement generator.

4.8.1 Discussion of Max-Gain+Min-Loss Heuristics

In addition to FN and FP which we defined above, we need the notions of a True Positive, or *TP*, and a True Negative, or *TN*. If PDX(case)=CDX(case)=dx, then the knowledge base has made a TP judgment with respect to dx in case; if dx≠PDX(case)≠CDX(case), then the knowledge base has made a TN judgment with respect to dx in case. Formally we define the following r-functions:

```
TP(dx,case)  = T if PDX(case)=CDX(case)=dx
             = F otherwise


TN(dx,case)  = T if dx≠PDX(case)≠CDX(case)
             = F otherwise.
```

For the purposes of the present discussion we may fix dx to be some constant endpoint, and the set of cases in M=M(dx) (see p.61).

The goal of the overall knowledge base refinement process is to *minimize the number of FP and FN judgments of the knowledge base,* consistent with the spirit of conservatism. (Minimizing FPs is equivalent to maximizing TN and minimizing FNs is equivalent to maximizing TP.) Given this overall goal, a generalization refinement may be seen as an attempt to contribute to it by *increasing the number of TPs* for an endpoint (equivalently, decreasing the number of FNs for that endpoint, and possibly, but not necessarily, decreasing the number of FPs for other endpoints). A specialization refinement is an attempt to contribute to the overall goal by *decreasing the number of FPs* for an endpoint (equivalently, increasing the number of TNs for that endpoint, and possibly, but not necessarily, increasing the number of TPs for other endpoints.)

However, anytime a generalization is made there is a possibility that the refinement will lead to an *increase in the number of FPs for the endpoint in question as well,* which is clearly at odds with our goal. Anytime a specialization is made there is a possibility that the refinement will lead to an *increase in the number of FNs (equivalently, a decrease in the number of TPs) for the endpoint in question as well*, which is also at odds with our goal.

From the max-gain+min-loss point of view it is the role of the refinement generator to produce refinements that not only have the chance of reducing the number of FPs and FNs over M, but that also have the least chance of generating new FPs and FNs over other currently correctly diagnosed cases in C.

In order to discover how we may attempt to generate such refinements using the information in the view of σ, consider the following notions. Let ΔTP represent the total net change (over all cases and all endpoints) in TPs that *will occur* due to a generalization refinement γ_g; let ΔFP represent the total net change in FPs that will occur due to γ_g. Then the refinement γ_g contributes to our overall goal iff

$$\Delta TP > 0$$

and

$$\Delta TP > \Delta FP \quad (1).$$

Similarly, let ΔTN represent the total net change (over all cases and all endpoints) in TNs that *will occur* due to a specialization refinement γ_s; let ΔFN represent the total net change in FNs that will occur due to γ_s. Then the refinement γ_s contributes to our overall goal if:

$$\Delta TN > 0$$

and

$$\Delta TN > \Delta FN \quad (2).$$

In terms of Max-gain+Min-loss way of looking at refinement generation, an optimal heuristic for generating generalization refinements would be one that never suggested a refinement that violates condition (1), and, an optimal heuristic for generating specializations would never suggest a refinement that violates condition (2). It is doubtful that there are any *truly heuristic principles* that are optimal in this sense. (Obviously a "heuristic" that says, "Incorporate such-and-such a refinement, then recalculate the knowledge base's performance, and accept the refinement only if either (1) or (2) is satisfied," is not the sort of thing that we have in mind. Such a "heuristic" pertains to the problem of experimentation and selection of refinements for incorporation of into the knowledge base, not to refinement generation.) One has to settle for something that is less than optimal, and computationally feasible as well.

This is where r-functions come into the picture. The r-functions, such as Gen, have a twofold character: they can be used as indicators of pathological rule behavior, but they can also be used as *estimators* of expected gains due to refinements. Thus Gen and GenCF can be used as estimators of ΔTP for appropriate generalization refinement operations, and, intuitively, this seems plausible. Therefore, if we can find a plausible estimator of ΔFP for generalization refinements then we will be able construct heuristics for generating generalizations that use these estimators as an approximation to condition (1). A seemingly good concept for this role would be something like the following:

BadGen(r) = the number of *correctly diagnosed cases* in which, if r *had been satisfied (or had a higher confidence factor)* the case would have been misdiagnosed.

The problem with BadGen, however, is that from a computational point of view it is not consistent with a general divide and conquer strategy. To compute BadGen(r) requires one to analyze every case in the data base having a PDX that does *not* match the conclusion of r (to see whether the satisfaction of r, or an increase in its confidence factor would lead to a false positive). In general, for any endpoint there will be far more cases in which it is the wrong conclusion, than cases in which it is the right conclusion. (Nevertheless, it might be worthwhile to implement something like BadGen on the grounds that its potential for yielding savings by filtering out more unacceptable refinements at the generation phase might be worth the additional cost; in general there is a trade-off between the amount of time one is willing to invest in the refinement generation process and the amount of work one will have to do in the experimentation process. This is an example of an option that is made available by utilizing a metalinguistic approach.)

We therefore have settled on the quantity [SpecA(r) + SpecB(r)] as an estimator of ΔFP due to a generalization refinement, and as such the conditions

$$Gen(r) > [SpecA(r)+SpecB(r)]$$

and

$$GenCf(r) > [SpecA(r)+SpecB(r)]$$

in our generalization heuristics for SEEK2 are our approximations to condition (1). In this context we are using [SpecA(r) + SpecB(r)] as a estimator on the grounds that the "future will resemble will the past," i.e., generalizing a rule that is *already* responsible for [SpecA(r) + SpecB(r)] FPs will cause the rule to generate another [SpecA(r) + SpecB(r)] FPs.

A similar account of the role of the conditions

$$SpecA(r) > Signif(r)$$

and

$$[SpecA(r)+SpecB(r)] > Signif\text{–}Level(r, Mean\text{–}PDX\text{–}CF([SpecA\text{–}mcases(r)+SpecB\text{–}mcases(r)]))$$

as approximations to condition (2) can be given. In this case we use SpecA and [SpecA + SpecB] as estimators of ΔTN due to a specialization refinement, and Signif and Signif-Level as an estimators of ΔFN for the same refinement; these correspondences are intuitively plausible. (Signif-Level is used only for evaluating confidence lowering refinements).

4.8.2 Discussion of Max-Gain Heuristics

Taking the Max-gain approach to refinement generation means not worrying about the possibility of increasing the number of FP's and FN's over Ccases when generating refinements to reduce their number over the mcases. Given our analysis for the Max-gain+Min-loss approach, it is a simple matter to recover from it an analysis for the pure Max-gain approach. The basic alterations to the analysis are to ignore the second clauses in conditions (1) and (2). Therefore, for generalizations we want predictors of ΔTP only, and for specializations we want predictors of ΔTN only. The same estimators of these quantities that were used in the Max-gain+Min-loss approach can obviously be used in the Max-gain approach as well. Thus, e.g., instead of comparing *Gen(r)* with *SpecA(r)+SpecB(r)*, we simply check whether *Gen(r)* is greater than 0, to determine whether generalization refinement experiments for *r* should be generated. Note that, for any r-situation, the experiments suggested by this Max-Gain approach must be a *superset* of the experiments suggested by the Max-Gain+Min-Loss approach.

4.8.2.1 Mixed Approaches

There is, however, a third possibility. Signif and Signif-Level are two r-functions for rule conservation that are basically intended to be estimators of ΔFN that can occur as a result of a specialization refinement. One might therefore use these r-functions as before, but eschew the use of SpecA, SpecB as estimators of ΔFP for generalizations, since we know that the latter are not particularly suited for this role. This approach is a mixture of max-gain and max-gain+min-loss.[9]

4.8.3 Specification of Refinement Experiments

Actually the analysis so far provides only one piece of information, viz., for which rules should have we generate refinements? Depending upon whether one adopts max-gain or max-gain+min-loss, one may get different answers to this question for a given r-situation, but the next questions are the same no matter which approach we use: given an implicated rule, which of its components should be revised, and in what manner?

Sometimes the answers are obvious given the information that implicated the rule in the first place, e.g., genCF rules should have their confidence factors raised, where the new value can be determined in the manner we discussed earlier (p.71). When the answers are not obvious we can try to answer the first question by using additional relevant r-function calls in an attempt to

---

[9]A version of SEEK2 that uses a mixed approach has been implemented and compared with the currently used Max-gain+Min-loss approach. The results agreed with our expectations: the set of experiments suggested by the latter approach was a subset of the experiments suggested by the former. However, in the cases tested, the additional experiments generated by the mixed approach did not lead to any net gain in performance.

localize the problem to certain components in the rule. For example, for implicated gen rules, a natural thing to do in first-order analysis is to find Mfmc. (For implicated Spec rules a natural thing is to find the components with minimum DSMs, but as we mentioned earlier this measure is not currently implemented in SEEK2).

At this point we have either managed to localize our concern to a single component of the rule, or not. In the latter case - which will generally arise for Spec rules - since our goal is to generate refinements with the largest On-target sets, the best thing we can do is to select a component of a type that has the least radical generic refinement operators applicable to it. Once a component has been selected in this manner, we proceed in the same way we do for the former case.

In whatever manner we have managed to localize our considerations to a single component c, our choices for γ are obviously constrained by the nature of c, the refinement operators applicable to it, and the type - generalization or specialization- of refinement to be generated. As we have seen in our discussion of r-functions, in some cases, e.g., a numerical finding, additional r-function calls can provide useful information in formulating an effective refinement operation. If such additional information is not available, we make an educated guess on the basis of the aforementioned constraints and conservatism constraints. For example, if we have localized to a choice component of a *gen* rule, and we have no further information, a conservative educated guess is to decrease the choice-number by 1.

There is one special case. If the localized component is an intermediate hypothesis H, then besides possibly generating a refinement to H itself, we definitely want to back-chain the analysis to the intermediate rules that conclude H. As we have seen above, back-chained analysis of intermediate rules closely resembles the initial analysis of endpoint rules. (Recall that SEEK2 does not back-chain on intermediate hypothesis in Spec situations.)

The reader is now in a position to fully understand the r-knowledge, or r-heuristics, that we have incorporated in SEEK2, and that is exhibited in below.

4.8.3.1 SEEK2's R-Knowledge

VR-Generalization Heuristics

(These are called VR heuristics because they contain only r-function calls in there premises).

1. If: Gen(rule) > [SpecA(rule) + SpecB(rule)] &
   Mfmc(rule) is equal to CHOICE c

   Then: Decrease the choice-number of CHOICE c in rule.

2. If: Gen(rule) > [SpecA(rule) + SpecB(rule)] &

Mfmc(rule) is some NON-CHOICE component

Then: Delete this NON-CHOICE component in rule.

3. If: GenCF(rule) > [SpecA(rule) + SpecB(rule)]

Then: raise the confidence level of the rule to
Mean-CDX-CF(GenCF-mcases(rule)).

RR-Generalization Heuristics

(These are called RR-heuristics because their premises make reference to the conclusions of VR or RR heuristics.)

4. Refine Confidence Range of Intermediate Hypothesis

i) If: the NON-CHOICE component that has been suggested to be deleted from rule r1 is an INTERMEDIATE-HYPOTHESIS H with associated confidence range (L:U) &
the majority of Gen-mcases(r1) in which H is not set in the range (L:U) are ones in which H's confidence factor is set below L

Then: lower the value of L in the range (L:U) in r1 to
Mean-value(H, {case| case is a member of Gen(r1) & the confidence for H in case is less than L})

ii) If: the NON-CHOICE component that has been suggested to be deleted from rule r1 is an INTERMEDIATE-HYPOTHESIS H with associated confidence range (L:U) &
the majority of Gen-mcases(r1) in which H is not set in the range (L:U) are ones in which H's confidence factor is set above U

Then: raise the value of U in the range (L:U) in r1 to
Mean-value(H, {case| case is a member of Gen(r1) & the confidence for H in case is greater than U})

5. Refine Range of Numerical Finding

i) If: the NON-CHOICE component that has been suggested to be deleted from rule r1 is a NUMERICAL-FINDING F with associated range (L:U) &
the majority of Gen-mcases(r1) in which F does not have a value in the range (L:U) are ones in which F's value is less than L

Then: lower the value of L in the range (L:U) in r1 to
Mean-value(F, {case| case is a member of Gen(r1) & the value for F in case is less than L})

ii) If: the NON-CHOICE component that has been suggested to be deleted from rule r1 is a NUMERICAL-FINDING F with associated range (L:U) &
the majority of Gen-mcases(r1) in which F does not have a value in the range (L:U) are ones in which F's value is greater than U

Then: raise the value of U in the range (L:U) in r1 to
Mean-value(F, {case| case is a member of Gen(r1) & the value for F in case is greater than U})

Control Heuristics

(The following is said to be a control heuristic because it specifies under what circumstances analysis should be backchained to intermediate rules.)

6. If: the NON-CHOICE component that has been suggested to be deleted from the rule r1 is an INTERMEDIATE-HYPOTHESIS &
r2 is a rule that concludes the INTERMEDIATE-HYPOTHESIS (at the indicated confidence range) &
r2 is closest to being satisfied in a plurality of Gen-mcases(r1)

Then: Identify the most frequently missing component of r2 relative to the cases in which r1 was chosen to be generalized; if it is a CHOICE, lower the choice-number, if it is a NON-CHOICE, delete it, or, if it is an INTERMEDIATE HYPOTHESIS, apply this heuristic again.

Specialization Heuristics

7. If: SpecA(rule) > Signif(rule) &
there is a CHOICE in rule

Then: Increase the choice-number of CHOICE in rule.

8. If: SpecA(rule) > Signif(rule) > 0 &
c component with range [L:U] in rule &
L′=Mean(c,Signif-cases(rule))-2*(Standard-deviation) &
L < L′ < Mean(c,Signif-cases(rule))

Then: raise L to L′

9. If: SpecA(rule) > Signif(rule) > 0 &

c component with range [L:U] in rule &
U′=Mean(c,Signif-cases(rule))+2*(Standard-deviation) &
Mean(c,Signif-cases(rule)) < U′ < U

Then: lower U to U′

10. If: [SpecA(rule) + SpecB(rule)] >
Signif-Level(rule,Mean-PDX-CF([SpecA-mcases(rule) +
SpecB-mcases(rule)])

Then: lower the confidence level of the rule to
Mean-PDX-CF([SpecA-mcases(rule) + SpecB-mcases(rule)]).

4.9 Failure of Refinability, Component/Rule Addition, and Failure-Driven Higher-Order Analysis

As we mentioned earlier (section 3.1.5), SEEK2 does not utilize an expressively complete set of refinement operators. In particular, our heuristics will never suggest addition of new components to rules or addition/deletion of rules from the knowledge base. In this section we briefly address some of the issues involved in integrating such operations into a refinement system. In particular we consider the connections among the issues of 1) what to do when first-order refinement fails, 2) ways of augmenting a first-order system with failure-driven higher-order heuristics that allow for addition of components to rules (or addition of new rules to the knowledge base), and 3) identifying situations in which a knowledge base has problems that cannot (or should not) be solved by refinement techniques at all.

It is easy to construct example refinement situations in which component/rule addition is necessary in order to correct a problem. For example, suppose that r has the form $f \rightarrow H$, where f is a boolean-valued finding, and suppose that r is the *only* rule that concludes H. Suppose that H is the PDX in several mcases M, none of which contain f as a case finding. There is nothing that the current SEEK2 can do to correct the false negatives for H in these cases. Clearly it is necessary to construct one or more new rules for H if the mcases are to corrected.

It is worthwhile to distinguish between two very different sorts of situations that involve addition of components/rules. In one sort of scenario - let us call this the *new-connection* scenario - addition of a new component/rule will involve the positing of a correlation between a finding and a hypothesis that is not implied by the initial knowledge base. Speaking loosely, a finding f and a hypothesis H are uncorrelated in a knowledge base if no rule-chain for H contains f. Thus adding a new-connection posits some degree of correlation between items that were completely independent in the initial knowledge base. From the point of view of the current work, such an operation may be viewed as being "too radical" to be suggested as a refinement. This point of view seems to be more or less reasonable in direct proportion to the degree of maturity of the knowledge base: the more mature the knowledge base the less likely it is that such a fundamental error has gone unnoticed. For less mature knowledge bases, however, it is possible that positing new-connections may be a worthwhile feature. While we might expect a robust refinement system to incorporate such a feature, from the point of view of the current work, this expectation should be understood as a desire to call upon an *inductive learning* subsystem to deal with situations in which the refinement system proper comes to grief.

The second sort of scenario in which component/rule addition may be involved - let us call it the *strengthen-connection* scenario - encompasses situations in which the intention in adding the component/rule is to strengthen correlations between items that are already correlated in the knowledge base. Davis's use of *rule-models* in the TEIRESIAS program [5], is a good example of this sort of scenario: rule-models contain information regarding the frequency of occurrence of components in the rules for certain conclusions or classes of conclusions. While Davis was interested in the *interactive transfer* of expertise, it is clear that the sort of information contained in his rule-models can be used in automatic knowledge base refinement. For example, if we want to specialize a rule r that reaches conclusion H we may consider adding a component c to r, if, among other things, c has a high frequency of occurrence in the other rule-chains leading to H.

The strengthen-connection scenario clearly is less radical than the new-connection scenario. In fact, the original SEEK program [30, 31] contained a specialization heuristic that generated component-addition refinements for such scenarios. Although a SEEK2 version of this heuristic was formulated, it was not incorporated into the program because from a computational point of view it was not consistent with the basic divide-and-conquer strategy.

4.9.1 First and Higher-Order Component/Rule Addition

Refinement operations involving the addition of components to existing rules, or the addition of new rules to the knowledge base may intuitively be seen as falling into our first versus higher-order classification. Adding a total of *n* findings or hypotheses components to an existing rule, or adding a new rule having a total of *n* finding or hypotheses components in its antecedent, may be viewed as an *n*th-order refinement operation. Adding a choice-component C to an existing rule or introducing a new rule with a choice-component as its antecedent, may be considered to be a first-order operation *provided* other rules in the knowledge base already contain C, i.e., C is already a "recognized" component in the knowledge base. The rest of the cases of choice-component addition may be assigned orders on the basis of the degree to which C differs from the "most similar" existing choice-component in the knowledge base.

4.9.2 Failure-Driven Higher-Order Analysis: Outline of a Scenario

We conclude this section by briefly outlining the sort of reasoning that one might use in attempting to deal with refinability failure in a first-order system. This outline will be fleshed out in section 6.5, after certain related issues have been addressed.

Suppose that r is the *only* gen rule for a given refinement situation σ=<R,M>, and c is its Mfmc. Suppose that we have generated and tested every (first-order) plausible refinement to c, and that in each case no improvement in empirical adequacy resulted. At this point, the first step is to find out whether these failures resulted because actual gains in TPs over M were offset by new FPs over Ccases, or because these refinements were not effective in increasing TPs over M itself. We analyze the latter case first.

Obviously, if even deletion of c from r did not increase TPs over M, there must be at least one other component of r missing in each of the mcases in the on-target set. This is a situation reminiscent of our discussion above (page 74) of the more sophisticated higher-order approach to localizing likely components of gen rules. At this point therefore, some version of that idea might be used identify either a single component other than Mfmc to generalize, or some combination of components.

If we are in the former situation, however, there is no point in looking for better ways to generalize r, since the refinements already generated are known to increase TPs over M. The problem is to prevent their increasing FPs over Ccases. Let μ be the set of former ccases that become mcases when r is generalized. On the face of it, it seems that we have a dilemma: either we generalize r and lose the μ ccases, or we fail to generalize r and continue to lose the gen-mcases(r). Does this failure of first-order refinability call for rule acquisition or higher-order analysis?

There are higher-order procedures that can be attempted in this situation. For example, maybe the problem can be alleviated by lowering r's confidence in tandem with one of the original refinements that was successful over M. The idea is to lower r's confidence to a point where it still corrects as many cases in M as possible, but reduces the size of μ as far as possible. To do this we could take the mean of PDX over the cases in $\mu=m_1$ and the mean of the CDX over the cases in gen-mcases(r)=m_2. We know that we can drop the confidence of r to a value somewhere above m_2, and still correct the majority and perhaps most of the cases in gen-mcases(r). If $m_1<m_2$, this lowering of confidence will still result in the majority of cases in μ being lost. On the other hand, if $m_1>m_2$, then it is possible that lowering r's confidence to a value closer to m_2 and farther from m_1, will have the effect of correcting the majority of cases in gen-mcases(r) without causing major loses over the current ccases.

This is also a point, however, at which component-addition (for specialization purposes) may be a reasonable alternative. Using the rule-model approach, one may try to identify a component c that is strongly correlated with the desired PDX in the mcases M but uncorrelated or weakly correlated with the PDXs in the Ccases in μ. By combining one of the original successful generalization refinements over M with the specialization refinement of adding c to the rule in question, one may arrive at a compound-refinement that preserves enough of the increase in TPs while generating sufficiently few new FPs that the net-gain will be positive. Alternatively, or in addition, one can try to select a component c that is known to be satisfied in a sufficiently large percentage of the desired PDX cases (including the mcases M) and unsatisfied in a sufficiently large percentage of the cases in μ or in some broader class of cases that are not supposed to conclude this PDX.

4.10 Summary

In this chapter we have presented the viewfinder of SEEK2's first-order heuristic refinement generator. In part this was done in order to pave the way for discussions of the role of a metalinguistic framework in the design of refinement systems; the exposition was also intended to show the power of the metalinguistic primitives selected.

We have also presented an architecture for extending or deepening the simple or "flat" model of heuristic refinement generation. We have discussed situations in which the notion of failure-driven higher-order refinement has applicability, and have given some idea of heuristics and procedures that can be applied in these situations. The question of when to look for and attempt to take advantage of such situations, is a key issue in contemplating higher-order refinement. For example, should a refinement system "always" attempt to discover situations amenable to higher-order refinement, i.e., in every cycle of refinement generation, or should it only make such an attempt when it reaches a point where all of its proposed first-order refinements are known to fail? These are issues involving the overall control strategy and tactics employed by a refinement system, which is the subject of the next chapter. Once we have discussed general questions concerning control we will be in a position to discuss some of the concrete issues involved in implementing a failure-driven approach to higher-order refinement (see chapter 6).

5 Strategy and Tactics

5.1 Integration of The Three Strategic Components

There are essentially three distinct strategic aims one usually wants to accomplish in one way or another with a refinement system.

The first aim is to *locate*, as well as possible, and to as fine a grain as is possible, "places" in the knowledge base where errors are present. This is analogous to the problems of locating hardware flaws in an actual circuit or a design flaw in a circuit schematic. All of these problems can be considered as instances of a class of problems that we may call *fault localization problems*. I therefore call the first component of our strategy the *fault localization* component. The localization issue is one that we have already touched upon in our discussion of refinement generation; we will have a brief discussion of it below.

Given that we have reason to believe that certain rules or rule-components are faulty, our second aim is to suggest ways of correcting these errors. This is the issue addressed by the second component of the overall strategy, and we will call it the *refinement generation* component. This strategic aim is truly at the heart of the problem, but since it is an issue to which we have already devoted much attention (Chapter 4), we have little to add here.

The third component addresses the issue of *refinement verification and selection*. Once we have generated some refinement possibilities, we want to know which of them, or which combinations of them, improve the empirical adequacy of the knowledge base, and which ought to be recommended for adoption, or tentatively incorporated in the knowledge base. This is the strategic aim that we have said the least about up until this point, and will therefore concentrate on in this chapter.

The main task of this chapter is to consider ways in which these three components may be integrated in a unified coherent strategy for doing knowledge base refinement.

5.2 Fault Localization

5.2.1 Philosophical Prelude

The analogy between the strategic aims of fault localization in knowledge base refinement and hardware fault diagnosis, also carries over to a certain degree at the level of strategic principles in the two problem domains. For example, in both problems one tries to use the inherent hierarchical relationships among the components of the entire (domain) system in order to aid in the search for flaws [13].

But the analogy has its limits and can be misleading if carried too far. In hardware (or design) fault diagnosis the issues of where the fault is and what to do about it, are not only conceptually distinct, they can be attacked separately in practice, and successfully so. This is because there are, in general, definitive observable criteria by which it can be determined that a fault exists at a certain location in the circuit. For example, if a circuit module is supposed to output a 1 at a port when a 0 is input at another port, then if the expected behavior is not observed we know that the module is faulty. Of course, to know this with "absolute certainty" in the case of an actual piece of hardware we have to know certain other things with absolute certainty, e.g., the failure was not a transient effect of random interference from a distant source. Clearly we are never in a position to rule out every other possible explanation of the failure with absolute certainty, but rarely is anything remotely approaching such certainty desired. If we are willing to make some assumptions, that may often be justified in ordinary circumstances, then we can say that obtaining *conclusive evidence of faultiness* is not only a real possibility in hardware fault diagnosis, but is in fact often obtained. This observation is even more pertinent with respect to fault diagnosis at the design level. This means that, for most intents and purposes, one can drive a fairly sharp wedge between the strategic goals of fault localization (where is the fault?) and fault classification (what is its nature?) and correction (how to fix it?) in hardware fault diagnosis.

The situation in knowledge base refinement is usually quite different, depending upon the nature of the domain of expertise the knowledge base is intended to capture. In the usual case, the rules in an expert system represent inductive rules of inference, and this is what we assume in our work. (If a knowledge base, however, contained rules that were intended to represent relations between premises and conclusions that could be made with deductive or mathematical validity, the analogy to fault localization in hardware fault diagnosis would be that much deeper, since putative logical or mathematical relationships must hold universally, i.e., one counterexample is proof of invalidity.) In a typical expert system domain, e.g., a branch of medical diagnosis, the rules will represent empirical associations of varying degrees of "necessity." Often the necessity of the association is purely a matter of statistical relevance of certain features to others; sometimes there is an understanding of the association in terms of underlying causal mechanisms, but more often than not the complexity of the problem together with limitations in the experts' understanding of these mechanisms is such that they must be regarded as non-deterministic, i.e., the corresponding associations must still be expressed in statistical laws. In such a domain the fact that a single case is known in which a rule sanctioned an inference that is incorrect, is usually *not conclusive* evidence that the rule is suitable for refinement. What is worse, definitive criteria for such evidence cannot be given. If we observe ten counterexamples and no positive instances to a rule which has a confidence factor of, say .7, is that *definitive* evidence that the rule is flawed in any way? The answer is no, for a very simple reason: the problem can always in principle be attributed to a failure to acquire other rules, rather than to a flaw in this rule.

In knowledge base refinement, therefore, while we can drive a *conceptual* wedge between the strategic aims of fault localization and fault correction, in practice this distinction can be sometimes obscured. The best evidence that we have located a faulty rule is the knowledge that if we refine it in a certain way then empirical adequacy is improved. If case evidence leads us to believe that a rule is flawed and we find that a certain refinement to the rule improves empirical adequacy, and we find no other refinement to another rule that does equally well, then we have even more reason to believe that we located a "real" flaw to begin with. If the expert approves of this refinement, then we are finally justified in concluding with relative certainty that a flaw was located. However, even after the refinement has been given expert approval, we can still pose doubts concerning its appropriateness or validity. Conversely, if we find that all plausible refinements to the rule in question fail to lead to adequate gains in empirical adequacy, etc., we may consider this as evidence that the rule was "OK" to begin with after all. Knowledge base refinement is truly an exercise in pragmatism.

The result of this discussion is that our division of the problem into three components does not mean that solutions to each component can be given in complete isolation from the others. Thus while we may offer certain strategic principles in relation to the interpretation of one strategic component, in many cases the principle will have implications for the entire problem.

5.2.2 Strategic Principles for Initial Fault Localization

While we can't hope to localize faults all the way down to the component level without doing refinement generation, we can hope to initially localize faults to the rule level, i.e., to sets of rules, by using other criteria. The details of how this is done for a first-order refinement system have already been discussed in chapter 4. To review briefly, given any mcase we can localize the rules responsible for it to those in rule-chains for either PDX(mcase) = the expert's conclusion in mcase, or CDX(mcase) = the knowledge base's conclusion in mcase. This criterion is sufficient to enable us to divide the overall problem of improving the knowledge base's performance into subproblems involving one dx, i.e., we deal with r-situations <R,M> in which $M=M(dx)=\{mcase|FP(dx,mcase) \vee FN(dx,mcase)\}$, and R is defined as in chapter 4, i.e., the set of rules that are in some rule-chain with dx as the endpoint. Note that R is also a function of dx, so we can write R(dx). It is then up to the refinement generator to further localize the problem.

One must be clear, however, as to how far this application of the strategy of divide-and-conquer goes. One could understand it as extending through all three strategic components of the refinement process. Viewing it in this way would mean that one would deal with each r-situation independently of the others even in the verification and selection phases of the process. In other words, for each endpoint dx, one would refine the rules for it with the goal that the cases in M(dx) should be corrected, without worrying about the other cases.

In the general case this wholesale adoption of divide-and-conquer is misguided. If we reduce the size of $M(dx_1)$ by refining the rules involved in concluding dx_1, while ignoring the effects of the refinements on other cases, then we have no way of knowing that we haven't created more mcases than we have gained. Divide-and-conquer makes sense for localization and refinement generation. To use it in verification and selection is, in general, a waste of time, and likely to be counterproductive. Only if we have special knowledge to the effect that the rules and cases for each dx have minimal "interaction" with one another, is wholesale use of divide-and-conquer justifiable.

Another important strategic principle for fault localization is also already familiar from our previous discussions. This is the idea of using the hierarchical logical structure of the knowledge base to guide our search for faulty rules. Thus, in heuristic refinement generation, we begin our analysis with endpoint rules and proceed to intermediate rules only when hypotheses components are implicated in the former. As noted before, back-chaining up a rule-chain may be repeated as many times as warranted.

There is another manner in which this strategic principle may be applied in knowledge base refinement. In some knowledge bases, the endpoints themselves are ordered in hierarchical fashion; we call such an ordering a *taxonomy* ([39]). To use automobile fault diagnosis as an example, while both dx_1= *car has electrical system problems* and dx_2= *battery is discharged* are both endpoints, if we employ a taxonomy we will designate dx_1 as a "predecessor" of dx_2, i.e., dx_2 is one type of electrical problem. Such a taxonomy is a hierarchical structure whose logical properties can be exploited for the purpose of more efficient fault localization. For example, if $PDX(mcase)=dx_2$, but $CDX(mcase)=dx_1$, where, as above dx_2 falls under dx_1 in the taxonomy, then we can localize the fault in this mcase to the rules that conclude dx_2.

5.3 Verification and Selection

We now move on to the topic of strategies for *verification and selection* of refinements. In contrast to fault localization, the situation here is somewhat less clear. Aside from the knowledge that it is wise to test refinements over a range of cases and not merely those they are designed to correct, there are no obvious strategic principles that determine the basic outlines of the process. In large part, the choice of verification and selection regime depends on the sort of performance we would like our refinement system to achieve, and the nature of the search algorithm used to achieve that level of performance. The nature of this connection will become clear below. But the fact that the connection exists makes it difficult to discuss verification and selection in a vacuum, i.e., without assuming something about the overall search strategy employed.

Therefore in this section we will discuss the issues of verification and selection of refinements in relation to three very general, mutually exclusive, and exhaustive options for doing knowledge base refinement. The three options are i) *ground-zero* systems: these work solely with the initial knowledge base, i.e., they do not tentatively incorporate refinements, ii) *single-generation* systems: these incorporate refinements, analyzing successive versions of the original knowledge base, but at any time have access only to the latest version, iii) *multiple-generation* systems: these are like single-generation systems except that they have access to multiple versions of the knowledge base at any time.

5.3.1 An Important Ground Rule

Before discussing the three options, we first need to state a "ground rule" that all three of them will be understood to obey.

The ground rule is the rule of *complete case analysis*. This is a shorthand way of referring to the principle that no selection (or final ranking) of refinements generated for *any* r-situation is to be done prior to the generation and testing of refinements for *every* r-situation involving the current knowledge base. In other words, before selecting any refinement for tentative incorporation, the refinement system must first do refinement generation *and* testing (of every refinement so generated) for every $dx \in DX$, i.e., every $<R(dx),M(dx)>$ must be analyzed. (Of course if $M(dx)=\phi$ for a dx, then the "analysis" of the corresponding r-situation is trivial.)

In a work where we have usually expended considerable effort in order to keep our analysis as general and flexible as possible one might wonder why we choose to impose such a seemingly arbitrary ground rule. For one thing the assumption of complete case analysis makes it much easier to conduct a meaningful comparative discussion of the three strategies to be presented. The main reason, however, is that no matter which strategy we use, the assumption of complete case analysis makes good sense. Clearly, for ground-zero and single-generation systems it would be reckless to change the only version of the knowledge base we have before completing our analysis of it. In the case of multi-generation systems, since multiple versions of the knowledge base are in hand, failure to adhere to the principle of complete case analysis would not be disastrous. However, as we shall see below, there are nonetheless good strategic reasons for adhering to this principle.

5.3.2 Verification and Selection in Ground-Zero Refinement Systems

A ground-zero system is one that never selects refinements for tentative incorporation in kb_0 (the initially given knowledge base), rather its analysis is always conducted with respect to kb_0. As output a ground-zero system will, at the very least, produce a list of refinements to kb_0 that have been verified to yield such-and-such a gain in empirical adequacy.

Failure to incorporate refinements is not, in itself, a failing, since the expert is always the final judge over the admissibility of refinements. However, while a ground-zero system does not need to worry about selection issues as such, if the system is to be of maximum utility, it has to be all the more concerned with verification issues. In other words, if all the system does is report findings of the form "refinement γ yields net gain of n cases," where the list of such findings is potentially large, the system is less useful than one that could say something more about the relative merits of these refinements. Simply reporting the results in order of decreasing net gain would be of some use. However, what we have in mind is something much more useful. Suppose that refinements γ_1 and γ_2 are known to result in (positive) net gains n_1 and n_2 respectively. This information still leaves open the question of what the *combined effect* of incorporating both γ_1 and γ_2 in kb_0 will be. The simple way of obtaining this information is to do a test of this joint refinement over the entire data base of cases, just as we have already done for each refinement separately.

Let G(γ,kb,C) be a function that for a given refinement to the kb, whether simple or complex, returns the net gain in cases in C that results. For $\gamma=\{\gamma_1,\gamma_2\}$, there are four possibilities of interest:

Empirical non-interference

$$G(\gamma,kb,C) = G(\gamma_1,kb,C) + G(\gamma_2,kb,C)$$

Constructive interference:

$$G(\gamma,kb,C) > G(\gamma_1,kb,C) + G(\gamma_2,kb,C)$$

Destructive interference:

$$G(\gamma,kb,C) < \mathrm{Max}\{G(\gamma_1,kb,C), G(\gamma_2,kb,C)\}$$

Indeterminate:

$$G(\gamma,kb,C) \geq Max\{G(\gamma_1,kb,C), G(\gamma_2,kb,C)\}$$
and
$$G(\gamma,kb,C) < G(\gamma_1,kb,C) + G(\gamma_2,kb,C)$$

Let us examine each of these in turn. If γ_1 and γ_2 are *empirically non-interfering*, the net effect of their joint incorporation is simply the sum of the net effect of their single incorporation. It is important to note that empirical non-interference of refinements, as well as the three other properties listed, is not a function solely of the refinements and the kb but also of the current composition of C. Two refinements that are empirically independent with respect to C might fail to be so if new cases were added to C.

If it turns out that the net effect of joint incorporation is greater than the sum of the two refinements taken singly, then we have *constructive interference.* If it turns out that the net effect of joint incorporation is less than the *maximum* of the two refinements taken singly, then we have *destructive interference.* In this case, and only in this case, can we say with certainty that somehow one or more cases that would have been gained by one of the refinements singly, is lost as a result of the joint refinement. If the joint result is greater than or equal to the maximum of the two but less than their sum, this circumstance could be the result of one refinement counteracting the other, but it could just as easily be the result of the two refinements being redundant over some cases, i.e., there is some overlap in the cases they correct singly; for this reason we label the results *indeterminate.*

Common sense seems to dictate the following precepts. Empirically non-interfering and constructively interfering refinements ought to be grouped together and recommended for joint incorporation. Destructively interfering and indeterminate refinements should be kept apart.

There is no reason to limit this joint verification idea to two refinements. Given a set Γ of n refinements of positive net gain, we would like to know all the "maximal" joint subsets of Γ, i.e., *subsets of* Γ *consisting of refinements whose joint incorporation into kb results in a net gain that is greater than or equal to the sum of the single gains, and such that no other member of* Γ *can be added to the subset without violation of this condition.*

A sophisticated ground-zero system might therefore work something like this. First it will generate and test refinements for each current r-situation over C, keeping a list of those that have positive net gain. At the end of this phase it will compute all the maximal joint subsets of refinements from this list, and then rank the resulting maximal sets in order of decreasing net gain.

Such a procedure might seem to be too costly. If there are n members of the initial list, then 2^n subsets will have to be tested. Note that we cannot cut down on the cost by making use of assumptions concerning the above properties that may seem natural, but are in fact not justified. There is no reason to believe, for example, that empirical independence is a transitive property, i.e., if α and β are empirically independent and β and γ are empirically independent, it does *not* follow that α and γ are.

Given that this procedure is too costly, what are the alternatives? An *approximation algorithm* that I find attractive will now be discussed. Intuitively, the idea behind the algorithm is to find one or more maximal subsets in an incremental fashion, although none of the maximal subsets generated is guaranteed to be among the best in terms of overall net gain. Let $\Gamma=\gamma_1...\gamma_n$ be the initial set of refinements ordered (from 1 to n) in terms of decreasing net gain. Let ω be initialized to $\{\gamma_1\}$. Let ζ be initialized to γ_1. Now for every other γ_i, i=2,...,n we do the following.

If

$$G(\omega \cup \{\gamma_i\},kb,C) \geq G(\omega,kb,C) + G(\gamma_i,kb,C)$$

(adding γ_i to ω leads to an increase over $G(\omega,kb,C)$ as least as great as $G(\gamma_i,kb,C)$)

then

$$\omega \leftarrow \omega \cup \{\gamma_i\}$$

(add γ_i to ω)

else

$$\zeta \leftarrow \zeta \cup \{\gamma_i\}$$

At this point ω is a maximal set in the above sense - this is obvious by its construction - although it need not be one with the greatest net gain. At this point we can repeat the procedure using ζ as the initial set. We continue until every member of the initial set belongs to some maximal set, i.e., until a pass yields $\zeta=\phi$. In the worst case this procedure will require on the order of n^2 verification runs over C. When we are done we may not have discovered all the maximal sets, nor those with greatest net gain, but we have succeeded in imposing some order on what is otherwise a mass of unrelated results. As we shall see below, this procedure is also useful in single and multi-generation systems.

The general point to be made here is that a good refinement system cannot avoid the issue of selection. A good ground-zero system will present its findings in a way that is more or less the same as a system that does tentative selection. Therefore the issue of choice of a selection criterion, which we discuss below, has implications for the verification component of a ground-zero system.

The main advantage of a ground-zero system is also its main disadvantage. By eschewing tentative incorporation of refinements a ground-zero system eliminates the problem of "dependency chains" of refinements, that is, the final results reported by a ground-zero system are independent, in the sense that the net gain engendered by one refinement does not depend upon incorporation of any other refinements presented. This is true even if the results are in the form of maximal sets as we have advocated, i.e., incorporation of any non-empty subset of a maximal set will result in a net gain. But there is another sense in which these refinements are independent: each refinement is discovered by doing refinement generation over kb_0. In a generational system, on the other hand, after doing some tentative incorporation, one may be working only with knowledge bases that are refined versions of kb_0. The results of refinement generation over these refined knowledge bases may depend upon earlier changes made to kb_0. If the earlier changes are later rejected by the expert, the work done in latter phases was for nought.

But the whole point of a generational system *is* to introduce changes in kb_0 that will "loosen things up a bit" and thus lead to new possibilities for refinement generation, and discovery of proven refinements. If tentative incorporation of refinements to kb_0 does not *ipso facto* lead to new refinement generation possibilities, or positive verification for refinements that previously resulted in zero or negative net gain, then we may as well use a ground-zero system. Therefore, the main disadvantage of a ground-zero system is that it misses out on the discovery of new refinement generation possibilities that could come from tentative incorporation.

How much of a loss or disadvantage this is depends upon the level of analysis carried out by a ground-zero system's refinement generator. The higher the order of the analysis, the more complex the generated refinement operations can be, and therefore the less likely it is that a useful refinement will be missed.

5.3.3 Verification and Selection in Single-Generation Refinement Systems

A single-generation refinement system is one that at any time has only one version of the knowledge base available for analysis. Whenever a tentative incorporation is made, the old version of the knowledge base is no longer available. A single-generation system that does tentative incorporation is said to be *cyclic*, where the cycles are demarcated by the sequence of successive knowledge bases.

As we remarked in the previous section, the intent of such a system is to follow up on new refinement generation possibilities, as well as retest old refinements in a new environment, created by incorporating proven refinements. The fact is that no matter what the level of analysis conducted by the refinement generator, one cannot rule out the possibility that incorporation of a proven refinement will result in r-situations that will yield new plausible refinements when analyzed by the same mechanism. Moreover, once some tentative incorporation is made, old refinements that previously led to little or no gain, may now produce positive net gains.

SEEK2 [17] is a cyclic system. In each cycle it does a complete case analysis, as defined above, and then it tentatively incorporates the single refinement that yields the greatest net gain over the current version of the knowledge base. It halts when none of the refinements generated in a cycle lead to a positive net gain. The output of the program is the set of refinements that have been discovered to lead to this result, together with the appropriate statistics on net gain and overall performance breakdown.

Given our previous discussion, there is one way in which a cyclic system such as SEEK2 can be augmented by additional useful information. When the system halts and has selected a set of refinements $\gamma_1 ... \gamma_n$ (listed here in order of *selection*) the user is not told whether or not there are any dependencies among these refinements. Since γ_1 was selected with respect to kb_0, we know that it can be incorporated into kb_0 with a resulting net gain. But we don't know whether the same can or cannot be said of γ_2 through γ_n. A simple way in which information concerning this question can be obtained is the following. Let O_1 be the *set* of refinements generated and tested in the *first cycle* that are verified to lead to a positive net gain. Note that if any of the selected refinements γ_i is a member of O_1, this entails that γ_i can be incorporated directly into kb_0 with a resulting positive net gain. On the other hand, if γ_i is *not* a member of O_1 then it may be concluded that γ_i's positive contribution to empirical adequacy is dependent upon at least one of the earlier refinements γ_j, $j<i$. Therefore, by keeping a record of O_1 a cyclic system can give the user some information concerning the relative dependence or independence of the final set of refinements selected.

This point also raises a question concerning the selection policy of a cyclic system. Instead of incorporating the single best refinement in a cycle, one could incorporate a maximal subset of all generated refinements in the cycle that have positive net gain. The approximation algorithm given above could be used for this purpose. In terms of cost-effectiveness, the idea is that while the cost per cycle would increase, one would avoid re-generation and re-testing of the same refinements over and over again in successive cycles.

An interesting question concerning this procedure is whether it has a good, bad, or no effect on the nature of the final refined version of the knowledge base produced. Assuming that both the simple selection policy and the complex policy can be employed in such a way as to always lead to a local maximum - this is an assumption we will investigate and justify below (see section 5.5) - can one be said to generally reach a better local maximum than the other? We will consider this once we have examined further how either of these procedures can be said to reach a local maximum.

5.3.4 Verification and Selection in Multiple-Generation Refinement Systems

In a multiple-generation refinement system at any given time the system has access to an, in principle, unlimited number of refined versions of kb_0. Data structures and procedures for implementing such a scheme have been design and utilized in RM (see chapter 6). At this point the basic fact to keep in mind is that any refined version kb' of kb_0 is completed determined by the set of refinement operations that lead from the latter to the former.

The new possibilities for verification and selection policies opened up by a multiple-generation system are legion. For example, suppose all the "old" versions of the knowledge base are accessible, along with several "current" versions (see figure 5-1), i.e., we have a lattice of knowledge bases rooted at kb_0. Essentially, at any time, we now have an historical record of how the refinement session has proceeded. Looking up the paths in the lattice, we can access (perhaps by re-generating) the earlier views of the knowledge base. This allows for the possibility of *strategic c-heuristics* (see chapter 4) that take account of the *evolution* of the *views* associated with the various versions of kb_0, and not just the knowledge bases themselves. Perhaps by comparing information from earlier views with a current view, and using feedback information generated by the earlier testing of refinements, one might be in a position to *predict* the effect of a currently suggested refinement. This idea is speculation, but it a potential topic for future investigation.

At a less speculative level, there are several advantages to using a multiple-generation control strategy, as opposed to a cyclic system. First, such a strategy can be used to decrease the number of arbitrary choices that must be made by a cyclic system. In a cyclic system it can happen that within a given cycle two or more refinements are tied for first place in net gain. We must choose one. (A similar arbitrary choice between maximal subsets of refinements can also arise in the case of the more complex selection strategy). If these refinements are empirically equivalent or destructively interfering we may never again have the opportunity to choose the refinement that was rejected, since under such circumstances it is unlikely that it will be re-generated in ensuing cycles. Perhaps if we had chosen differently, the final results might be different. Moreover, who is to say that the refinement we rejected, quite arbitrarily, is not a good one in the eyes of the expert? By allowing for multiple current version of the knowledge base one can adjudicate such conflicts in a perfectly fair manner: every time such a choice would have to be made in a cyclic system, a multiple-generation system will create a new version of the knowledge base corresponding to each of the possible choices. Of course, this means that the number of current knowledge bases available for further analysis will increase by the same number.

Taking the logic of this argument to an extreme, one can argue that the policy of selecting the *single* best refinement (or single best maximal subset of refinements) generated in a cycle is

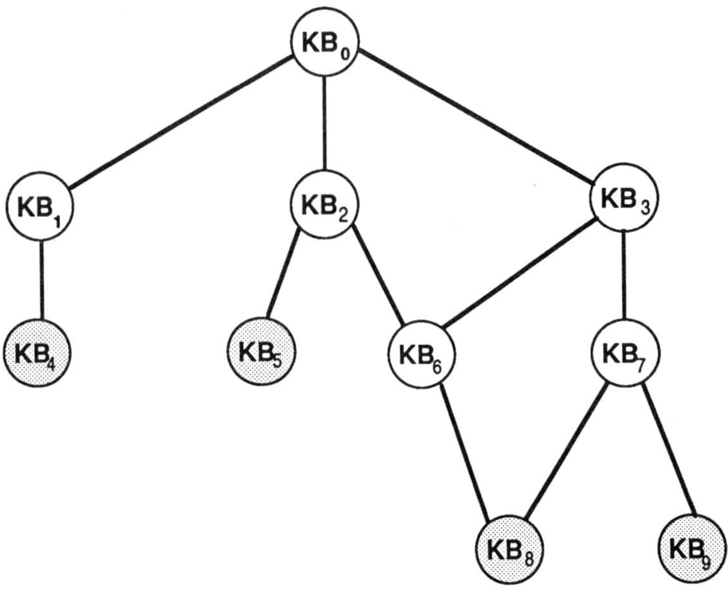

Figure 5-1: Multiple-Generation System

also somewhat arbitrary. For example, if the best refinement has a net gain of +25, and the next best has a net gain of +24, why select the former over the latter? A response to this criticism would lead us in the direction of a type of breadth-first search algorithm. This would work as follows. Starting with kb_0 as the root node, we generate all refinements, as required by the principle of complete case analysis, test them over C, and for *each refinement that has a positive net gain* we generate a successor node representing the kb that results from refining kb_0 in the specified way. We now do the same thing for every successor node, etc.

Besides the fact that this approach will be too costly to use in general, it suffers from the problem we have mentioned in connection with cyclic systems, viz., there could be concealed dependencies among the refinements generated in successive nodes. This problem can be addressed by incorporating something like the approximation algorithm given above into the current procedure. Thus given a node kb that has already been generated, using the approximation algorithm we would generate kb's successors as follows. Let Γ be the set of refinements with positive net gain generated at node kb. We apply our approximation algorithm for generating maximal subsets of Γ. *For each such subset* Γ' *generated we create a successor node kb′ that represents the knowledge base resulting from application of Γ′ to kb.* We now generate refinements for kb′ and all the other successors of kb and proceed as before.

Neither the simple breadth-first search technique, nor the complex version of it just presented are likely to be computationally practical. However, it would be premature to rule out such procedures on grounds of complexity, without first looking into the expected improvements that would ensue via exploitation of the inherent parallelism of the procedure. Again, this is a topic for future investigation.

5.4 Selection Criteria

Up until now we have used size of the (positive) net gain of a refinement as the sole selection criterion for both tentative incorporation in generational systems, and for ranking of maximal sets in a ground-zero system. This is the obvious choice, is it the only choice?

First of all, what happened to the spirit of conservatism? The first answer to this question is to remember that considerations of conservatism are already taken to account in the refinement generation process, so that highly radical refinements with relatively small on-target sets are not likely to be offered in the first place (given that more plausible refinements exist). But one wonders whether the selection criterion should not provide a second line of defense against radicalism? Recall our earlier discussions of this topic (especially in chapter 3) which assumed that *other things being equal*, a less radical refinement is preferable to a more radical one. Thus if two refinements are known to yield not only the same net gain in terms of numbers of cases, but also in terms of the actual cases they gain, then conservatism will surely lead us to select only the less radical of the two. But once we compare situations that are different in some way there are bound to be differing views as to how radicality versus net gain should be weighed and balanced against one another. Moreover, it may be that each of the possible attitudes towards the issue of radicality vs net gain trade-off is most appropriate at a certain point in the evolution of a knowledge base.

Ideally, therefore we would like to expand our metalanguage for knowledge base refinement with primitives that are useful for customizing a system's commitment to conservatism to suit the occasion and the expert's or knowledge engineer's tastes. An obvious and simple idea is to allow for the specification of thresholds on net gains, so that a refinement whose net gain falls below the threshold will not be selected. A more sophisticated idea is to comparatively evaluate refinements not only on the basis of the size of their net gains, but also on the basis of how the net gain is produced. For example, suppose in r-situation <R,M> refinement r_1 has a net gain of three cases that results entirely from the correction of three cases in M, while r_2 has a net gain of three cases also but it results from six cases in M being corrected but three cases in C being lost. Even from this information alone, conservatism constraints can be used to justify a preference for r_1 over r_2. To make the case stronger, one can add, let us suppose, the fact that the three lost cases were present from the "very beginning" of the enterprise of knowledge base construction and figured crucially in the acquisition and refinement of the rules that accounted for their correct diagnosis. A complete conservative with regard to the preservation of correct diagnoses might argue that once the expert has sanctioned a version of the knowledge base that correctly diagnoses a set of cases D, no refinement that loses any of the cases in D should be selected no matter how many new cases it gains. (Though, I, for one, am not *that* conservative.)

In order to allow for the metalinguistic specification of selection criteria that embody these constraints, we introduce the notion of a *paradigm*. A paradigm is a relationship between a set of rules $R_p \subseteq kb$ and a set of cases C_p that are known to be correctly diagnosed by kb "in virtue of" R_p, i.e., these rules were intended to deal with these cases. Specification of one or more paradigms for a knowledge base is an instance of the use of domain-specific metaknowledge. We stipulate that a single rule can belong at most to one paradigm. Intuitively a paradigm should be stipulated only when the defining condition of the relation is *both* known to hold for a $<R_p,C_p>$ pair and it is desired that any refinement to R_p,or perhaps even to other rules, will preserve the paradigm. In other words, there is an option here. We can be wary of violating paradigms only when refining rules in the paradigm, or also when refining rules outside the paradigm. There seem to be no good reasons for using paradigms in the latter way, so we ignore it here.

Whenever a refinement for a rule r is to be evaluated for selection we check to see if r belongs to a paradigm. If it does, we must check to see whether r causes kb to lose any of the cases in the paradigm. If so, we can take appropriate action according to the dictates of our brand of conservatism, e.g. automatically reject r, reject r if some other refinement gains some/most/all of the cases it gains without violating the refinement otherwise accept r, etc.

5.5 Searching The Universe of Knowledge Bases

Knowledge base refinement may be thought of as an "optimization" problem *in the following sense*: our goal is to maximize the empirical adequacy of the knowledge base subject to the constraints of conservatism. As we have seen, a number of general conservatism constraints hold for any knowledge base refinement problem, e.g., the number of rules does not change, the conclusions of rules do not change, etc., while other conservatism constraints may be chosen on a problem-by-problem basis.

Mathematical optimization problems involve a search through a well-defined space or graph of possible solutions with the goal of discovering a point or a node that maximizes a given "objective" function. In chapter 1 we indicated that while a well-defined search space, *kb-space*, exists for knowledge base refinement, the representation is not one that is amenable to the application of mathematical optimization techniques. It is nevertheless useful to show precisely how knowledge base refinement may be viewed as search through a space of possible solutions. By doing so we will, for one thing, be able to give more precise meaning to the notions of local/global maxima in the present context.

5.5.1 KB-Space: The Universe of Knowledge Bases

According to our assumptions, every knowledge base contains a finite set of rules which are "built out of" a finite set of elements. For the rule representation language we are considering, these elements fall in one of the following types: 1) findings, 2) hypotheses (as premises), 3) choice components, 4) conclusions, and 5) confidence factors.

By assumption every finding corresponds to a domain feature that can either be present or absent in a case, or take on some numerical value in a specified range. At this point we invoke certain assumptions on numerical features and their corresponding findings. The basic point of these assumptions is to aid in "breaking up" one numerical feature ϕ with range of possible values [l:h], into a finite set of true/false features ϕ_i each representing the presence/absence of the value of ϕ in a specified *sub-interval* of [l:h]. This break-up then induces a restriction on the way in which the corresponding finding may appear in a rule of the knowledge base. The assumptions are the following. Let F be a numerical finding, let ϕ be its corresponding feature with range [l:h], and let C be the ordered sequence of cells corresponding to the ϕ_i that are produced by breaking up the [l:h] using the step-size δ. We stipulate that whenever finding F appears in a rule of the knowledge base it must be accompanied by a range [a:b] that satisfies the following conditions: i) $a<b$, ii) both a and b are equal to a boundary of one of the cells in C.

Given our assumptions it follows that for any numerical finding F, there are only a finite number of ways in which it can appear as a component of a rule in either the original knowledge base or any refined version of it, i.e., it must take on the form F[a:b] for a and b that satisfy the stated restrictions. Moreover, for any numerical finding, we can construct and enumerate its possible ranges.

It follows from these remarks that, in principle, an exhaustive list of all the finding components that can ever appear in any refined version of the knowledge base can be enumerated. An analogous set of assumptions and remarks can be made concerning the possible forms of appearance of hypotheses in the premises of rules, i.e., we assume each hypothesis has a specified or "legal" range of values, and that a step-size is given, etc. Therefore for any hypothesis we can construct and enumerate its possible ranges. Furthermore, we will also assume that when a hypothesis appears as a rule conclusion, then the confidence factor of that rule can be raised/lowered only in multiples of the step-size specified for that hypothesis. A step-size is also provided for each *endpoint*. Therefore, for any rule, there are a finite number of confidence factors that it can take on.

Suppose that for a given knowledge base KB, we have indeed constructed a list L of all the ways in which findings and hypotheses can appear in the rules, i.e. we have a finite list with entries of the F[a:b] and H[c:d]. Now all the choice-components that can ever appear in any rule in the knowledge base must have a choice-list whose elements come from L. Let n be the number of elements in the list. Then there are 2^n-1 non-empty subsets of the elements in L, and hence the same number of possible choice-lists. For each choice-list <C> of length *l*, there correspond *l*+1 well-formed choice components, i.e., [0: <C>], [1: <C>],...,[*l*: <C>]. Thus we can construct and enumerate all the possible choice components that can occur in any rule, and add them to our list of possible rule components.

Given any initial knowledge base kb_0 - together with boundary values for every numerical findings - it is clear that from it we can, in principle, recover the complete list of all possible rule components, as defined above. Let us denote this list $C(kb_0)$. Using this list, we can define the set of all possible rule left-hand-sides by first enumerating all left-hand-side that can be formed from exactly 1 component in $C(kb_0)$, then all left-hand-sides that can be formed from exactly 2 *distinct* members of $C(kb_0)$, ..., and finally all left-hand-sides that can be formed from all the components of $C(kb_0)$. Since the repetition of identical components is not allowed, the resulting list of left-hand-sides - denote it by $L^i(kb_0)$, where the superscript is an index into the list - must be finite. We imagine that the construction proceeds in such a way that exact duplications and left-hand-sides that are permutations of one another are avoided.

Finally we can enumerate all possible rules by combining each member of $L^i(kb_0)$ with each possible conclusion, i.e., any hypothesis or endpoint with any possible confidence-factor. Since, by our assumption, the possible values for confidence-factors are finite, the resulting list of rules - denote it by $R^i(kb_0)$ - is finite.

Let n be the number of rules in $R^i(kb_0)$. A point, kb, in the n-dimensional kb-space based on kb_0 will be determined by specifying for every rule in $R^i(kb_0)$ whether it is contained in the knowledge base represented by kb. Formally a point in kb-space has the following form:

$$<r_1,...,r_n>$$

where the variable r_i takes the value 1 iff the *i*th rule in $R^i(kb_0)$ is included in the knowledge base, otherwise r_i has the value 0.

Clearly kb_0 is represented by a unique point in its kb-space, and it is also clear that any kb obtainable from kb_0 by application of refinement operations will have a representative point in kb-space. The fact there are many points in kb-space representing "knowledge bases" that are logically contradictory or semantically absurd is not an issue.

A typical knowledge base will generally contain relatively few rules *compared* to n, the dimensionality of kb-space. Therefore most of the entries r_i will be 0. This sparsity or "waste of space" of the proposed representation is a non-issue, since kb-space is important to us as an abstract mathematical tool for analysis, and not as a potential computer data structure. A good feature of this representation is that it defines a space of fixed dimensionality, while accommodating the full range of refinement possibilities associated with kb_0 (including addition and deletion of entire rules).

5.5.2 Maximization: Local and Global

Given a kb_0, we have seen how a kb-space that represents its "space of possible refinements" may be defined. In terms of kb-space, the process of knowledge base refinement may be described as the exploration of portions of kb-space with the point corresponding to kb_0 as the starting point of the search. Ignoring considerations of conservatism for the moment, the basic goal of this search may be seen as the maximization of an "objective function" that measures knowledge base performance over the data base of cases.

If c is a case and kb a point in kb-space then CDX(kb,c) returns the dx that is concluded by kb with highest confidence in case c; if no dx is concluded with positive confidence in case c, then CDX(kb,c) returns a distinguished "null value." A case c is diagnosed correctly by kb if and only if PDX(c)=CDX(kb,c). What we want to maximize is the number of cases for which this condition holds.

Let σ be the *microstate* that characterizes the r-system (see chapter 3). Then the function we want to maximize may be written as:

$f(kb,\sigma) = |\{case|PDX(case)=CDX(kb,case)\}|$

= the number of cases correctly diagnosed by kb.

Let kb be a point in kb_0's kb-space. Then kb is a *global maximum* if and only if $f(kb,\sigma) \geq f(kb',\sigma)$ for any other point kb′. For $n \geq 1$ we define *the nth-order neighborhood* of a point kb as the set of points that can be obtained from kb by the application of a single refinement operation of order $\leq n$. Then a point kb is an *nth-order local maximum* if and only if for any point kb′ in the nth-order neighborhood of kb, $f(kb,\sigma) \geq f(kb',\sigma)$.

It immediately follows from the definitions that an nth-order local maximum is an ith-order local maximum for all $i \leq n$.

To see why we relativize the notion of a local maximum in this way, let us consider what the intuitive mathematical notion of a local maximum is. A local maximum with respect to a function f(p) is a point p such that no matter in what direction around p one looks, all the points p′ in the "immediate neighborhood" of p have a value $f(p') \leq f(p)$. In other words, to talk about a local maximum *simpliciter*, one has to have a *metric* or *distance-function* on the points of the space, according to which it is possible to define the set of points that are "closest" to any given point.

We have not defined a metric on the points of kb-space. Such a metric would in fact seem to be nothing more nor less than the previously discussed *radicality metric* (see chapter 3). Any two points in kb-space may be obtained from one another via a (possibly complex) refinement operation γ. Rad(γ) may therefore be used as a distance measure on points in kb-space that are related by means of γ.

Just as the specification of a radicality metric is a domain-specific, and perhaps somewhat subjective matter, the same must therefore be said concerning a distance metric on kb-space. Thus we do not assume the existence of such a metric. Therefore the notion of a local maximum in kb-space *simpliciter* is not well-defined, and we must employ notions that are relativized, such as those defined above.

Note, however, that if we had a metric on kb-space then the goal of knowledge base refinement could be formulated in very elegant fashion as the search for the local maxima *closest* to kb_0. This formulation automatically takes account of the idea that conservatism is an important constraint on solutions.

5.5.3 Maximization in First-Order Systems

Let us consider a first-order refinement system that operates in the following manner. Starting with kb_0, such a system generates, tests, and perhaps incorporates first-order refinements until it reaches a point in kb-space at which all the refinements it generates fail to result in improved empirical adequacy, at which point the system halts. In this section we determine what sort of performance may reasonably be expected from such systems.

It is not surprising, and easy to show, that any first-order refinement system can *at most* guarantee that it always reaches a first-order local maximum. To see this let kb_f be the point in kb-space at which the system halts. Before halting at kb_f, the system will have investigated a subset of the first-order neighborhood surrounding kb_f, perhaps the entire first-order neighborhood. In addition, if the system employs an approximation algorithm for determining maximal subsets of refinements (see above p.101), or if it employs some form of failure-driven higher-order analysis, then it will also have examined certain selected points in higher-order neighborhoods surrounding kb_f. Thus it is quite possible that there is an *unexamined* point kb′ in the second-order neighborhood surrounding kb_f such that $f(kb',\sigma) > f(kb_f,\sigma)$.

The interesting question is under what conditions a first-order refinement system *can actually guarantee* that when it halts it has found a true first-order local maximum? It is obvious that if the system always examines the *entire* first-order neighborhood surrounding the current point in kb-space, then when it halts a first-order local maximum is reached. But is it *necessary* for the entire first-order neighborhood to be searched in order for such a guarantee to be given?

The answer is *no*. If a system has a *first-order complete refinement generator* (see section 4.4) that it can limit its search to a proper subset of the first-order neighborhood surrounding the current point in kb-space and still guarantee the attainment of a first-order local maximum. In order to prove this we first need to prove two lemmas.

The first lemma is a special case of a result that we proved earlier (see p.45).

> **Lemma 1:** Let Φ be an accurate viewfinder. Let <R,M> be an r-situation. Let γ be a first-order refinement that corrects every case in mcases$\subseteq$M. Then On-target(γ,Φ(<R,M>),mcases) is true.

The second lemma is the following:

> **Lemma 2:** Let kb be the knowledge base represented by the current kb-space point. Let m be any currently misdiagnosed case in the data base of cases, i.e., PDX(m)$\neq$CDX(kb,m). Let γ be any first-order refinement operation on a rule r *in* kb (or any first-order refinement that adds a new rule to kb) *that corrects* m. Then there exists an endpoint dx, and an r-situation <R(dx),M(dx)> with respect to kb, such that r$\in$ R(dx) and m$\in$ M(dx) (or, in case r is a new rule, r *would* be in R(dx) if it were added to kb).

To appreciate the need for lemma 2 consider the following line of reasoning. Basically we need to show that every refinement that can *really* correct any of the currently misdiagnosed cases will be considered in the current cycle. Lemma 1 guarantees that these refinements are a subset of all the on-target refinements for the current kb. Since a first-order complete refinement generator will generate all on-target refinements, it would seem that our result is forthcoming. But there is a problem with the preceding statement. A first-order complete refinement generator will generate all on-target refinements *with respect to some view of some r-situation*. How do we know that our way of defining r-situations guarantees that all relevant views, and therefore all on-target refinements, will be generated? What lemma 2 says is that our definition of r-situations - using the functions R(dx) and M(dx) (see section 4.6.1) - is sufficiently broad that any refinement that can really correct an mcase can be detected by examining some such r-situation.

Another point concerning lemma 2 is the need for special consideration of refinement operations involving addition of a new rule r to the kb. The problem here is that since r is not in the kb when r-situations are determined how can it be in R(dx) for any dx? Let kb′=kb$\cup${r}. According to lemma 2 if addition of r to kb is a refinement that can really correct some mcase, then r will be in R(dx) for some dx when R(dx) is computed with respect to kb′. If this is correct then we can be assured that by taking the views of the r-situations as we have defined them we will not miss any real first-order refinement possibilities.

Proof of Lemma 2:

Let PDX=PDX(m), let CDX=CDX(kb,m) (the CDX could be null). Then clearly m$\in$ M(PDX) because m is a false negative for PDX, and also, if CDX is not null, then m$\in$ M(CDX) because m is a false positive for CDX.

To show that either r$\in$ R(PDX) or r$\in$ R(CDX), assume that this is *not* true (we will show that any refinement to r cannot possibly correct m). (Recall that R(dx) is the set of all rules that are in some rule-chain whose last rule concludes dx.) By hypothesis, r is either an endpoint-rule concluding some endpoint dx′ not identical to PDX or CDX, or a rule concluding some hypothesis H. Suppose the former is the case. Then no matter whether γ represents a generalization or a specialization of r, or r is a new rule to be added to kb, the only changes that can obtain involve dx′, e.g., perhaps dx′ will now be concluded with stronger confidence. Since dx′ is neither PDX nor CDX, these changes cannot correct m. Suppose, on the other hand, that r concludes hypothesis H. Since r is not in any rule-chain leading to PDX or CDX - if r is a new rule then, by hypothesis, it does not occur in any rule-chain leading to PDX or CDX when R(PDX) and R(CDX) are evaluated with respect to kb$\cup${r} - then by definition it follows that H cannot occur in any rule that is a member of any rule-chain leading to PDX or CDX. Then no matter what γ does to r, or even if r is a new rule to be added to kb, the only changes that can obtain occur in rule-chains that can in no way effect the satisfaction or dissatisfaction of any rule-chain leading to PDX or CDX. Therefore γ cannot correct m.

Therefore if γ corrects m, it must be true that r$\in$ R(PDX) or r$\in$ R(CDX), or if r is a new rule to added to kb, one of these cases must be true when R(PDX) and R(CDX) are evaluated with respect to kb$\cup${r}. If r$\in$ R(PDX) is true then <R(PDX),M(PDX)> is an r-situation that satisfies the conclusion of the lemma. If r$\in$ R(CDX) is true then <R(CDX),M(CDX)> is. Q.E.D.

Using these two lemmas we now show the following. Let Σ be a refinement system with a first-order heuristic refinement generator Γ=<Φ,K> such that i) the viewfinder Φ is *accurate*, and ii) Γ is *first-order complete* (see section 4.4), iii) Σ obeys the principle of complete case analysis (see p.99 above). Then if a point p in kb-space is such that Σ halts at p, i.e., Σ can find no first-order refinement at p that improves empirical adequacy, then p is a *first-order local maximum.*

Proof:

We will show that if kb is the current kb-space point, then any first-order refinement on kb that improves empirical adequacy, i.e., leads to a higher value for the "objective function," will be generated (and hence tested) by Σ.

First note that any refinement that improves empirical adequacy must by definition *correct at least one currently misdiagnosed case.* Let m be an mcase corrected by γ, where γ is a first-order refinement to some rule r. Then by lemma 2, there is an r-situation <R,M> such that

$r \in R$ and $m \in M$. By lemma 1 and the fact that Φ is accurate it follows that On-target(γ,Φ(<R,M>),m) is true. Since Γ is first-order complete, and obeys the principle of complete case analysis, it follows that γ will be generated, and hence tested by Σ. Since γ was arbitrary it follows that Σ will generate and test every first-order refinement that corrects at least one case currently misdiagnosed at point kb. If none of these actually lead to an improvement in empirical adequacy (because they lose more cases than they gain) then there is no first-order refinement on kb that improves empirical adequacy, i.e., the point kb is a first-order local maximum. Q.E.D

5.5.4 Higher-Order Refinement Systems

We have seen that a first-order refinement system that meets the conditions stated above can be designed so as to always reach a first-order local maximum without searching entire first-order neighborhoods. One would expect that a similar result should hold for nth-order systems, viz., that for any n, an nth-order system that has an an accurate and *up-to-nth-order complete* refinement generator can be designed so as to always reach an nth-order local maximum without searching entire nth-order neighborhoods. In fact this is true, but the proof does not immediately follow from the proof for the first-order case.

The reason is that a suitably generalized version of lemma 2 is not true for higher-order refinements. As an example we will consider the case of second-order refinements. Let m be an mcase such that CDX(m)=dx_1, CDX-2(m)=dx_2, and that CDX-3(m)=PDX(m), where CDX-n(case) is the nth highest dx concluded in case. Let γ be a second-order refinement that corrects m by causing a rule r_1 for dx_1 *and* a rule r_2 for dx_2 to become unsatisfied, so that the conclusion formerly in third place becomes CDX(m). Then *if r_2 is not a member of any rule-chain that leads to dx_1 or PDX(m)* - which is certainly a possibility - then there is *no* dx such that both r_1 and r_2 are members of R(dx) and m is a member of M(dx). Thus lemma 2 is false.

The source of the difficulty is that the definition of an r-situation <R(dx),M(dx)> that we have been using is too narrow to account for the sort of analyses that would be necessary to generate higher-order refinements. This is not surprising, since the functions R(dx) and M(dx) were devised with first-order systems in mind. In order for the desired proof to go through the definition of an r-situation has to be altered. Note that the lemma is trivially satisfied if we take <KB,MCASES> as our definition of an r-situation, since no matter what the order of γ, all the rules on which it operates are in KB, and every mcase is in MCASES. This trick allows for the generalized version of the proof to succeed without additional complications, as the reader may verify.

5.5.5 Comparison of First-Order Selection Regimes

Let Σ be a refinement system with a first-order heuristic refinement generator Γ with viewfinder Φ such that i) Φ is *accurate*, and ii) Γ is *first-order complete* (see chapter 6), iii) Σ obeys the principle of complete case analysis, iv) Σ halts only when it finds no first-order refinement that improves empirical adequacy. Given our proof above, we now know that when such a system halts then it has found a first-order local maximum. Since the proof does not depend upon specific assumptions concerning the system's selection policy, it follows that any selection policy that involves choosing refinements that are verified to have a positive net gain is compatible with the conditions of the proof. In other words, whether Σ selects only a single refinement in a cycle or a maximal subset of refinements, as described above (see p.101), Σ will reach a first-order local maximum.

But this still leaves it an open question whether one of these selection policies necessarily, or on the average, *dominates* the other, i.e., leads to a first-order local maximum that is at least as great and perhaps greater than the other?

These questions are a great deal more difficult to answer than might appear to be the case. To understand why this is so, it is important to realize that once a knowledge base kb has been refined to kb′ - even via a single first-order refinement γ - it is as though one has entered an entirely new "universe." For example, it is entirely within the realm of possibility that every refinement that previously led to a positive net gain with respect to kb, is not even *generated* by a complete first-order analysis of kb′. In general, we do not expect changes induced by selected refinements to be so severe, but we cannot rule out such a possibility *a priori*.

We can, however, use just this consideration to give an admittedly non-rigorous argument that neither of the two selection policies dominates the other in general. In following the argument the reader should refer to figure 5-2. Suppose that, starting at kb_0, the complex selection strategy incorporates several first-order refinements on kb_0 that are verified to lead to a positive net gain. This selection is indicated by the bold arrow from kb_0 to kb_k. The simple selection procedure, on the other hand, will only incorporate one such refinement, which is indicated by the light arrow from kb_0 to kb_1. The lightest arrows in the figure going from kb_1 to kb_k are drawn to indicate that the simple selection procedure might eventually reach the node kb_k as well. For the sake of argument, however, we will assume that this does not happen on this occasion. Instead the simple procedure goes from kb_1 on a path to the final state kb_f^s, and the complex procedure eventually halts in state kb_f^c. Both of these final states are first-order local maxima.

Now one might argue that the state kb_f^s is likely to dominate kb_f^c using the following reasoning. In moving *directly* from kb_1 to kb_k, the complex procedure fails to conduct any analysis of the intervening states. In keeping with the intuition that even a single refinement

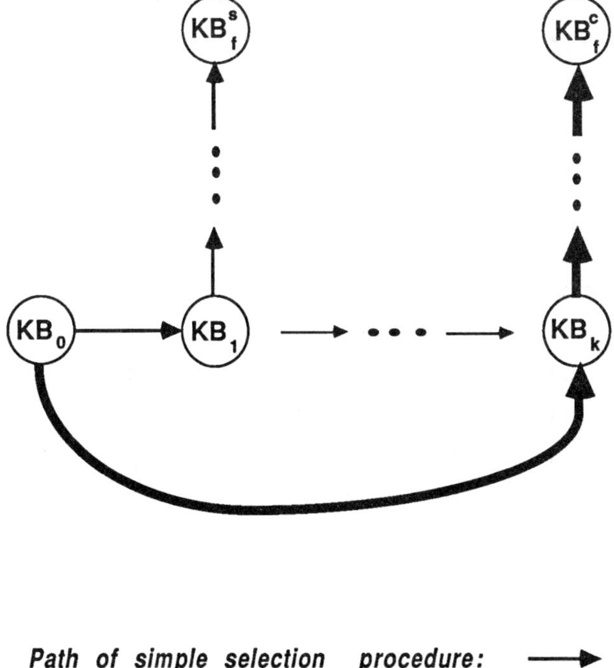

Figure 5-2: Comparison of Selection Procedures

can open up new possibilities, it is possible that in state kb_1 either new refinement experiments will yield generous increases, or that experiments that failed in state kb_0 may now succeed. These possibilities may be lost in kb_k due to the interactive effect of the several refinements incorporated. Therefore, it is quite possible that the local maximum in kb_f^s will be greater than that of kb_f^c.

On the other hand, one can give an analogous argument for the opposite conclusion, viz. that the state kb_f^c is likely to dominate kb_f^s. Just as it can happen that a single refinement to kb_0 opens up possibilities that were not originally available, so too it can happen that the *interactive effect* of several refinements, B, *simultaneously incorporated* can open up possibilities that are not opened up by selecting *any proper subset* of B. If, after the simple selection procedure moves to kb_1, it then moves off in direction that does not lead to kb_k, it will miss out on the possibilities present in that state. Therefore, it is quite possible that the local maximum in kb_f^c will be greater than that of kb_f^s.

Now if one views these two arguments as pointing out that on some occasions one procedure will dominate the other, and on other occasion the opposite will be true, then the arguments and conclusions are compatible. On the other, if they are both interpreted as arguing that *on the average* one procedure will dominate the other, then they are clearly incompatible. However, it seems that neither argument is good enough to warrant the stronger interpretation. It would seem that a much more sophisticated mathematically rigorous argument is needed to establish either claim. The final judgment on this question must therefore await the results of future investigation.

5.5.6 First-Order Multiple-Generation Systems

In section 5.3.4 above, we discussed a species of breadth-first search using a multiple-generation control strategy. Suppose that such a system is a first-order system and meets the assumptions listed in our proof above. Then it is easy to show that whenever this procedure reaches a terminal state - this is a state in which a cyclic system would simply halt operation altogether - then it has found a first-order local maximum.

Suppose, intuitively speaking, that such a multiple-generation system takes every path possible starting from kb_0. The question is whether, when the multiple-generation procedure halts, is one of the first-order local maxima it has found *guaranteed* to be a first-order *global* maximum? The answer is no, and the reason for it is that it is possible for an nth-order local maximum to be "unreachable" from kb_0 using an nth-order refinement system. In order to prove the point, and illustrate what it means, we give a simple example.

Let kb_0 contain the following rules: $abcd \rightarrow DX_1$, $ac \rightarrow DX_2$, and $bc \rightarrow DX_3$, where all the lower cases letters represent boolean-valued findings. Suppose the set of cases is the following: case-1: {a,b} ($PDX=DX_1$), case-2: {a,c} ($PDX=DX_2$), and case-3: {b,c} ($PDX=DX_3$). Case-1 is an mcase, case-2 and case-3 are ccases. In this scenario no first-order refinement yields a positive net gain. The only way to try to correct case-1 using an existing rule is to try to generalize the rule $abcd \rightarrow DX_1$. But this will not succeed since component deletion is the only applicable operation and *two* components must be deleted in tandem in order to get any gain. No performance gain can be had by performing a first-order rule addition operation. The rule $a \rightarrow DX_1$ would correct case-1 but it would simultaneously generate a new FP in case-2; the rule $b \rightarrow DX_1$ would also correct case-1 but it would generate a new FP in case-3.

In this example kb_0 already is a first-order local maximum. While it is clear that a global maximum, and therefore a first-order global maximum exists - replace the first rule in kb_0 with the rule $ab \rightarrow DX_1$ - there is no way that it can be reached from kb_0 using first-order refinement.

Should we infer from this that a second-order refinement system would be able to guarantee the discovery of a first-order global maximum? This is the wrong conclusion to draw from our example. It is clear that we could contrive an example of a kb_0 and a kb_x such that the latter is reachable from the former only by a third-order, or fourth-order, etc. refinement. The moral to draw from our example is rather the following. In the first place, we should draw a distinction between nth-order local maxima that are *nth-order-reachable* from kb_0 *via* the successive incorporation of positive net gain refinements of order $\leq$n (or maximal sets of such), and those that are not. It is then easily verified that the multiple-generation breadth-first search procedure we are discussing will discover *every* first-order local maximum *first-order-reachable* from kb_0. The ones among these with the best performance may then be thought of as first-order-reachable global maxima, i.e., not necessarily true first-order global maxima, but the greatest first-order local maxima that can be reached from kb_0.

5.6 Conclusion

As we pointed out in chapter 4, one reason we use the term *heuristic* refinement generation to describe our approach, is because we do not intend to design systems that generate *every* refinement in R that has a chance of correcting any misdiagnosed case in M. It is easy to show that SEEK2 is not a first-order complete system; in fact this immediately follows from the fact that SEEK2 uses a max-gain+min-loss refinement generation approach. In a nutshell, the idea of generating *all* first-order on-target refinements *heuristically* - although not a logical contradiction - is like trying to give a useful prediction of what, say, the weather will be like tomorrow, by providing a list of every scenario that has the slightest possibility of occurring. However, the idea of designing an *algorithmic* approach to refinement generation that *is* first-order complete does not suffer from the same sort of incongruity. Whether such approaches to refinement generation can be practical, is not clear at this time, and is a subject for future investigation. At the present time, however, it would seem that the combination of a heuristic (incomplete) first-order refinement generator with an architecture allowing for higher-order failure-driven refinement is more likely to yield useful results.

6 A Metalanguage for Knowledge Base Refinement

In the two preceding chapters we saw, among other things, concrete detailed expositions of the structure of an actual automatic refinement system, SEEK2. A good part of this exposition made use of a metalinguistic framework for refinement specification. This mirrors the fact that the metalinguistic approach was actually used in designing SEEK2's r-functions and heuristics, albeit "by hand."

A metalinguistic approach has several virtues as a research tool. First of all, it allows for generality: the same metalinguistic framework can be used in the specification of many alternative refinement systems. Such an approach also maximizes flexibility: to alter a feature of a refinement system specified within a metalinguistic framework is a much simpler affair than altering a hard-coded system. Finally a properly designed system of high-level metalinguistic primitives makes it much easier to experiment with alternative refinement systems, since the user need only be concerned with *what* he wants a refinement system to do, not with the internal details of *how* it is to be done.

In the context of knowledge base refinement, the idea of doing *experimental research* involves several possibilities, including: 1) designing, implementing, and comparing the performance of viewfinders, heuristics, and architectures for refinement generation, 2) designing, implementing, and comparing the performance of verification, selection, and control strategies, and 3) finding ways of expressing and utilizing domain-specific metaknowledge in the refinement process.

The metalanguage RM - short for **Refinement Metalanguage** - is a system that is intended to aid the researcher in doing experimental research in all of the aforementioned areas. RM may be used to define and utilize r-functions interactively, or will read and process a file containing definitions written in the language. In either case, the definitions are first translated into common lisp and may then be compiled into machine code. In interactive mode, both the primitive and user-defined r-functions may be used to obtain information concerning knowledge base performance, or the data base of cases in interactive fashion. For example, if one types **PDX(1)** to RM's command interpreter, then the expert's conclusion in the case whose id is 1 will be returned.

RM is intended to facilitate experimental research in knowledge base refinement by making it possible for the research scientist to quickly translate ideas into working definitions in the language. In this way the results of using alternative r-functions in a viewfinder may be compared without doing any programming in the traditional sense.

While the intended use of RM is as a research tool, such a system could be used as a framework for the specification of refinement systems in the same manner that EXPERT is used as a framework for the specification of expert systems. If the system is to be used for this purpose it would be useful to have an "optimizing compiler" for the language. Currently, in the time it takes RM to compute a view of an r-situation, the "hard-coded" SEEK2 system has not only computed the view but suggested and tested refinements for it. This "performance gap" may be partially attributable to some of the idiosyncrasies of the current hardware and software configuration. But it is also partially attributable to the fact that the declarative set-theoretic style of r-function definition, while useful for its intended purpose, is not easily translated into highly efficient code.

The preceding remarks lead up to a final virtue of a system like RM. It is generally easier to verify that a two or three line set-theoretic definition meets its intended design specification, than a programming language equivalent that may be spread over several pages of code. Thus RM can be used as a verification tool. Once we are satisfied that an RM definition captures its intended design specification, we can test a hard-coded version of the definition against the RM version. In fact, using RM in this fashion led to the discovery of a bug in the hard-coded SEEK2 with respect to the definitions of **SpecA** and **SpecB** (see chapter 4).

6.1 RM Primitives

In this section we discuss the key features of the metalanguage RM. A list of the most important primitives of RM may be found in appendix I.

6.1.1 The Interface

In order for a language like RM - or any metalanguage for studying and manipulating knowledge bases - to be implemented, certain software capabilities must exist vis-a-vis the software that implements the rule representation language. We say that an *interface* between the metalanguage and the rule representation language (or expert system framework) must exist, or be built. The interface will allow the user of the metalanguage to 1) access the knowledge base and cases, and 2) modify the knowledge base and create new versions of it, in a way that does not presuppose knowledge of the internal representations and procedures used by the rule representation language. The construction of such an interface may be a relatively simple matter or not, depending upon the nature of the underlying rule representation framework, but it is something that can always, in principle, be done.

RM uses an interface to EXPERT [39]. The high-level primitives described below enable a user of RM to design and test rule refinement heuristics and strategies for knowledge bases written in EXPERT, without requiring any knowledge of the internal representations or procedures used in the EXPERT framework. In other words, a user is expected to know what rules in EXPERT look like, and how confidence factors work, and other high-level matters, but he is not expected to know, for example, that EXPERT uses a "compiled" internal representation of knowledge base rules, rather than a rule interpreter.

6.1.2 Primitive R-Functions

Some primitive variables are needed to provide the system or a user with the ability to "access" various "objects" in the (available versions of the) knowledge base and the data base of cases. For example **kb** is a variable over the currently accessible versions of the knowledge base; $\mathbf{kb_0}$ is a *constant* that refers to the initial knowledge base. The term **rule** is a variable whose range is the set of rules in the domain knowledge base, **case** is a variable whose range is the set of cases in the data base of cases, and **dx** is a variable whose range is the set of possible final diagnostic conclusions in the knowledge base. In addition some primitive *functions* are needed to allow one to refer to selected parts or aspects of a rule or a case, e.g., **RuleCF(rule)** is a function whose value is the confidence factor associated with **rule**, **PDX(case)** is a function whose value is the expert's conclusion in **case** ("PDX" stands for "Presumed Diagnosis"), and **CDX(case)** is a function whose value is the conclusion reached by the knowledge base in **case** ("CDX" stands for "Computer's Diagnosis"). **Value(finding,case)**, is a function that returns the value of (numerical) **finding** in **case**.

Some of the primitives have, as it were, an implicit "knowledge base" argument. For example, **CDX(case)** must return *some* **kb**'s conclusion in **case**, but which one? While RM allows several versions of the knowledge base to be accessible at any given time, only one **kb** is designated as *active* at any given time. Basically this means that any functions that require an implicit **kb** argument will always be interpreted as referring to the active **kb**, whichever one that may be. Initially kb_0 is the active kb. The RM command **Activate(kb)** is used to make **kb** the active kb.

Some primitives can be used to return information concerning either 1) rules, 2) rule components, or 3) rule subcomponents. (In EXPERT the only subcomponents are the elements of choice-lists.) Rules are identified by numbers corresponding to their order of occurrence in the knowledge base. Rule components are identified by two numbers: the rule number and a number giving the position of the component in the rule (starting with 1 for the leftmost component). Rule subcomponents are specified by three numbers: rule number, component number, and a number giving the position of the subcomponent in the component. Thus, for example, the primitive **Range** can be used in two ways:

Range(rule,component) :

```
returns the [L:H] boundaries of the range
associated with rule component
```

Range(rule,component,subcomponent) :

```
returns the [L:H] boundaries of the range
associated with rule subcomponent
```

Certain special sets of objects are of importance in the knowledge base refinement process, and it is therefore useful to have primitives that refer to them, e.g., **Rules-For(hypothesis)** is a function whose value is the set of rules that have **hypothesis** as their conclusion (**hypothesis** is, of course, a primitive variable ranging over the set of hypotheses in the knowledge base). In addition, it is desirable to have the ability to refer to *subsets* of various objects. Thus, in RM, **cases** is a primitive variable over subsets of cases, **rules** is a primitive variable over subsets of rules.

Various primitives that in some way involve *semantic* properties of rules, or the *performance characteristics* of the knowledge base as a whole are clearly required. **Satisfied(rule,case)** is a predicate that is true *iff* **rule** is satisfied by the findings in **case**, and false otherwise. (This primitive can also be used with optional component and subcomponent arguments). **ModelCF(hypothesis,case)** is a function whose value is the system's confidence factor accorded to **hypothesis** in **case**.

6.1.3 Primitive Actions

6.1.3.1 Primitive Operators

A refinement metalanguage must provide operators for combining primitive r-functions in order to form sophisticated r-functions. The basic operators that are needed are familiar from set theory, logic, and arithmetic. Chapter 4 shows how all the r-functions used in SEEK2 may be defined using simple primitives such as set abstraction, i.e., forming a set of objects that meet a certain condition, boolean operations such as conjunction, disjunction, etc., and arithmetic operations such as addition, summation, etc. Some procedural or algorithmic primitives are needed as well, e.g. the **select** operator.

Since RM is built "on top" of common lisp, most of the primitive operations needed are already available as lisp primitives, and may be used in RM commands and definitions.

6.1.3.2 Modifying the Knowledge Base

A metalanguage for rule refinement must provide an adequate set of *primitive rule refinement operators* (see chapter 3). It should allow for these operators to be composed, so that higher-order refinement is possible (see chapter 4). Again, the internal mechanisms that implement these ideas ought to be hidden from the user.

RM offers a set of primitive operators that is not only sufficient for the definition of SEEK2, but also goes beyond the current implementation of SEEK2 in power. For example, in SEEK2 all refinement operators apply only to rule components (including confidence factors); there is no way SEEK2 can apply an operator to a rule subcomponent, i.e., to an element of a choice-list. In RM, on the other hand, rule subcomponents can be accessed and manipulated in the same manner as top-level components.

Higher-order refinements can be incorporated in heuristics by simply compounding primitive operators together, e.g.

```
(Operation
     (Operation decrease-choice-number n r1 c1)
     (Operation decrease-CF r2 x))
```

defines a second order operation: decrease the choice-number of component c1 in rule r1 by n, and at the same time decrease the confidence factor of rule r2 by x. When satisfied for specific bindings of the variables r1,c1, r2, and x, a heuristic that contains this complex operator expression in its consequent or "then" clause will suggest this second-order refinement for the objects bound by the variables.

6.1.3.3 Creating Mathematical Objects

A refinement metalanguage must give a user the ability to define r-functions using the primitives. In order for this to be possible a user must be able to *create* new sets, functions, and variables over both individuals and sets. RM provides several primitive commands that allows these tasks to be accomplished. The basic commands relevant to the design of r-functions are: define-set, define-variable, define-set-variable, and define-function.

As an example consider the following RM commands:

```
define-variable r1 rule

define-variable r2 rule

define-variable c1 component

define-variable c2 component
```

```
define-variable sub1 subcomponent

define-variable sub2 subcomponent
```

The first two commands define two new variables of type **rule**, the second two define two new variables of type **component**, and the last two define two new variables of type **subcomponent**. Since these are primitive types, RM, using frame-based property-inheritance, is able to determine what the properties of these newly defined objects should be.

It is also possible to define variables over *user-defined* objects. Consider, for example, the following RM commands:

```
define-set Misdiagnosed-Cases {case| (/= (pdx case) (cdx case))}

define-set-variable mcases Misdiagnosed-Cases
```

The first command defines a new set *misdiagnosed-cases*, i.e., the set of all **case** such that (Pdx case)≠(Cdx case). The second command then establishes **mcases** as a variable over *subsets* of *misdiagnosed-cases*. These defined variables may then be used to define a new r-function as follows:

```
[define-function joint-unsatisfied (r1 c1 r2 c2 mcases)
      {case in mcases| (= 0 (satisfied r1 c1 case)
                             (satisfied r2 c2 case))}].
```

This command defines a function *joint-unsatisfied* which is potentially useful in designing heuristics for second-order refinement. When called with actual arguments, or bindings, for r1, c1, r2, c2, and mcases, this function will return the set of all those cases in mcases in which *both* rule component r1 c1 and rule component r2 c2 are unsatisfied.

6.1.3.4 Creating Refinement Objects

A refinement metalanguage must allow the user to define heuristics for recommending refinements, and it must also provide facilities for the definition of *viewfinders* - see chapter 3 - that contain the r-functions called by the heuristics. RM provides commands and primitive data structures that are sufficient for the implementation of the general architecture for heuristic refinement generation described in chapter 4. For example, **vr-heuristics** and **rr-heuristics** are tables that contain heuristics of the appropriate sorts (see chapter 4), and the commands **define-vr-heuristic** and **define-rr-heuristics** are used to define the heuristics that will occupy these tables. Thus the following command adds a vr-heuristic to the table of vr-heuristics:

```
[define-vr-heuristic

  (if (and (> (gen rule) 0)
           (is-choice rule (Mfmc rule)))
   (decrease-choice-number 1 rule (mfmc rule)))].
```

```
(English translation: if Gen(rule) > 0 and Mfmc(rule) is a
 choice-component c then decrease the choice-number of c by 1.)
```

According to the general model of heuristic refinement generation, one will typically associate a set of heuristics with a set of r-functions that are called by the heuristics. Collectively, these r-functions make up a *viewfinder*. The idea is that there is a certain natural sequence of events in generating refinements heuristically: first the r-functions in the viewfinder are evaluated for every rule in the given r-situation, and these values are stored (these stored values are what we call the *view*); then the refinement heuristics are evaluated for every rule making use of these stored r-function values. In RM the **define-viewfinder** command allows the user to specify a set of (already defined) r-functions that are to form such a collection. Consider the following two examples:

```
[define-viewfinder rule-statistics number
     (signif speca specb gencf gen mfmc)]

[define-viewfinder set-valued-functions set
     (signif-cases speca-mcases specb-mcases gencf-mcases
            gen-mcases mfmc-mcases)]
```

The first command instructs RM to build a table (2-dimensional array) called *rule-statistics*, whose elements will be numbers, and whose columns will be labelled signif, speca, etc. The second command instructs RM to build a table called *set-valued-functions*, whose elements will be sets (lists), and whose columns will be labelled signif-cases, etc. The *n*th row of these tables will contain the values of these r-functions for rule *n*.

6.1.3.5 Using Refinement Objects

Finally, a refinement metalanguage must allow the user to evaluate viewfinders and heuristics, try suggested refinement experiments, and create new versions of the knowledge base if desired. The metalanguage should also allow the user to put all these primitive actions together into an overall control strategy for the refinement process.

There are several major RM primitives for performing these tasks. **Compute-View(viewfinder,rule-set)** is a procedure that, given a subset of rules, **rule-set**, computes the values of the r-functions in **viewfinder** for each of these rules. (The values are stored in the table **viewfinder**). **Evaluate-vr-heuristics(rule-set)** and **Evaluate-rr-heuristics(rule-set)** are procedures that evaluates all the heuristics in the tables

vr-heuristics and **rr-heuristics** respectively. Each of these procedures may also take an optional argument specifying a particular subset of the heuristics to be evaluated as opposed to the entire table.

Suppose that $\mathbf{kb_a}$ is the *active knowledge base* (see section 6.1.2 above). **Try-Experiment(operation)** is a procedure that 1) applies the refinement, **operation,** to $\mathbf{kb_a}$, 2) calculates the result of running this refined version of $\mathbf{kb_a}$ over all the cases, and returns a data-structure, called a *case-vector,* containing the new results (i.e., the endpoints concluded along with their confidences), and 3) applies the *inverse* of **operation** to $\mathbf{kb_a}$ in order to return it to its original form. Thus this procedure does not change $\mathbf{kb_a}$ permanently; rather the case-vector it returns is used to determine the effectiveness of **operation.** By comparing this returned case-vector with the case-vector for $\mathbf{kb_a}$ one can determine the exact effect of **operation** on a case-by-case basis, if desired. The function **Result-Experiment(operation)** will return the net gain (or loss) in cases due to **operation,** leaving $\mathbf{kb_a}$ unchanged.

In order to create a refined knowledge base that can be available for future analysis the procedure **Create-Kb(operation)** must be invoked. This procedure "creates a knowledge base" **kb** that is the result of applying **operation** to $\mathbf{kb_a}$ (the active kb). The data structure that represents **kb** contains a) **operation,** b) a pointer to $\mathbf{kb_a}$, c) a slot for pointers to **kb**'s potential successors, c) a table summarizing the basic performance characteristics of this knowledge base, including, for example, the total number of cases this knowledge base diagnoses correctly.

In virtue of these predecessors and successors links, at any time the set of available knowledge bases forms a tree rooted at $\mathbf{kb_0}$. When RM is instructed to *activate* a knowledge base $\mathbf{kb} \neq \mathbf{kb_a}$, RM traces back through the ancestors of **kb** until either $\mathbf{kb_a}$ or $\mathbf{kb_0}$ is reached (one of these events must occur). If $\mathbf{kb_a}$ is reached then in order to activate **kb** all the refinement-operations occurring in the path from $\mathbf{kb_a}$ to **kb** are performed on the current internal version of the knowledge base. If $\mathbf{kb_0}$ is reached, the operator information in the path from $\mathbf{kb_0}$ to **kb** is used to activate **kb.** (Note that RM never requires more than one internal copy of the knowledge base; to activate a refined version of $\mathbf{kb_a}$, the current internal copy is modified in the specified manner using the information in the "tree of knowledge bases.")

6.1.4 Adequacy of the Primitives

Ideally a set of primitive r-functions should allow for the definition of any conceivable (computable) r-function, and hence any conceivable viewfinder. A set of primitive refinement actions should allow for the definition of any conceivable refinement strategy. In general a refinement metalanguage should be of sufficient power to express anything that would come under the rubric of *generic refinement metaknowledge.*

The characterization of this ideal is, however, too imprecise to allow for a proof that a system of primitives meets it. The problem is that we do not have a precise independent characterization of what generic refinement metaknowledge is. For this reason, just as it can never be proven - but only refuted by means of counterexample - that the set of *computable* functions, in the *intuitive* sense, is, in fact identical to the set of Turing machine computable functions, so too it can never be proven that any refinement metalanguage is sufficiently rich to capture all possible generic refinement metaknowledge.

The best we can do at this time is to devise a system of primitives that is sufficient to account for the refinement metaknowledge that we either actually employ (in SEEK2), or that we know to be of possible interest. That the primitives in RM are sufficient to express the r-functions and heuristics used in SEEK2 is demonstrated by the analysis of chapter 4. In section 6.3 below we will see that the entire structure of SEEK2, including control strategy, can be expressed in RM. A system of primitives that meets these goals is likely to be a good starting point, and can, if necessary, be incrementally modified to account for new forms of refinement metaknowledge as they are discovered.

6.2 Designing R-Functions and Heuristics

The methodology that led to the development of RM had already proven to be of use in the design of SEEK2. Although SEEK2's viewfinder is "hard-coded," the fact is that the r-functions comprising it were designed using the metalinguistic framework that has now been implemented in RM.

Concrete instances of the use of RM in designing r-functions and heuristics can be given. The discovery of the r-function **signif-level** (see chapter 4, p.79) was aided by the interactive experimental use of RM. In this section we will exhibit another concrete and detailed example of how RM can be used in designing r-functions and heuristics for knowledge base refinement.

In order to present the example it might be helpful to review certain r-functions and heuristics used in SEEK2. A *gencf situation* was defined as an r-situation in which mcases can be corrected by boosting the confidence of a satisfied rule for the correct conclusion. SEEK2 makes use of the r-function **gencf(rule)**, defined below, in its analysis of such situations.

```
genCF-rule(mcase)
          =  the rule such that
                  a) PDX(mcase)=conclusion(rule)
                  b) rule is satisfied in mcase
                  c) of all the rules satisfying conditions
                    (a) and (b) in mcase, none has a greater
                     confidence factor than rule.

          =  Select rule ∈ Satisfied-rules-for(PDX(mcase),mcase)
                      with Max RuleCf(rule).
```

```
genCF-mcases(rule)
            = {mcase| rule = genCF-rule(mcase)}

genCF(rule)
            = |genCF-mcases(rule)|


Mean-CDX-CF(cases)
            = the mean value of the confidence of CDX(case)
              over cases


            = Mean(CDX(case),cases)
```

In particular, we are interested in:

```
Mean-CDX-CF(gencf-mcases(rule))

            = the mean value of the CDX in the gencf-mcases(rule)
              (this is the value to which we plan to raise the cf
              of rule)
```

A SEEK2 heuristic that makes use of these r-functions is the following:

```
   If:   GenCF(rule) > [SpecA(rule) + SpecB(rule)]

 Then:   raise the confidence level of the rule to
         Mean-CDX-CF(GenCF-mcases(rule)).
```

In chapter 4 we justified the if-clause of this heuristic in terms of the max-gain+min-loss approach to heuristic refinement generation (see p.85). As was pointed out, the quantity [specA(rule) + specB(rule)] is certainly not the best estimator of the number of currently correctly diagnosed cases that might be lost as a result of raising the confidence factor of the rule. That quantity was chosen to play this role in the interest of efficiency.

I now want to discuss the possibility of designing a better estimator of the loss that can result from raising the confidence of a rule. The point of this discussion is to show how the interactive use of RM can facilitate the construction of such an r-function.

Let us suppose we are interested in raising the confidence of endpoint-rule r. If we want to know how many cases we may lose by doing so, we will have to examine all currently correctly diagnosed cases with PDX≠rule-conclusion(r) to see whether r is satisfied in these cases. Only in these cases does the contemplated refinement pose a danger. So far this suggests the following definitions:

```
define-variable ccase {case| (= (pdx case) (cdx case))}

[define-function antigenCF-ccases (rule)
     {ccase| (and (/= (rule-conclusion rule) (pdx ccase))
          (= (satisfied rule ccase) 1))}]
```

The first command defines a variable, **ccase**, over the set of all currently correctly diagnosed cases. The second command defines a function **antigenCF-ccases(rule)** that returns the set of all **ccase** such that **rule** concludes an incorrect conclusion in **ccase** and **rule** is satisfied in **ccase**.

One of the refinements suggested by SEEK2 involved raising the confidence factor of a certain rule, number 49 to be exact. This refinement was suggested in virtue of the satisfaction of the preceding heuristic. SEEK2 tries the experiment and discovers that it leads to a net loss of nine cases. Examination of this situation in RM yields the following information (comments appear in italics):

mcases we are liable to win by raising the CF of rule 49

```
RM>  (gencf-mcases 49)
(11 60 74 84)
```

Ccases we are liable to lose by raising the CF of rule 49

```
RM>  (antigenCF-ccases 49)

(39 50 51 53 54 65 68 69 76 82 85 101)
```

We see that there are far more **ccases** that are liable to be lost than there are **mcases** that are liable to be won by this refinement.

However, it would be wrong to conclude that raising the confidence factor of a rule will cause a net loss in cases whenever |antigenCF-ccases(rule)| is greater than |genCF-mcases(rule)|. Whether a loss will result depends on two other values: 1) the value to which we have to raise the rule's confidence in order to win (half or more) of the gen-mcases(rule), i.e., mean-cdx-cf(gen-mcases(rule)), and 2) the average value of PDX(ccase) in antigenCF-ccases(rule), or what we defined (in chapter 4) as mean-pdx-cf(cases), i.e.,

```
Mean-PDX-CF(mcases)
            = the mean value of the confidence of PDX(mcase)
              over mcases

            = Mean(PDX(mcase),mcases)
```

Now, continuing with our RM session, we see that:

find mean value of CF of current highest conclusion in genCF-mcases of rule 49; must raise CF to this value to win 1/2 of mcases

```
RM>  (mean-cdx-cf (gencf-mcases 49))
0.75
```

find mean value of CF of PDX in Ccases we are liable to lose

```
RM>  (mean-pdx-cf (antigencf-ccases 49))
0.575
```

This information indicates that while we can expect to win 2 or so cases by raising the confidence of rule 49 to .75, we can also expect to lose 6 or so antigenCF-ccases(rule) at the same time, because these cases conclude PDX at a confidence level around .575.

The lesson of this example can now be generalized into the following refinement heuristic:

```
[define-vr-heuristic
  (if (and (> (gencf rule) 0)
           (< (mean-cdx-cf (gencf-mcases rule))
              (mean-pdx-cf (antigencf-ccases rule))))
  (raise-cf rule (mean-cdx-cf (gencf-mcases rule))))]
```

```
(In English this heuristic says: if gencf(rule) is greater
 than 0 and the mean-cdx-cf in the gencf-mcases(rule) is less
 than mean-pdx-cf in the antigencf-ccases(rule), then raise
 the confidence factor of the rule to mean-cdx-cf in the
 gencf-mcases(rule).)
```

The claim here is not that this is the optimal heuristic for suggesting confidence-boosting refinements, only that the new heuristic does have certain advantages over the original SEEK2 version. (In fact, in testing over various refinement situations the new heuristic suggests every useful refinement suggested by the original, and succeeds in preventing the suggestion of several poor experiments that are generated by the original.) The main point is that RM offers an environment within which such investigations may be carried out with relative ease.

6.3 Designing Refinement Strategies

In this section we show how the control strategy used by SEEK2 can be specified in RM.

Recall that SEEK2 uses a quasi-hill-climbing cyclic control strategy (see chapter 1). Within each cycle the single refinement with the highest actual net gain in performance is incorporated into the knowledge base. The procedure halts when no refinement yielding a positive net gain is found.

In presenting the RM specification of SEEK2, we use an ALGOL-like programming notation, since this is the most natural mode of representation in this case. The actual RM specification makes use of common-lisp constructs, which although structurally similar to those used below, are less readable. The main procedure is called SEEK2, and it calls several procedures that are also presented below.

Variables with delimiting asterisks are global variables. Note that the procedure SEEK2 determines the number of MCASES={case|(/= (pdx case) (cdx case)} at the start of each cycle. As with any r-function that does not contain an explicit kb argument MCASES is always computed with respect to the currently *active* knowledge base. Therefore in the first cycle SEEK2 will compute {case|(/= (pdx case) (cdx case kb_0))}, since kb_0 is the active knowledge base to start with. In subsequent cycles other knowledge bases will be active as a result of the **activate(kb)** command that is invoked at the end of any cycle, and MCASES will then be computed with respect to these knowledge bases. The function M(dx) was defined in chapter 5. This function returns the set of all *false positives* and *false negatives* for a given dx with respect to the active knowledge base.

Control Strategy for SEEK2

```
PROCEDURE SEEK2
BEGIN
DO WHILE |MCASES| >0
 ;start of current cycle
 *Best-Experiment* ← ϕ
 *Best-Net-Gain* ← 0
 FOR EVERY dx in ENDPOINTS DO
  dx-mcases=M(dx)
  IF dx-mcases≠ϕ THEN
   FOR EVERY rule IN Rules-For(dx) DO
    endpoint-experiments
              ←FIND-ENDPOINT-EXPERIMENTS(rule,dx-mcases)
    intermediate-experiments
              ←FIND-INTERMEDIATE-EXPERIMENTS(rule,endpoint-experiments)
    Suggestions
              ←Endpoint-Experiments∪Intermediate-Experiments
    TEST-EXPERIMENTS(suggestions)
   END FOR ;end analysis of current endpoint-rule-chain for dx
 END FOR ;end of analysis for current dx
 IF *Best-Experiment*=ϕ THEN STOP
 kb←CREATE-KNOWLEDGE-BASE(*Best-Experiment*,*active-kb*)
 ACTIVATE(kb)
END WHILE ;end of current cycle
END Seek2
```

```
PROCEDURE FIND-ENDPOINT-EXPERIMENTS(rule)
BEGIN
 Compute-View(first-order-viewfinder,endpoint-rules)
 Endpoint-Experiments←Evaluate-VR-Heuristics(endpoint-rules)
 Endpoint-experiments←
      Endpoint-Experiments∪Evaluate-RR-Heuristics(endpoint-rules)
END

PROCEDURE FIND-INTERMEDIATE-EXPERIMENTS(Experiments,mcases)
BEGIN
  FOR EVERY experiment in Experiments DO
    IF r-operation in experiment involves a hypothesis component
       THEN
          Intermediate-Experiments←BackChain(hypothesis,mcases)
  END FOR
END

PROCEDURE TEST-EXPERIMENTS(suggestions)
BEGIN
  FOR EVERY experiment in Suggestions DO
    Net-Gain←Result-Experiment(experiment,kb)
    IF Net-Gain>*Best-Net-Gain* THEN
       *Best-Net-Gain*←Net-Gain
       *Best-Experiment*←Experiment
  END FOR   ;end of tests for current rule-chain leading to
            ;current endpoint-rule for dx
END

PROCEDURE BackChain(hypothesis,mcases)
BEGIN
Compute-view(first-order-viewfinder,Rules-for(hypothesis))
FOR EVERY rule IN Rules-For(hypothesis) DO
  Intermediate-Experiments←Evaluate-VR-Heuristics(rule)
  Intermediate-Experiments←
    Intermediate-Experiments∪Evaluate-RR-Heuristics(rule)
  ;recursive backchain on implicated intermediate hypothesis
  FOR EVERY experiment in Intermediate-Experiments DO
        IF r-operation in experiment involves a hypo component
          THEN
             Intermediate-Experiments
               ←Intermediate-Experiments∪BackChain(hypo,mcases)
  END FOR
RETURN Intermediate-Experiments
END BackChain
```

The preceding specification is not intended to function as a guide to the workings of SEEK2, which was given in chapter 1. The point is that using this specification, which - together with the RM specification of the SEEK2 viewfinder and heuristics - takes up about five printed pages of text, RM carries out the same procedure as the hard-coded SEEK2, which takes up about fifty printed pages of source code. In RM the user need only understand and manipulate functions, variables, commands, etc., that are really part of the "essence" of knowledge base refinement, and the user need only be concerned with *what* he wants done, e.g., try an experiment, not with the internal details of *how* these actions are to be carried out. The "dirty work" is taken care of by RM.

6.4 Domain-Specific Metaknowledge in RM

Certain forms of domain-specific metaknowledge can be incorporated into RM with little additional effort. For example, consider the following set definition:

```
define-set NO-TOUCH {25 33 34 55}
```

where the set {25 33 34 55} contains the id-numbers of rules that are, for one reason or another not to be refined under any circumstances. (Set definition via enumeration is available in RM). The way such information would be used is obvious: one would like to be able to instruct the refinement system's control strategy that no refinements should be generated for these rules. This would be done by putting a check in the procedure **Test-experiments** (see p.134), so that any refinement suggestion that involves an operation on any of the members of NO-TOUCH is automatically passed over.

In chapter 5 (p.108) we discussed the notion of a *paradigm*, i.e., a pair of the form **<rules,ccases>** where it is known that **ccases** are correctly diagnosed in virtue of the satisfaction of **rules**, and that this is a relationship that ought to be preserved in any refined versions of the knowledge base. If a refinement γ to the **rules** in a paradigm causes one or more **ccases** to be lost, then one may wish to reject γ no matter how great a gain in performance it achieves.

This sort of domain-specific metaknowledge can also be accommodated using RM's current stock of primitives. The following RM definitions illustrates a way in which this can be done:

```
define-set paradigm-1-rules {7 8 9}

define-set paradigm-1-ccases {1 2 3}

define-set paradigm-1 {paradigm-1-rules paradigm-1-ccases}

[define-function violates-paradigm-1 (experiment)
  (and
   (some #'member-of paradigm-1-rules  experiment)
   (some #'member-of  paradigm-1-cases
                        (lost-ccases experiment)))]
```

The first three **define-set** commands create a set named *paradigm-1* = {{7 8 9} {1 2 3}}, whose first member is the set of rules in the paradigm, and whose second member is the set of ccases in the paradigm. In this example we assume that the user has verified that the rules 7, 8, 9 are indeed each satisfied in ccases 1,2, and 3, and that they either conclude the endpoint of those cases or some intermediate hypothesis leading to the endpoint. (Functions that automatically perform this check can be designed using RM.) The **define-function** command then creates a function *violates-paradigm-1*, which will return the value T if and only if some member of **rules** is refined by **experiment**, *and* some member of **ccases** is lost by **experiment**, where the latter is determined by invoking a defined function **lost-ccases**, that returns the set of all ccases that "become" mcases through **experiment**. (This is accomplished by using **Try-experiment(experiment)** to return a case-vector for the effect of the refinement and comparing it case-by-case with the case-vector for the active knowledge base.)

In this example we have defined a *single* paradigm and a function that checks for violations of that paradigm *only*. If one intends to use this sort of domain-specific metaknowledge, however, it would be desirable to have a general command or "macro" **define-paradigm** that, given a set of rules and ccases, automatically generates the above sequence of commands (taking care, of course, that new names are used for each paradigm so defined). This is easily achieved in RM through use of the underlying common-lisp macro facility.

6.5 Incorporation of Failure-Driven Higher-Order Refinement

A general architecture for failure-driven higher-order refinement and an outline of a scenario where such ideas might be applied were presented in chapter 4. We are now in a position to consider in greater detail how a failure-driven approach to higher-order refinement may be incorporated in a first-order automatic refinement system.

There are four key questions that must be addressed: 1) at what point or points in a refinement process should higher-order refinements be generated and tested, 2) what information concerning failures of attempted refinements should be gathered, 3) when should such information be gathered, and 4) what heuristics for generating higher-order refinements should be employed? We shall refer to questions (1) and (3) together as *the timing issue*, and we shall refer to issues (2) and (4) together as *the epistemological issue*.

To answer all these questions in complete detail would be tantamount to specifying a complete higher-order refinement regime. Moreover, as is the case with first-order refinement, there is no one "best design" for such a regime; a full account should deal with the major alternatives and their relative advantages and disadvantages. Such an account is a subject for future investigation. In this chapter we will give concrete answers to the questions posed above by considering how an intuitively acceptable higher-order refinement heuristic could be implemented in a SEEK2-like first-order refinement system.

Stated in English, the heuristic for higher-order refinement we would like to employ is the following:

FDH-1

IF:

There is evidence that a generalization refinement γ_1 to the most frequently missing component c_1 of a rule r failed because other components of r are also unsatisfied in gen-mcases(r) &

c_2 is a component of r that maximizes the joint-unsatisfied count of <c_1,c_2> with respect to gen-mcases(r)

THEN:

Determine a set of generalization refinement experiments $\Gamma=\{\gamma_2 \ldots \gamma_n\}$ to c_2 by evaluating the set of heuristics in the table Basic-Heuristics &
Retry γ_1 in tandem with each of the experiments in Γ respectively.

The consequent of this heuristic, called **FDH-1** for "failure-driven-heuristic-1", refers to a table of **Basic-Heuristics.** This is a set of vr and rr heuristics of the form:

IF:

Component c of rule r is a <component-type> &
c is to <generalized|specialized> with respect to cases

THEN:

{<invoke r-functions> &}
<suggest refinement-operation>

The element <invoke r-functions> is enclosed in braces to indicate that it is an optional feature. The following is a concrete example of such a basic heuristic:

IF:

Component c of rule r is a *choice-component* &
c is to be *generalized* with respect to gen-mcases(r)

THEN:

Decrease the choice-number of c by 1.

In other words, these "basic" heuristics relate the structural features of rules and the desire to generalize or specialize a rule over a given set of cases, to classes of refinement operations that may achieve the desired result (and that may or may not require certain information to be gathered prior to being applied). Such heuristics are easily specified in RM. The role of Basic-Heuristics in FDH-1 will become clear in the course of our explication.

FDH-1 concerns a situation in which generalization of Mfmc(r) (the most frequently missing component of r) is *suspected of having failed because other components are also unsatisfied in* gen-mcases(r) (the misdiagnosed cases for which r is a generalization candidate). Below we will see how evidence supporting this suspected cause of failure can be gathered. The second clause in the antecedent of FDH-1 selects a second component c_2 of r such that the pair $<c_1,c_2>$ maximizes the joint-unsatisfied function over such pairs in r. This function was defined above (see section 6.1.3.3). The consequent of FDH-1 then instructs us to evaluate the table of Basic-Heuristics for component c_2, with *generalization* as the refinement goal. Evaluation of these heuristics will yield a set $\Gamma = \{\gamma_2 ... \gamma_n\}$ of generalization refinement experiments for c_2. FDH-1 then instructs us to test every joint experiment of the form $<\gamma_1,\gamma_i>$ for $2 \leq i \leq n$.

The second higher-order heuristic, FDH-2, is more specialized than FDH-1; it illustrates one way in which component/rule addition refinement experiments may be generated.

FDH-2

```
IF:
      There is evidence that a generalization refinement γ1 to
      the most frequently missing component c1 of a rule r
      succeeds in correcting mcases ε in gen-mcases(r)
      but fails to provide a positive net-gain because a
      larger number of new mcases μ were generated &

      The ratio |ε|/|gen-mcases(r)| ≥ α &

      There is a finding f that is present in all the cases
      in ε and not present in any of the cases in μ

THEN:
      Add a new rule r' to the kb, where r' is formed
      from r by applying the refinement γ1 to r and then
      adding f to the resulting rule.
```

The parameter α is a threshold on the fraction of the gen-mcases(r) that must be corrected by γ_1 in order for FDH-2 to be applied. This parameter is left unspecified: depending on time constraints, complexity of the knowledge base, the number of mcases, and other factors, α may be set to a lower or higher value. To understand why FDH-2 recommends *adding* a new rule, rather than replacement of an old rule, let us consider a very simple example. Suppose $ab \rightarrow H$ is the rule r, and b is the most frequently missing component (a and b are boolean-valued findings). Suppose there are 3 cases with PDX=H, where case-1={a,b}, case-2=case-3={a,c}, and 4 correctly diagnosed cases that have *some other* PDX, where case-4=case-5=case-6=case-7={a,d}. Our first-order heuristics will suggest deletion of component b from r. This experiment will lead to a net gain of -2: case-2 and case-3 will be corrected, but cases 4-7 will become new FPs for H. In this situation FDH-2 will fire and suggest adding the rule $ac \rightarrow H$ to the knowledge base. By *adding* this rule we *guarantee* that the ε cases (case-2 and case-3) will be corrected while none of μ cases (cases 4-7) will become new FPs. Note that if we instead *replace* r with the new rule we will get a net gain of +1, but we will cause case-1 to become a new FN for H. By adding the new rule we guarantee that no new FNs for H will be generated. We see, therefore, that FDH-2 is a "heuristic" that actually guarantees a positive net gain. Of course, the fact that it depends upon locating a finding that is present in *all* of the ε cases and not present in *any* of the μ cases, makes it less likely that FDH-2 will have a high degree of applicability. Note, however, that the constraint on the finding can be relaxed: as long as f is present in a greater number of ε cases than μ cases, the suggested refinement guarantees a positive net gain. (Also note that this heuristic allows for the positing of *new-connections* as defined in section 4.9.)

Let us now turn to the epistemological issue as it pertains to these heuristics. The first clauses in the antecedents of FDH-1 and FDH-2 both require a judgment *that* a given refinement has failed, and a judgment as to the reason for the failure. We already know *a* criterion of failure: the refinement leads to zero or negative net gain in performance. But this criterion is too coarse for the purposes of implementing failure-driven higher-order analysis. Not every refinement that "fails" according to the coarse criterion is one for which it is desirable to investigate higher-order possibilities. For example, if a generalization refinement that is intended to correct 2 mcases results in a net loss of 100 currently correctly diagnosed cases, then we are well-advised to abandon this refinement altogether: the evidence that this refinement is wrong is so overwhelming, that its failure is not an "interesting one." What is needed are features of unsuccessful refinements that make their failures "interesting," in the sense of offering some hope for an ultimate higher-order success. We also need to have clues as to where to look in attempting to generate a complex refinement operation.

We will now show how these problems can be addressed by means of a data-structure that we will call *the Outcome-Vector corresponding to a refinement experiment* γ. This can be thought of as a vector of elements indexed by the case identification numbers for the current stock of cases. Each element of an outcome-vector contains two items or cells: 1) an *outcome-type* cell, and 2) a *component-success* cell. We discuss the nature of the component-success cell first.

Every first-order refinement γ must operate on a single component c of a single rule r. Moreover, since every γ is either a generalization or a specialization, the "immediate" intended effect of γ with respect to a single case must always be to cause an unsatisfied component c to become satisfied (generalization) or to cause a satisfied component c to become unsatisfied (specialization). For example if γ involves decreasing a choice-number of choice-component c, then γ has its immediate intended effect with respect to a given mcase if and only if c changes from being unsatisfied to being satisfied in mcase. Whether any first-order generalization or specialization has its immediate intended effect in a case, is easily computable by means of RM primitives.

The important point is that even if γ fails to correct an mcase it was intended to correct, this information does not tell us whether γ achieved its immediate intended effect in mcase, i.e., caused component c to become satisfied or unsatisfied as the case may be. This is precisely the information that is contained in the *component-success* cells of the outcome-vector for γ. That is, if i is the identification number of mcase, then the ith element of the outcome-vector for γ will contain a 1 in its component-success cell if and only if γ has its intended immediate effect on component c with respect to mcase i; otherwise this cell contains a 0.

We now discuss the nature of the *outcome-type* cells. First of all, for any refinement experiment γ, generated heuristically, there is always a set of mcases that γ is *intended* to correct; we will call this set *the On-Target set of* γ, since γ is presumably On-target with respect to these mcases in the sense defined in chapter 3. For example, if γ is a component generalization refinement to rule r, the On-target set of γ will be given by gen-mcases(r). Now given a γ, its On-target set τ, and *any* **case** in the current stock of cases, a set of five mutually exclusive and jointly exhaustive outcome types can be identified for the purposes of failure-driven refinement:

1. γ *fails with respect to* **case**: **case** is a member of τ and γ does not correct **case** (**Fail-1**).
2. γ *causes a new loss with respect to* **case**: **case** is a ccase (correctly diagnosed case in the active knowledge base) and γ causes it to become an mcase (**Loss-2**).
3. γ *succeeds with respect to* **case**: **case** is a member of τ and γ corrects **case** (**Success-3**).
4. γ *causes a new win with respect to* **case**: **case** is an mcase but *not* a member of τ and γ corrects **case** (**Win-4**).
5. γ *is neutral with respect to* **case**: **case** is not a member of τ and γ does not change the endpoint of **case** (**Neutral-5**).

For the sake of brevity and clarity we will identify these outcomes by the accompanying mnemonics given in the above enumeration, e.g. if γ *fails with respect to* **case**, we will say that γ is a Fail-1 with respect to **case**. (Although uses for the outcomes Win-4 and Neutral-5 can be given, we list them here for the sake of completeness only.) Given a γ, its associated τ, and any **case** with identification number i, the ith element of the outcome-vector of γ will contain the code for the appropriate outcome type in its *outcome-type* cell. Again, the outcome type of any case is easily computed by means of RM primitives.

We are now in a position to see how the notion of a *refinement's having failed for a certain reason* can be given operational significance using the information contained in outcome-vectors. We will show this by giving a simple example pertaining to FDH-1.

Figure 6-1: A Portion of An Outcome-Vector

Case Number	Outcome-Type	Component-Success
•	•	•
3	Fail-1	1
•	•	•
5	Fail-1	1
•	•	•
8	Loss-2	1
•	•	•
10	Success-3	1
•	•	•

Let γ be a generalization refinement to component c of rule r. Suppose that the refinement is tested, is found to lead to zero or negative net gain in performance, and that we have obtained the outcome-vector V. A portion of V is displayed in figure 6-1. Notice that cases 3 and 5 are ones in which 1) γ failed to correct an mcase in its On-Target set (this is the meaning of outcome Fail-1), and 2) γ did, however, succeed in causing component c to become satisfied. Clearly these are cases that provide evidence that γ failed because there are other components of c that are unsatisfied in gen-mcases(r). Case 8, on the other hand, is of outcome-type Loss-2, and, therefore, is evidence that γ fails because it causes previously correctly diagnosed cases to become mcases. If there are more cases akin to 8 than there are cases akin to 3 and 5, we cannot logically expect to produce a successful higher-order refinement by looking for other components of r to generalize in tandem with c. (We cannot rule out the possibility that additional generalization of r may yield enough cases with outcome-type Win-4 to overcome the negative effect of cases with outcome-type Loss-2; this result would, however, be a matter of luck - Win-4 cases are not in the On-target set of the refinement - and is not something that one would expect to happen very often, or that is necessarily desirable.) On the other hand, if the number of cases akin to 3 and 5 is greater than the number of Loss-2 cases, the search for a higher-order refinement is warranted. And the greater the (positive) difference between cases of the former and latter types, the more we stand to gain.

This concludes our discussion of the epistemological issue. We have shown that Outcome-Vectors can be used to operationalize the notion of a refinement's having failed for a specified reason. We now briefly consider the *timing* issue: when should outcome-vectors be obtained and the pertinent failure-driven-heuristics (FD-heuristics) be evaluated?

There are many possible answers to this question. In the context of a SEEK2-like first-order refinement system, two of the obvious and "extreme" possibilities are: 1) gather outcome-vectors and invoke FD-heuristics for every first-order refinement experiment as it is attempted, and 2) invoke FD-heuristics only when a "performance plateau" (which may or may not be a first-order local maximum) has been attained, i.e., when every first-order refinement generated yields zero or negative net gain in performance (see chapter 5).

If option (1) is selected, one would gather an outcome-vector for a refinement γ at the same time it is being tested over the current stock of cases. One might then decide to evaluate the pertinent FD-heuristics only if the net gain achieved by γ was judged unsatisfactory. The higher-order refinements generated would then be tested before returning to the "normal" first-order regime. Note that the major additional overhead in space required by this option would be minimal: only one outcome-vector is needed at any given time.

If option (2) is selected one would proceed according to the "normal" first-order regime until a "dead end" is reached. In a SEEK2-like, i.e., single-generation system, the dead end would leave the refinement system with a final active knowledge base $\mathbf{kb_f}$ and no other accessible knowledge bases. At this point one would "rerun" the last first-order cycle - the one in which no refinement led to any improvement in performance - but this time one would proceed as described in the previous paragraph. That is, as each first-order experiment is attempted, an outcome-vector is obtained, the pertinent FD-heuristics are evaluated, and all generated higher-order refinements are attempted. If some of the latter lead to a net gain in performance then one could select the one with greatest net gain (as in the first-order regime). This would lead to a new active knowledge base, and then one could revert to the first-order regime until another plateau is reached, and so on. One would halt when invocation of the higher-regime at a first-order plateau also failed to yield any positive net gain refinements.

Finally, note that in a multiple-generation refinement system, one would not have to halt when such a "higher-order plateau" is reached. Rather one could then "back up" to the predecessor of $\mathbf{kb_f}$, or to anyone of its ancestors, or activate one of its "siblings" in the tree of knowledge bases, and attempt higher-order procedures with respect to this knowledge base.

6.6 Summary

In this chapter we exhibited a high-level metalanguage, RM, for specifying, developing, and studying alternative refinement concepts, heuristics, and strategies. Concrete examples of how RM can be used as a tool for experimental research, as a vehicle for the customization of refinement systems, and as a framework for the incorporation of certain forms of domain-specific metaknowledge were given. Finally, a detailed account of the use of RM for implementing a failure-driven approach to higher-order refinement was given.

The research on a metalinguistic framework presented here may be seen as an exploration of the consequences of applying the "knowledge is power" principle to the domain of knowledge acquisition itself, and more specifically, to knowledge base refinement. If domain knowledge gives a system problem-solving power, and if the domain of interest is itself the problem of making a given knowledge base fit certain given facts more closely, then it follows that *metaknowledge about knowledge representation itself* - e.g., knowledge of the ways in which formal objects can be used or altered to fit facts, knowledge of the sorts of evidence that can be gathered in support of certain classes of refinements, etc. - must be an essential ingredient of any successful automatic knowledge base refinement system, and *a fortiori* of any successful automatic knowledge acquisition system. It also follows that just as there is a knowledge acquisition problem for "object-level" systems, so too there must be a *metaknowledge acquisition* problem for knowledge refinement and acquisition systems. Therefore, just as the use of high-level formal languages has helped researchers to clarify issues and generalize from experiences with object-level knowledge acquisition, one would expect that the use of a high-level *metalanguage* would provide similar benefits with respect to the metaknowledge acquisition problem. It is hoped that the work presented here will be seen as justifying this expectation.

7 Conclusion

7.1 Research Significance

The broad objective of this research concerns the discovery, study, and implementation of principles, methods, and tools for the automatic refinement of expert system knowledge bases. Within this broader objective, the current research has made progress in demonstrating the feasibility and validity of an empirically-grounded heuristic approach to knowledge base refinement, and it has contributed to the formulation of a general methodology for facilitating the development of automatic refinement systems that utilize such an approach. In concrete terms an automatic refinement system, SEEK2, has been designed, implemented, tested, and studied, and a high-level metalanguage, RM, that allows for relatively easy experimentation with alternative refinement concepts, heuristics, and strategies has also been designed and implemented.

7.1.1 Feasibility and Validity of The Approach

To say that an approach to automatic knowledge base refinement is *feasible* is to say, at least, two things. First of all, the approach should presuppose as little specialized domain knowledge as possible. No matter how effective an approach to the problem is, if it presupposes domain knowledge or metaknowledge - whether from an expert or another source - that is just as difficult or costly to acquire as the desired knowledge base, the approach cannot be cost-effective. Secondly, the approach must be computationally cost-effective, i.e., it must produce results in a "reasonable" amount of time working on large-scale knowledge bases. To say an that an approach has *validity* is to say that, with a certain degree of reliability, it produces results that actually improve the overall empirical adequacy of a knowledge base and that are acceptable to the domain expert.

7.1.1.1 Evidence of Feasibility

In terms of the above desiderata, the empirically-grounded heuristic approach advocated here fares well. While it is true that *case knowledge* is required by our approach, it is also true that such knowledge is already a desideratum in expert systems work to begin with. As we pointed out in chapter 1, it is difficult, if not impossible, to verify the accuracy and adequacy of a putative expert system without comparing its performance to that of a domain expert's, or some alternative source of presumably correct diagnoses. However, while the approach advocated here does not *depend* on additional specialized domain knowledge, we have shown that general constructs that make use of such knowledge can be effectively utilized by this approach, e.g., radicality orderings (see chapter 3), the notion of *paradigms*, etc. (see chapter 5).

In terms of computational cost-effectiveness, we can offer both concrete and theoretical evidence for the feasibility of the current approach. First of all, as we have mentioned (see chapter 1.3), SEEK2 shows that the proposed approach can be relatively fast. In chapter 4 we showed one reason why this is the case: any purely first-order refinement system can be designed so that the analysis of an r-situation <R,M> - i.e., gathering the view and evaluating the heuristics - can, in the worst case, be achieved in time proportional to */M/*(the number of rules in R + the number of rule components in R).*[10] We have also seen that an extended general architecture for heuristic refinement generation which allows for a failure-driven approach to higher-order refinement can be devised. This gives us reason to believe that ever more powerful heuristic-based refinement systems can be developed that still exhibit a high degree of computational cost-effectiveness.

7.1.1.2 Evidence of Validity

The best evidence for the validity of an approach can come only from actual examples of its successful use. On this score, we can say that with respect to the rheumatology knowledge base we have used as a test case, SEEK2 has produced results that are similar to those produced by SEEK, some of which were found to be acceptable to the experts [30].

However, evidence of the *reliability* of the approach in producing refinements that improve the *general* empirical adequacy of a knowledge base (not just its empirical adequacy with respect to the given data base of cases) can be obtained via experimentation with a single knowledge base. Two experiments have been performed, and will be related below. The results of both experiments are encouraging.

The first experiment will be called *Train-and-Test*, and is actually a series of similar experiments. In a single typical train-and-test "run" the given data base of cases is divided into two disjoint subsets (not necessarily of equal size) preserving the distribution of cases by endpoint. Let us call these sets σ_1 and σ_2. The first phase of a train-and-test experiment involves running SEEK2 using σ_1 as case knowledge, or as the "training" set. SEEK2's refined version of the knowledge base is then *tested* over σ_2 and the combined set $\sigma_1 \cup \sigma_2$. In the second phase of the experiment the roles of σ_1 and σ_2 are interchanged.

---

[10]Another reason for the speed must be reckoned to be the internal structure of the underlying expert system framework itself, viz., EXPERT, which the RM interface utilizes in order to test refinements over the data base of cases.

	Training Set 1	Testing Set 1
Start	42/62 (69%)	46/59 (78%)
Finish	61/62 (98%)	55/59 (93%)

Overall: 116/121 (96%)

	Training Set 2	Testing Set 2
Start	46/59 (78%)	42/62 (69%)
Finish	59/59 (100%)	59/62 (95%)

Overall: 118/121 (98%)

Figure 7-1: Train and Test Experiment

Figure 7-1 gives the results of such a run with training and test samples of equal size. Training over σ_1 led to a performance increase of 29% (69% to 98%). When tested over the new set of cases in σ_2, there was an increase in performance of 15% (78% to 93%). The results of the second run are similar. While there was less improvement observed over the test sets than in the training sets in these runs, the fact is that the experiment shows that refinements that were "learned" by SEEK2 with respect to one set of cases also improved empirical adequacy with respect to a new set of cases.

This experiment has another interpretation. In terms of statistical pattern recognition techniques a single train-and-test experiment can be viewed as giving an *estimate* of the *probability of error* - i.e., the probability that the *refined* knowledge base (classifier) misdiagnoses a case [12]. Under this interpretation, the total performance ratio obtained in the test run, e.g., the 93% figure, estimates the probability of error to be .07. While this figure is certainly more conservative than the estimate, .01, that would be obtained by using the results of the training run as an estimate, it is only a *point-estimate.* To obtain a more reliable estimate, one needs to average over the results of many train-and-test experiments. Alternatively, a more accurate figure could also be obtained by employing a *leave-one-out* or so-called "jacknifing" technique for error estimation [12]. Unfortunately, the general application of these techniques in knowledge base refinement would appear to be computationally prohibitive for large-scale problems.

However, additional train-and-test runs for the rheumatology knowledge base have been performed and these results can be used to derive a more reliable estimate of the probability of error. In all, 15 train-and-test runs were conducted. In 6 runs, the size of the training sample was 50% of the cases; 3 runs each with training sample sizes of 33%, 67%, and 75%, respectively, were also conducted. The average performance increase observed in the test cases in these 15 runs was 21.2%. The average total performance over the test cases was 94.5%, which gives an estimate of probability of error of .055. The lowest overall performance over a test set obtained in any of these runs was 90% (this occurred in a run with training sample size 67%), which yields a .1 point estimate of probability of error. The highest overall performance over a test set obtained in any of these runs was 100% (this occurred in a run with training sample size 75%).

The second experiment will be called *Train-and-Train.* The sets σ_1 and σ_2 are defined as in the first experiment. In this experiment, however, after the initial training over σ_1, we take *the generated refined knowledge base* and use it in a *second training run* over the overall data base of cases $\sigma_1 \cup \sigma_2$. As before, the experiment is repeated interchanging the roles of σ_1 and σ_2.

Intuitively, this experiment is intended to capture certain aspects of the actual "standard" use of a refinement system that are not captured in the first experiment. Thus, in the process of knowledge base construction we can expect that *several,* perhaps many, refinement episodes will be necessary, and that *new* case knowledge may become available in latter refinement episodes. The new case knowledge will now become part of the the overall data base of cases used in subsequent refinement episodes, i.e., the size of the data base of cases is expected to be a monotonically non-decreasing function of time. Now an interesting question one might ask of a refinement system is this: if at time t_1 the system selects a set of refinements γ_1 using case knowledge C_1, then what do we expect the refinements γ_2 selected at time t_2 using case knowledge C_2 to look like, given that $C_1 \subseteq C_2$?

This is a question whose answer would seem to depend on what assumptions we make about the statistical distribution of cases received in each of the refinement episodes. In the train-and-train experiment, the distribution of cases by endpoint is the same in both sets σ_1 and σ_2. There is no reason to think that new case knowledge will always *arrive* in such fashion. However, this does not mean that the experiment is totally lacking in general significance. While we have assumed that neither the expert nor the knowledge engineer has knowledge of the prior probabilities of case breakdown by endpoint, we can imagine that as the *first* batch of cases is gathered, the expert and the knowledge engineer, by reviewing the case data, will be able to reach some hypothesis about the relative frequencies of the various endpoints with respect to the "local" population, i.e., the distribution of cases that *this* expert has experienced in his practice. Since our goal is to construct a knowledge base that reproduces the performance of *this* expert, it is reasonable to expect that we will be "tuning" the knowledge base in a way that reflects the case population with which he is most familiar. Therefore, as new cases come in, the knowledge engineer will not initiate a new refinement episode *until* such time as the overall distribution of cases again matches the postulated local frequencies. It must, however, be emphasized that this "policy" is not being required as a condition of the applicability of SEEK2, but only as an imagined condition for interpreting the significance of the train-and-train experiment.

Given this condition, what would be the "best" or "ideal" behavior of a refinement system over the course of time? Assuming that our system is a "perfect" refinement system and assuming that the initial batch of cases, σ_1, contains cases of every significant type that exists in the domain, we would expect that every useful refinement would be generated and selected in the initial training run, and that therefore no new refinements would be proposed in the subsequent training runs. In general, however, neither of these assumptions is justified. In general, the new cases in σ_2 will contain some cases that differ in one or more significant ways from every case in σ_2. Therefore, it is not unreasonable to expect a refinement system, even a perfect one, to discover new refinements in subsequent training runs.

One property we would find in a perfect refinement system, that would be displayed in such an experiment, is what we may call *soundness*. A refinement system may be said to be sound if it never selects a refinement γ in a session unless that refinement actually improves the general empirical adequacy of the system *in the long run*, i.e., the refinement is not significantly "retracted" by any possible subsequent refinement episode. Conversely, an unsound system might select a refinement in one training session, but in a later session it might find itself selecting the inverse refinement, i.e., simply undoing a modification it had previously selected. (Note that such a reversal might very well be a good thing to do in the presence of *biased* sequences of case knowledge, but this violates the assumption on case knowledge presentation that we are making.)

Whether *this* notion of soundness is ultimately a property of interest in knowledge base refinement is not at issue here. We introduce it simply to give the reader an idea of the *kind* of behavior that would seem to be desirable in a refinement system. A system that tends to select refinements that "stand the test of time," would seem to be preferable to one that habitually selects refinements that it later retracts.

RUN 1

	Training Set 1	Training Set 2
Start	42/62 (69%)	116/121 (96%)
Finish	61/62 (98%)	120/121 (99%)

RUN 2

	Training Set 1	Training Set 2
Start	46/59 (78%)	118/121 (98%)
Finish	59/59 (100%)	120/121 (99%)

Figure 7-2: Train and Train Again Experiment

With these remarks in mind, we are now ready to discuss the results of the train-and-train experiment (see figure 7-2). In both runs of this experiment seven refinements were selected in the first training phase. In both cases six of these seven refinements are ones that are selected by SEEK2 in the overall run using the entire data base of cases as the training set, the others are refinements considered by SEEK2 in the overall run but not selected. In one of these runs, two additional refinements were selected in the *second* training phase. These two refinements were also selected by SEEK2 in the overall run. In the other run, four refinements were selected in the second training phase, of these three were accepted in the overall run, and one was not. Thus in both of these runs the result of the double training experiment was nearly identical to the result of the overall run: in one run nine refinements were selected, eight of which were selected in the overall run; in the other run eleven refinements were selected, nine of which were selected in the overall run. Both of the double training runs ended with a total performance ratio exactly equal to the overall run.

First let us discuss what might seem to be a negative side of these results. The fact that the refinements selected by the double training sessions are not exactly identical to the single overall run is not surprising, since the order in which refinements are generated, as well as their computed net gain, is sensitive to the composition of the data base of cases. Since only one refinement is selected in a given cycle, *even in the case of ties in positive net gain*, the ordering of generated refinements can have an effect upon the refinements selected. This circumstance also accounts for the fact that at the conclusion of one of the double training sessions it turns out that two essentially redundant refinements were selected, viz., the run in which eleven refinements were selected, only nine of which are needed to reach the identical final performance situation. This does not mean that such redundancies can occur within the course of a *single* SEEK2 refinement session; in fact they cannot. It would seem fair to conclude, therefore, that these features of the result have no negative bearing on the validity of the basic approach, but only indicate some possibly avoidable side-effects of the current SEEK2 procedure.

The experiment does, however, seem to provide some evidence that the basic approach is sound: none of the refinements selected in either of the first training sessions is retracted in either of the second training sessions.

7.1.1.3 Some Remarks on Optimality and Convergence

Viewing the knowledge base as a classification system, we have seen that one can apply various pattern recognition techniques to estimate its error rate; knowledge base refinement involves an attempt to improve the error rate. The question is can we design a knowledge base refinement system such that the optimal error rate will be achieved "asymptotically" in all cases, i.e., that the error rate of the optimal Bayes classifier [7] will be approached in the limit?

This is a question that will not be addressed here, except to say the following. It is clear that since the current version of SEEK2 does not incorporate an expressively complete set of refinement operations (see p.35) there will be situations in which it cannot reach the optimal error rate. More important, by its very nature, a *heuristic* approach is usually not capable of reaching an optimal state in all cases. By the same token, this should not be viewed as a failing of the approach.

Convergence is another property that has received attention in formal approaches to learning (for example, [18, 36]); actually it seems to cover two distinct properties. One of these addresses the question of whether a procedure can guarantee that "the right answer" will eventually be reached. In this context the notion of "the right answer" is not defined in terms of the optimal error rate, but rather in terms of a particular object or representation in a given formal system. For example, can we ever guarantee that a system that attempts to induce definitions of concepts from positive/negative instances using a given set of primitive symbols will always converge to a particular definition, i.e., the pattern of primitive symbols that actually represents the concept?

The concept of "the right answer" is problematic when applied to the field of knowledge base refinement. Knowledge bases are essentially empirical theories, and it is a well known feature of such theories that they are *undetermined by all possible empirical evidence* (see, for example, [37]). That is, let T be a theory that always gives the desired results in all possible cases. Then there will always exist a non-equivalent theory T′ that also yields exactly the same results (in fact that there will be many such). As an example, note that any knowledge base that employs *intermediate hypotheses* can be translated into an "empirically equivalent" one in which all rules contain only findings on their left hand sides and directly conclude an endpoint [16]. The original and translated knowledge base are empirically equivalent because they always conclude exactly the same endpoints (and because intermediate hypotheses are not included as part of the PDX in the cases).

In "real world" knowledge base refinement we certainly never know what "the right answer" is ahead of time - otherwise there would be no refinement problem. What this discussion shows is that the belief that we ever attain "the right answer" as opposed to *one* of the many empirically equivalent "right answers" is a matter that can ultimately be judged, if at all, only by non-empirical criteria . Except for our remarks concerning radicality and plausibility, and the role of the expert, investigation of such criteria are beyond the scope of this work.

The other property denoted by "convergence" has to do with the notion of reaching a solution which one will never be forced to abandon as a result of confronting future cases. In terms of the search for a version of a given empirical theory (knowledge base) with improved empirical adequacy, this boils down to reaching *one* of the many empirical equivalent "right answers." In other words, can we design a refinement system with the guarantee that at some point, after having seen "enough" cases, the resulting knowledge base will never have to be changed, i.e., no future case will be misdiagnosed? (Of course, we assume that the relevant "real world" environment remains constant, as it were, during the course of the learning.) One should note that - even with such a guarantee - one can never know with certainty *when* the procedure has converged. However, empirical estimation of error rates could be used to indicate distance from the goal and as a measure of our confidence that convergence has taken place.

Gold [18] shows that, *in principle*, such a procedure exists (as long as a solution exists and we can recursively enumerate all the possible solutions). Clearly the question is whether such a guarantee can be given for any class of theories by *computationally tractable* procedures. To this question - which is essentially the question concerning attainment of the optimal error rate under the assumption that zero error is attainable - I do not know the answer.

7.1.2 General Methodology for Knowledge Base Refinement

In terms of general methodology, the work presented here can be seen, first of all, as providing a more general and powerful understanding of the nature and potential role of heuristic analysis in knowledge base refinement. Starting with the simple paradigm for heuristic refinement generation, we have shown that a general architecture for heuristic refinement generation that allows for the implementation of failure-driven higher-order refinement can be specified (see chapters 4 and 6). Moreover a concrete tool that provides the means to implement this type of architecture has been constructed, RM. With both the tools and the blueprint on hand, it is reasonable to expect that these ideas will eventually be realized.

The fact is, however, that RM has already proven to be a useful tool in facilitating research progress. The RM design methodology was an important factor in the design, development, growth, and debugging of the SEEK2 system. Concrete examples of its use have already been discussed in detail in chapter 6. Here we should note that the two experiments discussed in section 7.1.1.2 above, are also examples of the type of experimentation that can be easily carried out in RM. We should also mention that a complete version of SEEK2 has been specified in RM. Running on the same rheumatology knowledge base, the RM version achieves the same results as the hard-coded in approximately 2 hours of CPU time. RM has also been used to specify and run experiments using an alternative experimentation and selection regime.

Viewed as a testing and debugging tool, what SEEK and SEEK2 are to knowledge bases, RM is to knowledge base refinement systems: SEEK and SEEK2 help a knowledge engineer to test and debug the rules in a knowledge base, RM helps a researcher to test and debug refinement system design specifications. The difference is that RM is not just a single body of procedures, but a flexible high-level metalinguistic framework within which the design, testing, and debugging of refinement concepts, heuristics, and strategies are integrated into a single environment.

7.1.3 Generality of The Approach

In this section I will very briefly indicate how the basic ideas involved in SEEK2's refinement regime can be applied to an expert system framework other than EXPERT. The point of this exercise is to show that the ideas presented here are general in a concrete sense, i.e., nothing of importance ultimately hinges on some idiosyncrasy of EXPERT.

To this end we will show that, using a subset of OPS5 [9], let us call it EXOPS, one can write knowledge bases that are amenable to the SEEK2 approach to knowledge base refinement. To show this formally one would show that for any EXPERT knowledge base KB there is a suitable EXOPS "translation" KB′ that is *case equivalent* to KB, i.e., for any case c, KB reaches a conclusion H in c iff KB′ reaches H in c. (To say that an EXOPS knowledge base reaches conclusion c in a case is to say that c is in working memory when the conflict set is empty.) Rather than take a formal route, however, it will be easier to proceed by way of a simple example. (It is assumed the reader has familiarity with OPS5).

Consider the following EXOPS example:

```
;**** note that strategy can be LEX or MEA

(literalize finding name value)

(literalize hypothesis name value confidence-factor)

(literalize choice-component choice-number
        choice-list-id choice-number status)
(p yuppie-rule-1
   (finding ^name occupation ^value {banker lawyer doctor})
   (hypothesis ^name career-class ^confidence-factor < 1)
   -->
   (modify 2 ^value  up-mob-pro ^confidence-factor 1))

(p yuppie-rule-2
   (finding ^name age ^value <= 45)
   (hypothesis ^name age-class ^confidence-factor < .9)
   -->
   (modify 2 ^value young ^confidence-factor .9))

;if one out of three elements in list-1 are satisfied,
;then the choice-component is
(p yuppie-rule-3
   (hypothesis ^name age-class ^value young ^confidence-factor {>= .9 <= 1})
   (choice-component ^choice-number 1 ^choice-list-id list-1
                                              ^status unsatisfied)
   -->
   (modify 2 ^status satisfied))
```

```
;if one out of three elements in list-1 are satisfied,
;then the choice-component is
(p yuppie-rule-4
   (hypothesis ^name career-class  up-mob-pro)
   (choice-component ^choice-number 1 ^choice-list-id list-1
                                          ^status unsatisfied)
   -->
   (modify 2 ^status satisfied))

(p yuppie-rule-5
   (finding ^name salary ^value >= 50000)
   (choice-component ^choice-number 1 ^choice-list-id list-1
                                          ^status unsatisfied)
   -->
   (modify 2 ^status satisfied))

;if two out of three elements in list-1 are satisfied,
;then choice-component is
(p yuppie-rule-6
   (hypothesis ^name age-class ^value young ^confidence-factor {>= .9 <= 1})
   (hypothesis ^name career-class  up-mob-pro)
   (choice-component ^choice-number 2 ^choice-list-id list-1
                                          ^status unsatisfied)
   -->
   (modify 3 ^status satisfied))

(p yuppie-rule-7
   (hypothesis ^name age-class ^value young ^confidence-factor {>= .9 <= 1})
   (finding ^name salary ^value >= 50000)
   (choice-component ^choice-number 2 ^choice-list-id list-1
                                          ^status unsatisfied)
   -->
   (modify 3 ^status satisfied))

(p yuppie-rule-8
   (hypothesis ^name career-class  up-mob-pro)
   (finding ^name salary ^value >= 50000)
   (choice-component ^choice-number 2 ^choice-list-id list-1
                                          ^status unsatisfied)
   -->
   (modify 3 ^status satisfied))

(p yuppie-rule-9
   (choice-component ^choice-number 1 ^choice-list-id list-1
                                          ^status satisfied)
   (finding ^name make-of-car ^value BMW)
   (finding ^name work-location ^value NYC)
   (hypothesis ^name Socio-category ^confidence-factor < .7)
   -->
   (modify 4 ^value yuppie ^confidence-factor .7))

(p yuppie-rule-10
   (hypothesis ^name age-class ^value young ^confidence-factor {>= .8 <= 1})
   (hypothesis ^name career-class  up-mob-pro)
   (finding ^name salary ^value >= 50000)
   (hypothesis ^name Socio-category ^confidence-factor < .8)
   -->
   (modify 4 ^value yuppie ^confidence-factor .8))
```

```
;****  initialization of working memory *******

; default initializations for hypotheses

(make hypothesis ^name career-class ^confidence-factor 0)
(make hypothesis ^name age-class ^confidence-factor 0)
(make hypothesis ^name socio-category ^confidence-factor 0)

; initialize memory elements for choice-components
; note that list-1 is a short hand for the choice list:
;(hypothesis ^name age-class ^value young ^confidence-factor {>= .9 <= 1})
;(hypothesis ^name career-class  up-mob-pro)
;(finding ^name salary ^value >= 50000)

(make choice-component ^choice-number 1 ^choice-list-id list-1
                                                  ^status unsatisfied)
(make choice-component ^choice-number 2 ^choice-list-id list-1
                                                  ^status unsatisfied)

;case-1: PDX is
;    (hypothesis ^name socio-category ^value yuppie)

  (make finding ^name occupation ^value lawyer)
  (make finding ^name age 46)
  (make finding ^name salary ^value 100000)

; case-2: PDX  is null

  (make finding ^name age 33)
  (make finding ^name salary ^value 5000)
  (make finding ^name make-of-car ^value BMW)
  (make finding ^name work-location ^value NYC)
```

One immediately notes that no variables are allowed in the rules. In addition, it is clear that the knowledge base is intended to solve a classification problem in the sense we have been concerned with throughout this work: certain observable attributes - findings - concerning a fixed and predetermined number of objects (in this case, a single person) are given, and certain hypothesis can be reached to categorize the object(s) is a certain way. Once a case has been decided, the working memory is reinitialized in order to handle the next case.

The use of confidence-factors requires some comment. In EXPERT a satisfied rule can only be used to *increase* the *absolute value* of the current confidence in some hypothesis. For the sake of simplicity we have left negative confidence-factors out of consideration in our example, which means that the qualification about absolute values can be ignored. EXPERT's non-additive use of confidence-factors is simulated in EXOPS by including additional clauses in the left-hand-sides of rules. For example, yuppie-rule-2 can be used to assert that some person p is in the age-class young with confidence .9 only if p has not already been asserted to be in some age-class with confidence $\geq$ .9. (In addition, these clauses help to prevent the continual reintroduction of essentially identical instances of productions into the conflict set.)

Choice-components are "implemented" in EXOPS in a rather inefficient manner. It practice, it would be far better to simply rewrite the OPS5 interpreter to allow for choice-components as syntactic primitives. In EXOPS each choice-component of the form [*k:* C_1, ..., C_n] is represented by a memory element having the choice-number, *k*, a mnemonic for the choice-list C_1, ..., C_n, and a satisfaction status, as slot values. For each choice-component productions must be written that guarantee that satisfaction of the appropriate number of elements in the choice-list leads to a "satisfied" status for the appropriate memory element. In order to allow for the admissibility of SEEK2's choice-number refinement operations, one should also be sure to include memory elements and corresponding productions for all values of choice-numbers (except for zero and the *n*, i.e., the number of elements in the choice-list). Thus, in our example, even thought the condition element:

```
(choice-component ^choice-number 1 ^choice-list-id list-1
                                         ^status satisfied)
```

is not used in any production, yuppie-rules 3 through 5 are still included, in order to allow for refinement of the other choice-component.

To see how some of SEEK2's concepts can be applied to this example, consider the cases listed above. Case-1 would be correctly classified if either yuppie-rule-9 or yuppie-rule-10 fired. Note however, that yuppie-rule-10 is closer to being satisfied in this case than yuppie-rule-9. While yuppie-rule-9 is unsatisfied because the appropriate findings relating to possesion of a BMW, working in NYC *and* age are not present or false, yuppie-rule-10 is unsatisfied only because of the age finding. Therefore the latter production would be flagged as the Gen rule for case-1. Clearly, SEEK2's heuristics would suggest deletion of the first component of yuppie-rule-10; in addition, however, SEEK2 would recommend raising the upper bound on the age finding in yuppie-rule-2. The larger the number of cases available, the more likely it becomes that a bound-raising refinement will have a positive net gain, while the deletion refinement will have a negative net gain.

Case-2 illustrates application of some of the specialization concepts and heuristics. Here we find that yuppie-rule-9 is satisfied, but that its conclusion should not have been reached. In fact yuppie-rule-9 will be flagged as the specA rule for case-2. The only refinement suggestion offered by SEEK2 in this case will be to raise the choice-number of the choice-component in the rule.

Clearly the yuppie-KB is not intended to be viewed as a "real world" knowledge base. However, while it is a contrived example, it does serve to illustrate the point, viz., a version of SEEK2 that would work with appropriately restricted OPS5 knowledge bases could be written immediately. To do this, one would, of course, need to built an interface to OPS5 that would allow one to gather the necessary statistical data. But what has been shown by the discussion here is that one does not need to alter OPS5 in any essential way in order to carry out this program.

7.2 Future Directions

7.2.1 More Powerful Rule Representation Languages

Many of the concepts dealt with in this work may be seen as being generally applicable to *any* refinement system, and others can be easily extended to have greater applicability. In other words, the analysis is applicable not only to refinement systems that are intended to address a *particular subclass of refinement system design problems* - those involving expert system frameworks that are designed with classification problems in mind - but to the whole range of refinement systems imaginable. For example, let us consider rule representation frameworks designed for *planning problems*, i.e., the rules represent *precondition-action* pairs, and the job of a concrete system is to find a sequence of actions that will achieve a certain given goal (see, for example, [34]). A *case* would now be interpreted as consisting of data representing the *initial state* of the domain together with a specification of the desired *goal state*. The expert's conclusion in a case would be the sequence of actions *he* would carry out in that case to reach the desired goal. The expert system would be said to diagnose the case correctly if its "plan" matched the expert's, or deviated from it only in ways that are of no consequence, the latter being a determination that could only be made with the use of domain-specific knowledge. While refinement systems for these types of rule representation frameworks would certainly differ from those that deal with expert system frameworks for classification problems, they would also have much in common, e.g., there would certainly be overlap in the set of primitive refinement operations, r-functions and heuristics, and control strategies utilized.

However, a planning problem, or a design problem, typically requires a richer rule representation language than does a classification problem. Systems that solve planning problems will generally make non-trivial use of rules that contain variables, i.e., the bindings of these variables may be altered dynamically as the problem is solved and cannot be fixed once and for all for the course of the run-time session.

Therefore, a natural path for future research is to think about how the present paradigm may be generalized to deal with a richer rule representation language. The first step would be to specify a canonical grammar for such a language. It may very well be that the grammar given in chapter 3 is a good place to start. The next step is to think about new primitive refinement operators that could be added to the present stock. Then one must think about situations in which it would make sense to apply one of these operators in order to improve empirical adequacy. One must then try to isolate the features of these situations that may provide evidence for the application of the operator. Determining how, and with what cost, such evidence may be gathered is the next step. At this point one is well on the way to deriving r-functions and heuristics for the new operator. At the same time one would extend RM so as to include all the new primitives necessary for dealing with a richer language.

7.2.2 Parallelism

At the algorithmic level it is not difficult to see that all of the types of refinement systems we have talked about offer opportunities for the exploitation of parallelism. The hill-climbing approach of SEEK2, for example, is amenable to parallel computation at every level. In each cycle each dx can be pursued independently of the others. Within a cycle, each rule for each dx can be examined independently of all other rules. Most r-functions can be evaluated independently of all the others. And finally each experiment can be tested independently of all the others.

A direction for future research implied by these facts, involves the design of a realistic machine architecture, based on existing technological possibilities and limitations, for exploiting the inherent parallelism in the process to the fullest degree.

7.2.3 Growth, Maintenance, and Integration of Knowledge Bases

It is a well known fact that knowledge engineering does not come to end with the successful construction of a high-performance knowledge base. As with any software, such systems must be maintained, and are liable to grow as domain knowledge and techniques continue to improve. Moreover, from time to time users may find it worthwhile to attempt to integrate two distinct, but overlapping, high-performance knowledge bases into a single expert system. Such integration may initially cause a degradation in performance, and therefore refinement of the combined system may be required.

There is every reason to believe that the methodology of knowledge base refinement will prove to be applicable to these tasks as well.

7.2.4 Extending the Scope of the Metalanguage

A potentially fruitful direction for future research is to *integrate* a richer version of the metalanguage with the rule-representation language, i.e., rules in a knowledge base could contain metalinguistic constructs. This could probably be done in such a way that at least some *control knowledge* could be explicitly represented in rules. Thus one could, for example, write rules to capture the following sort of control advice: *if finding f is true and there are currently two or more rules for distinct endpoints satisfied, then do not allow any of these rules to fire - until told otherwise - but try to obtain further information regarding hypotheses* H_1 *and* H_2.

Perhaps the easiest and safest way of carrying out such a program is to devise a reasonable *layered* rule-based system architecture. For example, a knowledge base might consist of several levels operating in parallel and accessing a shared memory as well as their own local memory. Rules at a "higher" level could refer to rules at lower levels, and effect their invocation and firing, but rules at lower levels could not directly refer to higher level rules.

7.3 Concluding Remarks

The basic expert system paradigm would seem to be a relatively simple combination of ideas: rules, working memory, and inference procedure. In the view of some it may perhaps be *too* simple a model to be interesting. Controversy surrounding the degree to which expert systems have lived up - or can live up - to popular expectations, may contribute to this impression.

I would argue, however, that it is *precisely* the simplicity of the expert system paradigm that makes it an attractive vehicle for research in certain areas of artificial intelligence. Simple things are more amenable to precise analysis than complex things. Indeed it seems to me that our only hope of understanding more complex things is to first understand a sufficiently powerful set of simple things. Once we have the right level of understanding concerning the behavior of expert systems, we should be able to translate at least some of this understanding into programs that manipulate and create knowledge bases in order to reliably learn from experience. If the work presented here leads in the direction of such understanding, then it has achicvcd its purpose.

I List of RM Primitives and Some Constructs

Primitives

Constants

CASES The set of cases in the data base of cases

kb_0 The initial knowledge base

DX The set of endpoints in kb_0

Special Variables

case A variable over CASES

cases A variable over *subsets* of cases

rule A variable ranging over rules

kb A variable over knowledge bases

dx A variable over DX

component A variable over rule components and sub-components

finding A variable over finding components

hypothesis A variable over hypothesis components

Functions

PDX(case)
the expert's conclusion in case

CDX-Total(case,kb)
The set of dx concluded with positive confidence in case by kb

CDX(case,kb)
The dx concluded with greatest positive confidence

in case by kb

CDX-2(case,kb)
The dx concluded with the second greatest positive confidence in case by kb

RuleCF(rule)
The confidence factor of rule

ModelCF(hypothesis,case,kb)

The hypothesis confidence assigned to hypothesis in case by kb

Rules-for(hypothesis)

The set of rules with dx as their conclusion

Conclusion(rule)
The conclusion of rule

Satisfied(item,case,kb)

= T iff item is satisfied in case in kb
= F iff item is unsatisfied or *unknown* in case in kb,
where item is either a component of a rule or an entire rule

Value(numerical-finding,case)

The value of numerical finding in case

Mean(quantity,cases)

The mean value of quantity over the set of cases

Component-Parameters(component)
The type of component, and in addition
i) <choice-number, |choice-list|> if component is a choice
ii) <l,h> if component is a hypothesis with cf-range [l:h]
iii) <l,h> if component is a finding with range [l:h]

Special Operators

Select *item* **with Max/Min** *specification*

returns a *single item* that maximizes/minimizes the value of the condition in *specification*

Select {*item*} **with Max/Min** *specification*

returns the *set* of item that maximizes/minimizes
the value of the condition in *specification*

Useful Defined Notions

Constants

CCASES = {case| PDX(case)=CDX(case,kb)}
= the set of cases in which the kb's conclusion matches the expert's (correctly diagnosed cases).

MCASES = {case| PDX(case)≠CDX(case,kb)}
= the set of cases in which the kb's conclusion does not match the expert's (misdiagnosed cases).
Note that a null CDX is possible and considered a misdiagnosis.

Variables

ccase	A variable ranging over CCASES
ccases	A variable ranging over subsets of CCASES
mcase	A variable ranging over MCASES
mcases	A variable ranging over subsets of MCASES

Functions

(The following are defined in terms of a fixed kb.)

Satisfied-Rules-For(hypothesis,case)

= {rule∈ Rules-for(hypothesis)| Satisfied(rule,case)}

TP(dx,case)
= T if PDX(case)=CDX(case)=dx
= F otherwise

TN(dx,case)
= T if dx≠PDX(case)≠CDX(case)
= F otherwise.

FP(dx,case)
= T if PDX(case) $\neq$ CDX(case)=dx
= F otherwise

FN(dx,case)
= T if dx=PDX(case) $\neq$ CDX(case)
= F otherwise.

Primitives for Specifying Refinement Strategies

Variables and Sets

R-OPERATORS
The set of primitive refinement operations

r-operator
A variable over R-OPERATORS

Primitive-r-operation

A variable over 4-tuples of the form

<rule,component,r-operator,parameters>

where component is the component of rule to which r-operator is to be applied with the given parameters

Complex-r-operation

A variable over sets of primitive-r-operations

r-operation

A variable over primitive and complex r-operations

experiment
A variable ranging over 3-tuples of the form

<r-operation,kb,cases>

and ordered pairs of the form

<r-operation,kb>

where r-operation is to be applied to kb and then tested with respect to cases (3-tuples), or with respect to CASES (pair)

suggestions
A variable over sets of (untried) experiments, that have been generated by the refinement generator

r-situation
A variable over triples of the form <rules,mcases,CASES>

kb-object
A variable over kb-objects (see chapter 6)

VIEWFINDER
The set of r-functions used by the refinement generator

r-function
A variable over the r-functions in VIEWFINDER (see chapter 6)

r-functions
A variable over subsets of r-functions in VIEWFINDER

R-KNOWLEDGE
The set of heuristics used by the refinement generator

VR-HEURISTICS
The set of heuristics having only r-function calls in their left-hand-sides (see chapter 6)

RR-HEURISTICS
The set of heuristics referring to the results of evaluation of other heuristics (see chapter 6)

vr-heuristic
A variable over VR-HEURISTICS

rr-heuristic
A variable over RR-HEURISTICS

Operations and Functions

Compute(r-function,kb-object,mcases)

Returns the value of r-function(kb-object,mcases,CASES) if kb-object and cases are legitimate arguments for r-function, otherwise undefined (Recall that CASES is an optional argument in r-functions)

View(kb-object,mcases,CASES)

for every applicable r-function ∈ VIEWFINDER
    Compute(r-function,kb-object,mcases)
    and store results

performance(kb,dx,cases)

returns the ordered pair consisting of
<|{case ∈ cases|TP(dx,case,kb)}|,|{case ∈ |FP(dx,case,kb)}|>

Evaluate-Heuristics(heuristics,kb-object,View(kb-object,mcases))

returns the results of evaluating every heuristic in heuristics for kb-object using information in View(kb-object,mcases)

Try-Experiment(experiment,kb,cases)

Temporarily incorporates the r-operation in experiment into kb, then runs the resulting knowledge base over the specified set of cases; computes, and returns the net gain of the r-operation over these cases

Create-Kb(experiment,kb)

returns the knowledge base resulting from application of the r-operation in experiment to kb

II Generic Atomic Refinement Operators for EXPERT

Non-Structural Refinements

<u>Generalizations</u>

Concept Generalization

...[<find|hyp> <value|range>]... → ...[<G(find)|G(hyp)><value|range>]...

where G(item) is a more general concept than item.

Extend a Range From Below

...[<find|hyp> <n:m>]... → ...[<find|hyp> <k:m>]...

where k<n

Extend a Range From Above

...[<find|hyp> <n:m>]... → ...[<find|hyp> <n:k>]...

where m<k

<u>Non-Structural Specializations</u>

Concept Specialization

...[<find|hyp> <value|range>]... → ...[<S(find)|S(hyp)><value|range>]...

where S(item) is a less general concept than item.

Restrict a Range From Below

...[<find|hyp> <n:m>]... → ...[<find|hyp> <k:m>]...

where n<k

Restrict a Range From Above

...[<find|hyp> <n:m>]... → ...[<find|hyp> <n:k>]...

where k<m

Structural Refinements

<u>Generalizations</u>

Component Deletion

...[<comp>]... → ... ...

Decrement Choice-Number

...[n: <Choice-list>]... → ...[(n-1): <Choice-list>]...

Append Component to Choice-list

...[n: <Choice-list>]... → ...[n: <Choice-list><find|hyp>]...

Increase Confidence Factor

<Conclusion CF> → <Conclusion CF′>

where CF<CF′

<u>Structural Specializations</u>

Component Addition

... ... → ...[<comp>]...

Increment Choice-Number

...[n: <Choice-list>]... → ...[(n+1): <Choice-list>]...

Delete Component From Choice-list

...[n: <Choice-list><find|hyp>]... → ...[n: <Choice-list>]...

Decrease Confidence Factor

<Conclusion CF> → <Conclusion CF′>

where CF>CF′

III A Grammar for the Canonical Rule Representation Language

In using this grammar the following points must be kept in mind:

- Expressions in angle-brackets, such as *<Rule>*, are non-terminals; expressions in braces, such as *{<Range>}* represent optional constructs; expressions delimited by asterisks such as **Predicate-Symbol** represents valid sequences of terminal symbols, whose precise formal specification is unimportant for our purposes; every other symbol is a special symbol belonging to the vocabulary of the canonical language.
- The given grammar will accept quantified formulas in Prenex normal form only, i.e., quantifiers are not allowed within the scope of the boolean operations.
- The given grammar is important as an expository device and is certainly not the most elegant one that can be devised. The goal is to provide a grammar that parses all the formal notation that we intend to employ in a way that helps to clarify the formal nature of refinement operations.

<Rule>→ <Premises> **->** <Conclusion>[*Confidence-Factor*]

<Premises>→ <Component><Connective><Premises>|Λ

<Conclusion>→ <Simple-Component>

<Connective>→ &|∨ |→ |Λ

<Component>→ <Simple-Component>|<Compound-Component>|<Choice>
|<Quantified-Component>

<Quantified-Component>→ (∀ <*Variable*>)(<Component>)
|(∃ *Variable*)(<Component>)

<Simple-Component>→ {¬ }<Propositional-Form>|{¬ }<Predicate-form>

<Choice>→ [<Choice-Number>: <Choice-List>]

<Choice-Number>→ *positive-integer*

<Choice-List>→ <Choice-Element>, <Choice-list>|Λ

<Choice-Element>→ <Simple-Component>

```
<Compound-Component> → (<Simple-Component><Connective>
                        <Compound-Component>)
                       |Λ

<Propositional-Form> → (*Propositional-Constant*{<Range>})

<Predicate-Form> → (*Predicate-Constant* <Parameter-List>{<Range>})

<Parameter-List> → <Term>|<Term>,<Parameter-List>|Λ

<Term> → *Variable*|*Constant*|<Function-Term>

<Function-Term> → (*Function-Symbol* <Parameter-List>)

<Range> → *Truth-Value*|[*Number*:*Number*]
```

References

[1] Bazaraa,M., and Jarvis, J.
Linear Programming and Network Flows.
Wiley, New York, 1977.

[2] Boose, J.
Personal Construct Theory and The Transfer of Human Expertise.
In *Proceedings of the Fourth Annual National Conference on Artificial Intelligence,* pages 27-33. Austin, Texas, 1984.

[3] Chomsky, N.
Syntactic Structures.
Mouton, The Hague, 1957.

[4] Clancy, W.
The Epistemology of a Rule-Based Expert System: A Framework for Explanation.
Artificial Intelligence 20(3):215-251, 1983.

[5] Davis, R.
Interactive Transfer of Expertise: Acquisition of New Inference Rules.
Artificial Intelligence 12:121-157, 1979.

[6] Drastal, G., and, Kulikowski,C.
Knowledge-Based Acquisition of Rules for Medical Diagnosis.
Journal of Medical Systems 6(5), 1982.

[7] Duda, R., and Hart, P.
Pattern Classification and Scene Analysis.
Wiley, New York, 1973.

[8] Eshelman, L. and McDermott, J.
MOLE: A Knowledge Acquisition Tool That Uses Its Head.
In *Proceedings of the Fifth Annual National Conference on Artificial Intelligence*, pages 950-955. Philadelphia, Pa., 1986.

[9] Forgy, C., and McDermott, J.
OPS, A Domain-Independent Production System Language.
In *Proceedings of the Fifth International Joint Conference on Artificial Intelligence,* pages 933-939. 1977.

[10] Fu, K.S.
Syntactic Methods in Pattern Recognition.
Academic Press, New York, 1974.

[11] Li-Min, Fu and Buchanan, B.
Enhancing Performance of Expert System by Automated Discovery of Meta-Rules.
In *The First Conference on Artificial Intelligence Applications.* December, 1984.

[12] Fukunaga, K.
Introduction to Statistical Pattern Recognition.
Academic Press, New York, 1972.

[13] Genesereth, M.
Diagnosis Using Hierarchical Design Models.
In *Proceedings of the Second Annual National Conference on Artificial Intelligence*, pages 278-283. Pittsburg, Pa., 1982.

[14] Ginsberg, A.
Quantum Statistics, Quantum Field Theory, and The Interpretation Problem.
PhD thesis, Department of Philosophy, Rutgers University, 1983.

[15] Ginsberg, A.
A New Approach to Checking Knowledge Bases for Inconsistency and Redundancy.
In *Proceedings of The Third Annual Expert Systems in Government Conference.* Washington, D.C., 1987.

[16] Ginsberg, A.
Theory Revision via Prior Operationalization.
Technical Report, AT&T Bell Laboratories, 1988.

[17] Ginsberg,A., Weiss,S., and Politakis,P.
SEEK2: A Generalized Approach to Automatic Knowledge Base Refinement.
In *Proceedings of the Ninth International Joint Conference on Artificial Intelligence*, pages 367-374. Los Angeles, California, 1985.

[18] Gold, E.M.
Language Identification in the Limit.
Information and Control 10:447-474, 1967.

[19] Gonzalez, R. and Thomason, M.
Syntactic Pattern Recognition.
Addison-Wesley, Reading, Mass., 1978.

[20] Hall, R.
Learning By Failing to Explain.
In *Proceedings of the Fifth Annual National Conference on Artificial Intelligence.* 1986.

[21] Kahn, G., Nowlan, S., Mcdermott, J.
MORE: An Intelligent Knowledge Acquisition Tool.
In *Proceedings of the Ninth International Joint Conference on Artificial Intelligence*, pages 581-584. Los Angeles, CA, 1985.

[22] Langley, P., Bradshaw, G., and Simon, H.
Rediscovering Chemistry With the BACON System.
Machine Learning.
Tioga Publishing Company, 1983.

[23] Lee, W. and Ray, S.
Rule Refinement Using the Probabilistic Rule Generator.
In *Proceedings of the Fifth Annual National Conference on Artificial Intelligence*, pages 442-447. Philadelphia, Pa., 1986.

[24] Lenat, D.
The Role of Heuristics in Learning By Discovery: Three Case Studies.
Machine Learning.
Tioga Publishing Company, 1983.

[25] Michalski, R.
A Theory and Methodology of Inductive Learning.
Machine Learning.
Tioga Publishing Company, 1983, pages 83-134.

[26] Michalski, Carbonell, Mitchell (editors).
Machine Learning.
Tioga Publishing Company, Palo Alto, 1983.

[27] Mitchell, T.
Generalization as Search.
Artificial Intelligence 18:203-226, 1982.

[28] Mitchell, T., Utgoff, P., and Banerji, R.
Learning By Experimentation: Acquiring and Refining Problem-Solving Heuristics.
Machine Learning.
Tioga Publishing Company, 1983.

[29] T. Mitchell and R. Keller and S. Kedar-Cabelli.
Explanation-Based Generalization: A Unifying View.
Machine Learning 1:47-80, 1986.

[30] Politakis, P.
Empirical Analysis for Expert Systems.
Pitman and Morgan Kaufmann, London, UK, and Los Altos, Ca., 1985.

[31] Politakis, P. and Weiss, S.
Using Empirical Analysis to Refine Expert System Knowledge Bases.
Artificial Intelligence 22:23-48, 1984.

[32] Doyle, R.
Constructing and Refining Causal Explanations from An Inconsistent Domain Theory.
In *AAAI-86.* Philadelphia,Pa., 1986.

[33] Smith, R., Winston, H., Mitchell, T., and Buchanan, B.
Representation and Use of Explicit Justification for Knowledge Base Refinement.
In *Proceedings of the Ninth International Joint Conference on Artificial Intelligence,* pages 673-680. Los Angeles, California, 1985.

[34] Stefik, M.
Planning and Meta-Planning.
Artificial Intelligence 16:141-170, 1981.

[35] Tolman, R.
The Principles of Statistical Mechanics.
Dover, New York, 1979.

[36] Valiant, L.
Learning Disjunctions of Conjunctions.
In *Proceedings of the Ninth International Joint Conference on Artificial Intelligence*, pages 560-566. Los Angeles, California, 1985.

[37] Bas Van Fraassen.
The Scientific Image.
Clarendon Press, Oxford, 1980.

[38] Waters, R.
KBEmacs: A Step Toward the Programmer's Apprentice.
IEEE Transactions on Software Engineering 11:1296-1320, 1985.

[39] Weiss, S., and Kulikowski, C.
EXPERT: A System for Developing Consultation Models.
In *Proceedings of the Sixth International Joint Conference on Artificial Intelligence*, pages 942-947. Tokyo, Japan, 1979.

[40] Weiss, S. and Kulikowski, C.
A Practical Guide to Designing Expert Systems.
Rowman and Allanheld, Totowa, New Jersey, 1984.

[41] Wilkins, D. and Buchanan, B.
On Debugging Rule Sets When Reasoning Under Uncertainty.
In *Proceedings of the Fifth Annual National Conference on Artificial Intelligence*, pages 448-454. Philadelphia, Pa., 1986.